W9-ATP-470

ENGLISH REVIEW GRAMMAR

English Review Grammar

WALTER KAY SMART

Fourth Edition

Prentice-Hall, Inc., Englewood Cliffs, New Jersey

PE 1111
S 49
1940 X

© 1940
by PRENTICE-HALL, Inc.,
Englewood Cliffs, New Jersey

All rights reserved. No part of this book
may be reproduced in any form or by any means,
without permission in writing from the publisher.

Printed in the United States of America

ISBN: 0-13-282897-9

55   54   53   52   51   50   49   48   47   46

Copyright renewed, 1968, by M. Elizabeth Campbell
Copyright renewed 1958, 1959, by Mary Elizabeth Smart Campbell
Copyright renewed 1953, by Walter Kay Smart

PRENTICE-HALL INTERNATIONAL, INC., *London*
PRENTICE-HALL OF AUSTRALIA, PTY. LTD., *Sydney*
PRENTICE-HALL OF CANADA, LTD., *Toronto*
PRENTICE-HALL OF INDIA PRIVATE LIMITED, *New Delhi*
PRENTICE-HALL OF JAPAN, INC., *Tokyo*

PREFACE TO THE FOURTH EDITION

This fourth edition of *English Review Grammar*, with its complete resetting of type in new format, has offered the welcome opportunity to make revisions and amplifications throughout the book, wherever it seemed desirable. An entirely new chapter on Vocabulary has been added, which provides practice in the use of the dictionary; introduces the student to the structure of words and their development in meaning; and gives exercises in synonyms, pronunciation, and spelling. In addition, new exercises have been supplied throughout and in increased number, including many of the fill-in type.

The purpose of this book remains as before to furnish a review of English grammar for mature students who need a more thorough knowledge of the structure of the English language. Experience has shown that the prevailing lack of this knowledge is a serious handicap in composition courses, as well as in the study of foreign languages, and many institutions have found it necessary to require a systematic review of grammar to remedy this condition.

The book is divided into two parts. Part I contains a simplified review of the fundamental grammatical principles and forms. It is elementary enough for those who have practically forgotten their public school work in grammar, and at the same time it is complete enough to acquaint them with grammatical terminology and the standard constructions which constitute the framework or backbone of the language.

Part II supplements the material in Part I. English is a living language and is constantly changing. The result is that there have grown up a large number of constructions which do not conform to the ordinary rules. For instance, the ordinary statement of the formal use of tenses gives an incomplete and even erroneous idea of their actual use in modern English; cases of pronouns are subject to many irregularities; and adverbial elements show an aversion to formal classification. The more important of these variations from the standard forms are discussed in Part II.

This division of the book is intended to meet two needs.

(1) It may be used for reference by students who are covering Part I in class and want a more complete discussion of certain subjects.

(2) It may be used as a text for review in more advanced classes. Each chapter is provided with a summary of the essential features of the same subject as discussed in Part I, or this material is made accessible by means of cross references. In this way different points which were treated under various headings in the first part are brought together in one place, and combined with additional material.

Especial attention has been devoted to making the book teachable. The discussions in Part I have been made as simple and non-technical as possible, and the arrangement of material is such that the student is not confused by the introduction of exceptions and irregular constructions while he is engaged in mastering the standard forms.

The chapter on Punctuation treats the subject not as a series of isolated rules but as a vital factor in indicating thought relations between groups in a sentence. Emphasis is laid on showing *why* certain punctuation is needed in a given place. Since this is intended as a review of the subject, some of the more elementary rules have been omitted, such as the use of a period at the end of a declarative sentence and the use of a question mark after a question.

Acknowledgments are due to many instructors who have used the book, and especially to Mr. R. D. Highfill and Mr. Martin Ross, for constructive suggestions as to the presentation of the material.

W. K. S.

CONTENTS

PART I

PART II

CONTENTS

7

PART ONE

A sentence consists of words so combined as to express a thought. Each word has a particular function to perform in expressing that thought, and all words are classified according to these functions into eight classes or **Parts of Speech.**

The eight Parts of Speech are:

Nouns	Verbs	Prepositions
Pronouns	Adverbs	Conjunctions
Adjectives		Interjections

A Noun is the name of something: as, *house, man, liberty.*

> The *house* is burning.
> The *man* paid dearly for his *liberty.*

A Pronoun is a word used for a noun: as, *he, they, who.*

> *They* are here.
> *He* is the boy *who* won the prize.

An Adjective is a word that describes a noun or modifies its meaning: as, *black, small, first.*

> He wore a *black* hat.
> John was the *first* arrival.

A Verb is a word that makes a statement about the subject of the sentence. It expresses an action or state as, *run, climb, rest, think, is.*

> The boys *run* awkwardly.
> They *had rested* for an hour.

An Adverb is a word used to modify a verb, an adjective, or another adverb: as, *quickly, safely, very, too, soon.*

> They arrived *safely.*
> It was a *very* warm day.
> We left *too soon.*

A Preposition is a connecting word used to show the relation of a noun or pronoun to some other word in the sentence: as, *for, through, from, at, in, over.*

> The family came *from* the farm *to* the city.
> We sat *at* a table *in* the corner.

A Conjunction is a connecting word used to join words or groups of words in a sentence: as, *and, or, if, although, while.*

> The man *and* the child were lost.
>
> He must study *or* he will fail.
>
> You may go *if* you wish.

An Interjection is an exclamatory word which has little or no grammatical connection with the rest of the sentence: as, *alas, pshaw, oh, ah.*

> *Alas,* he has gone.

These eight classes fall naturally into four groups, divided according to the relation existing between the different Parts of Speech.

(1) Nouns; Pronouns (used for nouns); Adjectives (modifiers of nouns).

(2) Verbs; Adverbs (primarily modifiers of verbs).

(3) Prepositions and Conjunctions, which are connecting words.

(4) Interjections, which are usually without grammatical relation with the other Parts of Speech.

The following sentence contains seven of the Parts of Speech and illustrates their use.

> Two small boys crept silently to the door and opened it.

Boys and *door* are nouns—they are the names of things.

It is a pronoun standing for the noun *door.*

Two and *small* are adjectives modifying the noun *boys.*

The is an adjective (article, see Sec. 89), modifying the noun *door.*

Crept and *opened* are verbs—they tell what the boys did: that is, they make a statement about the boys.

Silently is an adverb modifying the verb *crept*—it describes the manner of their creeping.

To is a preposition—it shows the relation of the noun *door* to the verb *crept.*

And is a conjunction connecting the verbs *crept* and *opened.*

Chapter I   NOUNS

1. A Noun is the name of something.

The something which a noun names may be:

(1) A living or an inanimate thing having physical existence: as, *man, horse, tree, rock, victor, city.*

(2) A mental or spiritual concept: as, *mercy, patriotism, love, error, truth.*

(3) Some quality, property, or condition belonging to an object: as, *whiteness, weakness, strength, depth.*

(4) An action: as, *running, swimming, reading.*

Note. In the sentence, *"Running* is good exercise," *running* is a noun because it is the name of an act and is the subject of the verb *is;* but notice that in "He is *running* a race," *running* is not a noun: it is a part of the verb *is running,* which tells what he is doing.

CLASSIFICATION OF NOUNS

2. Nouns are divided into two classes: Common Nouns and Proper Nouns.

(1) A **Common Noun** is the name belonging to all the members of a class of objects—that is, the name is *common* to all members of that class: as, *city, ship, woman, religion, river.*

(2) A **Proper Noun** is the distinctive name of an individual member of a class: as, *Chicago* (a member of the class *city*); *Lusitania* (*ship*); *Mary* (*woman*); *Christianity* (*religion*).

The word "proper" is from the same root as "property," and conveys the idea of "one's own."

3. In writing, a proper noun is distinguished by beginning it with a capital letter. Such words as *Clydesdale* (That horse is a Clydesdale), the *English,* an *American,* a *Mason* (a member of the Masonic Order), *Republicans, Catholics,* etc., are also written with a capital letter. These

5

are really common nouns, since they are names common to all members of a class, but they are derived from proper nouns.

4. Special Classes. The two classes—common and proper—cover all nouns. Included in these two, however, are some special classes.

(1) An **Abstract Noun** is one that names a mental or spiritual concept, or some quality or condition of an object (see (2) and (3) in Sec. 1): as, *hatred, truth, strength, depth.*

(2) A **Collective Noun** is the name of a collection or group of similar objects: as, *army, flock, committee, nation, firm* (a commercial organization), *Union League Club, Democratic Party, Atlas Chemical Company.*

(3) A **Compound Noun** is made up of two or more nouns, or a noun and some other word or words, which form a unit-idea: as, *grandfather, stairway, washerwoman, commander-in-chief, sister-in-law, ticket office, Congress Hotel, Blake and Company.*

Note. A collective noun may also be compound.

PROPERTIES OF NOUNS

5. Nouns have Person, Number, Gender, and Case. The discussion of Person is reserved for the chapter on Pronouns (see Sec. 35), since this property is more closely connected with the use of Pronouns than with the use of Nouns.

NUMBER

6. Number is that property of a noun or pronoun which indicates whether one object, or more than one object, is designated.

Nouns have two numbers: the Singular and the Plural.

(1) The **Singular Number** indicates one object only: as, *boy, house, man.*

(2) The **Plural Number** indicates two or more objects: as, *boys, houses, men.*

The plural number of most nouns is formed by adding *-s* or *-es* to the singular: as, *park, parks; book, books; porch, porches; box, boxes.* (See Secs. 326 ff. for other methods of forming the plural, and for an exercise in making plural nouns.)

GENDER

7. Gender is that property of a noun or pronoun by which the sex of an object is distinguished.

There are three genders: Masculine, Feminine, and Neuter.

(1) The **Masculine Gender** indicates a being of the male sex: as, *man, boy, father, gander, Henry.*

(2) The **Feminine Gender** indicates a being of the female sex: as, *lady, niece, sister, hen, mare, Alice.*

(3) The **Neuter Gender** indicates an object without sex: as, *flower, stone, water, city.*

8. In addition to these three it is convenient to use the term **Common Gender** in referring to nouns which may be either masculine or feminine, but which do not designate the gender: as, *child, parent, animal, bird, cousin.*

Some inanimate objects, naturally of the neuter gender, are often treated as if they were masculine or feminine. A ship is commonly referred to as *she;* a locomotive engineer speaks affectionately of his engine as *she;* a machine operator, talking of his lathe or drill-press, says, *"She's* working well today"; semi-poetically the sun becomes *he*—the moon becomes *she.* This usage is chiefly colloquial or poetical; in ordinary prose, as in a scientific treatise, all these words are treated as neuter nouns, with perhaps the exception of *ship,* which rather persistently retains the feminine gender.

For differences in form in the masculine and feminine genders, see Sec. 324.

Exercise 1

Point out the nouns; tell whether they are common or proper nouns, collective, abstract, or compound nouns.

1. Each house was occupied by a family of refugees. 2. His two children —a son and a daughter—are living in Newark. 3. Nature has no kindness, no hospitality, during a rain. (Nathaniel Hawthorne.) 4. The conductor of the orchestra was the nephew of an Italian actress. 5. The English are, I suppose, the most unimaginative race in the whole world. (Hugh Walpole.) 6. This society was supported by a group of influential alumnae. 7. We worked out of the Thames under canvas, with a North Sea pilot on board. (Joseph Conrad.) 8. Among the trees the hunters saw three deer—a buck and two does. 9. Presently I ascended to the hurricane-deck and cast a

longing glance toward the pilot-house. (Mark Twain.) 10. The Earl was their hero; but they were loyal subjects of the Queen. (Lytton Strachey.)

11. The memoranda must first be translated into French. 12. Crowds of country-folk had come into town with the produce of field and garden. (George Gissing.) 13. The Stanton Inn is one of the oldest hotels in America. 14. The Democratic party has a large majority in the Senate. 15. A few Democrats refused to vote for the amendment. 16. The endowment of the school has been increased by gifts from the alumni. 17. Mary was the daughter-in-law of the president of the corporation. 18. Every alumnus will receive an invitation to the dinner.

(A) Name the number and gender of each noun in the sentences above.

Exercise 2

(A) Place each of the following words in its proper class, and give the corresponding forms for the other genders.

	MASCULINE	FEMININE	COMMON
deer			✓
boy	✓		
duck			✓
hen		✓	
sheep			✓
cattle			✓
goose		✓	
pig			✓
mother		✓	
daughter		✓	

(B) Give the corresponding masculine or feminine form.

landlord	M	bachelor	M	SPINENGTER
aunt	F	actor	M	
bride	F	belle BEAU	F	GIANTIST
hero	M	giant	M	
monk	M	tiger	F	COUNTIST (BRITAIN)
widow	F	duke	M	
nephew	M	earl	M	MADAM
emperor	M	Sir	M	
alumnus	N	queen	F	
heir	F	witch	F	
sultan	M	knight	M	LADY

SULTANA

MADINA

CASE

9. Case is a property of a noun or pronoun which helps <u>to show the relation of the noun or pronoun to the other words in the sentence.</u>
Nouns have three cases.

(1) The **Nominative Case** is the case used primarily in the subject of a verb and in the predicate noun (see Secs. 18, 19).

The *man* spoke earnestly. WHO
John is a *broker*. WHAT

(2) The **Objective Case** is the case used primarily in the object of a verb or of a preposition (see Secs. 20–22).

The boy broke the *window*. WHAT
They came from the *city*. WHERE

(3) The **Possessive Case** is the case which normally denotes possession.

This is the *girl's* hat.

10. Forms. The three cases have the following forms.

	SINGULAR	PLURAL	SINGULAR	PLURAL
Nominative	boy	boys	man	men
Possessive	boy's	boys'	man's	men's
Objective	boy	boys	man	men

11. The Nominative and the Objective Cases. The nominative case and the objective case of a noun have the same form. Hence there can be no confusion in the use of these two, and the discussion of them is therefore reserved for the chapter on Pronouns, in which a careful distinction is necessary because the two cases frequently have different forms (see Sec. 40).

12. The Possessive Case. The possessive case of a noun is distinguished by the use of an apostrophe (').

(1) The possessive case of a singular noun is regularly formed by adding *'s* to the simple noun: as, *man's, horse's, boy's.*

(2) The possessive case of a plural noun is formed:

(a) By adding only an apostrophe to the simple plural, when the plural ends in *s:* as, *horses'* (simple plural, *horses*), *boys'* (simple plural, *boys*).

(b) By adding *'s,* as in the singular, when the simple plural does not end in *s:* as, *men's* (simple plural, *men*), *children's* (simple plural, *children*).

In a few singular nouns which end in *s* or an *s*-sound (like *ce*) only the apostrophe is added, just as in the plural: as, for *Jesus'* sake, for *conscience'* sake. This is especially true when, as in the preceding examples, other *s*-sounds precede or follow. It is not, however, incorrect to use the regular *'s* in such instances.

(3) In compound nouns and in groups of words having a unit idea the sign of the possessive case is added to the last member of the group: as, *father-in-law's, the Princess of Wales', the Queen of England's.*

13. The possessive case usually denotes possession.
   Harry's hat was lost.
   A crowd had gathered before the *mayor's* house.
Sometimes a modified kind of possession is indicated. For instance, in the expressions, "Ohm's law" and "Kipling's poems," Ohm and Kipling are the possessors only in the sense that they are the discoverers or originators. Compare the two sorts of possession shown in the sentence, "This is *John's* copy of *Whittier's* poems."

14. In some uses of the possessive case the idea of ownership is entirely lacking: as, a *day's* work; a *year's* salary; a *penny's* worth; the *law's* delays; a *hand's* breadth. These mean "the work *of a day*," "the salary *for a year*," etc.

15. A noun in the possessive case is usually equivalent to a phrase beginning with *of*. Thus we may say either "*Kipling's* poems" or "the poems *of Kipling*"; "the *lawyer's* papers" or "the papers of *the lawyer*"; "the *mayor's* house" or "the house *of the mayor*."
We would not, however, say "the book *of Mary*" for "*Mary's* book," or "the law *of Ohm*" for "*Ohm's* law." For such distinctions in usage the student must be guided by his feeling for the proper "sound" of the expression.

16. As a general rule the possessive case is not used with inanimate objects, a phrase with *of* being employed in its place: thus, "the roof *of the house*" (not "the *house's* roof"); "the branches *of the tree*" (not "the *tree's* branches"). The use of the possessive in expressions like "a *day's* work" (see Sec. 14) is an exception to this rule. Exceptions occur also in *time's delay, earth's surface, sun's heat, ship's mast*, etc.

Exercise 3

Give the possessive case, singular and plural, for the following nouns.

	SINGULAR	PLURAL
boy	*BOY*	*BOY'S*
child	*CHILD*	*CHILDERN*
goose	*GOOSE*	*GEESE*
deer	*DEER*	*DEER*
friend	*FRIEND*	*FRIENDS*
month	*MONTH*	*MOONTHS*
lady	*LADY*	*LADIES*
woman	*WOMAN*	*WOMEN*
family	*FAMILY*	*FAMILIES*
hero	*HERO*	*HERO'S*
wife	*WIFE*	*WIVES*
son-in-law	*SON-IN-LAW*	*SONS-IN-LAWS*
editor-in-chief	*EDITOR-IN-CHIEF* / *EDITORS-IN-CHIEF*	

THE PRINCIPAL USES OF NOUNS

17. The principal uses of a noun in a sentence are:

1. Subject of a Verb
2. Predicate Noun *~ Sub) ect/Comp*
3. Direct Object of a Verb
4. Indirect Object of a Verb
5. Object of a Preposition
6. Apposition
7. Objective Complement
8. Nominative Absolute
9. Direct Address

For some less common uses, see Secs. 28, 300 ff.

18. Subject of a Verb. A noun may be used as the Subject of a Verb.

The *army* retreated
The *train* was wrecked.
Here comes the *bride*.

The subject names the person or thing about which something is said by the verb.

In some sentences the subject follows the verb, as in the last example above.

19. Predicate Noun. A noun may be used as a Predicate Noun.

The king became a *tyrant*.
The postmaster is *John Smith*.
My uncle was a *captain*.
The man has turned *traitor*.

A predicate noun is normally placed after the verb; it answers the question *what?* or *who?* and it represents the same person or thing as the subject. Thus, in the examples given, "The king became *what?*"—Answer, a *tyrant*. "The postmaster is *who?*"—Answer, *John Smith*. The *tyrant* is the same person as the *king* (subject); *John Smith* is the same person as the *postmaster* (subject).

20. Direct Object of a Verb. A noun may be used as the Direct Object of a Verb.

> The boy wrote the *letter.*
> The assassin killed the *tyrant.*

The direct object names the receiver of the action indicated by the verb. It is normally placed after the verb; it answers the question *what?* or *whom?* and it represents a person or thing *different* from the subject. Thus, "The boy wrote *what?*"—Answer, a *letter.* "The assassin killed *whom?*"—Answer, the *tyrant.* The *letter* is *not* the same person or thing as *boy* (subject); the *tyrant* is *not* the same person as *assassin* (subject).

Both the predicate noun and the direct object of a verb answer the same question, *what?* or *who? (whom?)*. They are readily distinguished, however, by their relations with the subject: the predicate noun represents the *same* person or thing as the subject; the direct object represents a *different* person or thing. The only exception to the latter statement occurs in the use of a reflexive pronoun as the object of a verb (see Sec. 51).

The direct object sometimes precedes the subject and the verb.

> This *picture* we bought in Paris.

21. Indirect Object of a Verb. A noun may be used as the Indirect Object of a Verb.

> The boy wrote his *mother* a letter.
> John bought the *child* some candy.

The indirect object tells *to whom* or *to what, for whom* or *for what* something was done. In the first sentence given above, the direct object *letter* tells *what* the boy wrote, and the indirect object *mother* tells *to whom* he wrote it; in the second sentence, the direct object *candy* tells *what* John bought, and the indirect object *child* tells *for whom* he bought it.

A phrase introduced by the preposition *to* or *for* can be used instead of an indirect object. Thus the first sentence would become "The boy wrote a letter *to his mother";* the second sentence would become "John bought some candy *for the child."* With an indirect object, however, the *to* or *for* is never expressed in the sentence; if it were expressed, the noun would be the object of the preposition (see Sec. 22), and not an indirect object.

We may also classify as indirect objects certain nouns which are equivalent to *of whom* when used after the verb *ask*. Thus the sentence, "The employer asked the *clerk* a question," is equivalent to "The employer asked a question *of the clerk*." Here, however, the idea of *to* is also present, for asking something *of* a person implies addressing one's self *to* him.

22. Object of a Preposition. A noun may be used as the Object of a Preposition.

> The merchant sent the coffee to the *customer*.
> The travelers found shelter under a *tree*.
> The train came from *Atlanta*.

Here *customer, tree,* and *Atlanta* are the objects of the prepositions *to, under,* and *from,* respectively. (Prepositions are words like *of, before, at, over, beside, behind, through, for, in, into, on,* etc.)

The object of a preposition answers the question *what?* or *whom?* after the preposition: thus, "He asked for a *dollar*." For *what?*—Answer, a *dollar*.

23. In Apposition. A noun may be used in Apposition with another Noun.

> My friend, the *lawyer*, has just arrived.
> I saw the butcher, *Mr. Jones*.
> We next visited Washington, the *capital* of the United States.

A noun in apposition with another noun represents the same person or thing as the other noun: that is, it is another name for the same person or thing. In a combination of two nouns in this relation, the second one is said to be in apposition with the first, not the first with the second.

Note. A predicate noun and a noun in apposition with the subject both represent the same person or thing as the subject. They are distinguished by the fact that the predicate noun is connected with the subject by a verb.

> My friend is a *lawyer* (predicate noun).
> My friend, the *lawyer*, has arrived (apposition).

A noun in apposition may be separated from its related noun by a number of intervening words, if the connection between the two nouns is clear.

> A lone *house* stood in the clearing, a tiny *cabin* built of rough logs.

24. Objective Complement. A noun may be used as an Objective Complement.

> They made his father *colonel*.
> We elected John *president*.

The objective complement is so called because it is added to the direct object to complete the meaning expressed by the verb ("complement" means something that completes). Thus, in the sentence just given, they didn't make his *father:* they made his *father colonel.* A simple test is to see whether *to be* can be inserted between the direct object and the noun following: for example, "They made his father *to be* colonel." If *to be* can thus be inserted without changing the meaning of the sentence, the second noun is an objective complement.

The objective complement is commonly used with verbs expressing the idea of *making, electing, appointing, choosing,* and similar ideas, but it sometimes occurs after other verbs.

> They considered the man a *genius.*
> We found the boy a raving *maniac.*

25. Nominative Absolute. A noun may be used Absolutely with a Participle, to form the so-called Nominative Absolute construction.

> The *time having come,* we went to the meeting.
> The *work being* easy, we soon finished it.
> He sprang from his chair, his *eyes flashing* with anger.

For the present, it is sufficient to say that a participle is a verb form ending in *-ing,* such as *being* or *having,* although later we shall have to modify that definition. The nominative absolute construction consists of a noun followed by a participle.

When a noun used absolutely with a participle is placed at the beginning of a sentence, it must be carefully distinguished from a noun used as the subject of the verb.

For example, in the sentence, "The guests being hungry, dinner was served," *guests* is in the nominative absolute construction with the participle *being,* and *dinner* is the subject of the verb *was served.* On the other hand, in "The guests, being hungry, took their places at the table," *guests* is not in the nominative absolute construction: it is the subject of the sentence (subject of the verb *took*).

Note. The word *absolute,* as used here, means "free" or "loose." The noun in a Nominative Absolute construction is "free" from the regular uses of a noun in a sentence, such as subject or object of a verb.

26. Direct Address. A noun may be used in Direct Address.

> *Harry,* it is time for dinner.
> This incident, my *friends,* must not be ignored.

John, come here.
Boys, listen to me.

Here *Harry, friends, John,* and *boys* are the names or words by which the persons are addressed. These nouns are not the subjects of the verbs. The subject in the first sentence is *it;* in the second, *incident;* in the third and fourth the subject is *you* understood (the subject is usually omitted in a direct command, since it is always *you*). With the third example compare "John comes here every day"—in which *John* is the subject.

Notice that a word in direct address is set off by a comma or commas.

27. Any word having one of these nine uses in a sentence is a noun or noun-equivalent in that sentence, although it may be another part of speech in another sentence.

Are is a verb.
He misspelled *among.*
The *poor* are always with us.

In the first sentence *are,* which is ordinarily a verb, is a noun-equivalent, for it is the subject of the verb *is.* In the second, the preposition *among* is a noun-equivalent, because it is the object of the verb. In the third, *poor*—regularly an adjective—is a noun-equivalent, the subject of the verb.

28. **Nouns Used as Other Parts of Speech.** Some words which are ordinarily nouns may be used:

(1) As Adverbs (adverb-equivalents), to denote *time, place, measure,* etc.

The ship sails *tomorrow.*
The clerk went *home.*
He walked a *mile.*

In origin these words are nouns, since they are names of things; but in these sentences they are used as adverbs (any word which tells *when, where, how, how much,* or *how far* is an adverb—see Sec. 174).

(2) As Adjectives (adjective-equivalents)—see Sec. 86.

This is the *girl's* hat
It happened on *Monday* night.

Exercise 4

Give the use of each noun (subject of a verb, object of a preposition, and the other uses in Secs. 17–28).

1. Few voters will endorse the platform of the new party. 2. This picture is a reproduction of Reynolds' famous painting. 3. The next few months showed me strange things. (Mark Twain.) 4. The president appointed Henry Adams secretary of the delegation. 5. During the past year, gentlemen, little progress has been made by the committee. 6. The morrow, being fairly fine, found Elizabeth-Jane again in the churchyard. (Thomas Hardy.) 7. The audience gave the distinguished visitor a hearty welcome. 8. Man is priest, and scholar, and statesman, and producer, and soldier. (R. W. Emerson.) 9. This plan having failed, some new measure must be devised. 10. The movement of settlers toward Dakota had now become an exodus, a stampede. (Hamlin Garland.)

11. Yesterday, they awarded the corporal a medal for bravery. 12. Hardy pedestrians leaned against the gale, their heavy coats flapping about them. (Edgar Lee Masters.) 13. You should remember, Fred, that knowledge is power. 14. Literature leaves her footsteps not on the sands, but on the quicksands of time. (John Galsworthy.) 15. Power companies build dams for one purpose—power. (Stuart Chase.) 16. Next year, Congress should make this vast area a national park. 17. The place had become home to him in the last three years. (Rudyard Kipling.) 18. Only occasionally are these accidents reported to the police. 19. His assistant, a newcomer in the organization, was responsible for the mistake. 20. Our preparations being completed, we sailed the next morning for the South Seas.

21. The coaches voted Jim Grove, the quarterback, the most valuable player on the team. 22. The class meets every Thursday at 2 o'clock. 23. The statute allows the complainant two alternatives. 24. Books are the treasured wealth of the world and the fit inheritance of generations and nations. (Henry Thoreau.) 25. In the anteroom sat two men in civilian clothes, evidently reporters for the morning papers. 26. Paris a man may understand thoroughly with a reasonable amount of study. (Arthur Machen.) 27. His parents named the boy Henry, in honor of his grandfather. 28. Only four or five houses, mostly humble shepherd dwellings, were visible in that wide circuit. (John Burroughs.) 29. With riches has come inexcusable waste. (Woodrow Wilson.) 30. Quincy is a notable example—a brisk, handsome, well-ordered city. (Mark Twain.)

Exercise 5

(A) Make original sentences showing uses of nouns as indicated (a separate sentence for each use).

1. Use *messenger* as: (a) subject of a verb; (b) direct object of a verb; (c) indirect object of a verb.

2. Use *evening* as: (a) nominative absolute; (b) object of a preposition.

3. Use *brother* in: (a) direct address; (b) apposition with a direct object; (c) apposition with a subject; (d) nominative absolute.

4. Use *member* as: (a) objective complement; (b) predicate noun; (c) indirect object of a verb.

5. Use *Saturday* as: (a) adjective; (b) adverb.

(B) Make *one* sentence containing different nouns used as subject; direct object of a verb; indirect object of a verb; in apposition; as object of a preposition.

(C) Make *one* sentence containing different nouns used as subject; predicate noun; nominative absolute; in direct address.

(D) Make *one* sentence containing different nouns used as subject; direct object of a verb; objective complement; adverb.

Chapter II ⭐ PRONOUNS

29. A Pronoun is a word used for a noun.

Its most common use is as a substitute word employed to prevent the awkward repetition of a noun.

Take, for instance, "John asked *his* mother to send *him* the book *which he* left in *his* room." If there were no pronouns, we should have to say, "John asked *John's* mother to send *John* the book, the *book John* left in *John's* room." The advantage gained by the use of the pronouns is obvious.

30. Antecedent of a Pronoun. The noun for which the pronoun stands is called the Antecedent of the pronoun.

Thus in the sentence given above, *John* is the antecedent of *his, him, he,* and *his;* and *book* is the antecedent of *which.*

"Antecedent" is derived from the Latin and means "going before."

The antecedent may be compound: that is, it may consist of two or more nouns.

Bring the *book* and the *tablet* if you find *them.*

31. A pronoun may also be used as the antecedent of another pronoun.

He who hesitates is lost (*he* is the antecedent of *who*).

Everyone will do *his* best (*everyone* is the antecedent of *his*).

32. Classes of Pronouns. Pronouns are divided into the following classes.

Personal Pronouns: *"He* knew *their* names." *"We* sent *you* the telegram."

Relative Pronouns: "John met the man *who* was here." "Here is the purse *which* was lost."

Interrogative Pronouns: *"What* was the answer?" *"Who* was the first speaker?"

Demonstrative Pronouns: *"That* is the best book." *"These* are the largest apples."

Indefinite Pronouns: *"Anything* will satisfy the boys." *"Somebody* must do the work."

33. **Properties and Uses of Pronouns.** Pronouns have Person, Number, Gender, and Case. With the exception of a few details, especially in matters of form, what has been said of Number, Gender, and Case of Nouns applies to Pronouns also.

Pronouns have, in general, the same uses as Nouns (see Sec. 17).

PERSONAL PRONOUNS

34. The Personal Pronouns are *I, you, he, she,* and *it,* together with their various forms for indicating the following properties.

First, second, and third person.
Singular and plural number.
Masculine, feminine, and neuter gender.
Nominative, possessive, and objective case.

	FIRST PERSON	SECOND PERSON	THIRD PERSON		
	MASC. OR FEM.	MASC. OR FEM.	MASC.	FEM.	NEUT.
		Singular Number			
Nom.	I	you	he	she	it
Poss.	my, mine	your, yours	his	her, hers	its
Obj.	me	you	him	her	it
		Plural Number			
Nom.	we	you		they	
Poss.	our, ours	your, your ҷ.		their, theirs	
Obj.	us	you		them	

The older second person forms, *thou, thy* or *thine, thee,* and *ye,* which were formerly in common use, belong to the so-called "solemn" style and are now employed rarely except in prayer and poetry. In ordinary speech they have been supplanted by the forms, *you, your* or *yours, you.*

Person

35. Personal pronouns are divided into three grammatical "persons" according to the relation existing between the individual who is speaking and the individual or thing to which the pronoun refers.

(1) The **First Person** indicates the *person speaking:* as, *I, me, we, us,* etc.

(2) The **Second Person** indicates the *person or thing spoken to:* as, *you, your, yours.*

(3) The **Third Person** indicates the *person or thing spoken of:* as, *he, she, it, him, her,* etc.

Note. Nouns also have three grammatical persons.

First Person: I, *Frank Brown,* have sworn to this statement.
Second Person: William, open the door.
Third Person: The *road* is rough.

NUMBER

36. The **First Person** pronouns in the singular number (*I, my, mine, me*) are used by the speaker in referring to himself.

The first person pronouns in the plural number (*we, our, ours, us*) are used by the speaker in referring to himself and some other person or persons with whom he is associated in a particular action: he is the speaker for the group.

The use of the so-called "editorial *we*" by editorial writers ("*we* believe," "*we* think," instead of "*I* believe," "*I* think") is based on the idea that the writer is supposedly expressing not his own opinions, but those of the organization and staff which he represents.

37. The **Second Person** pronoun has the same forms for both the singular and plural numbers: *you, your, yours, you.*

Since *you* was originally a plural form, the plural verb is always used when it is the subject, even when only one person is addressed: thus, "You *were* alone," never "You *was* alone."

38. The **Third Person** pronouns, as we have seen, have the same form in the plural for all genders: *they, their* or *theirs, them.*

GENDER

39. In the **First** and **Second Persons** there is no change in form to indicate gender, and the pronouns *I, me, we, us, you,* etc., are of masculine or feminine gender according to whether the persons or things to which they refer are male or female, respectively.

I am John (masculine).
I am Mary (feminine).
You are big boys (masculine).
You are big girls (feminine).

In the **Third Person** there are different pronouns for the different genders in the singular number—*he, she,* and *it,* with their various forms, being used when the person or thing spoken of is male, female, or without sex, respectively. In the plural, the forms are the same for all the genders.

Note. It is often used in referring to animals or to very small children, although they are male or female. See also Sec. 345 (6).

CASE AND USE

40. Most of the personal pronouns have different forms for the nominative, possessive, and objective cases.

NOMINATIVE	POSSESSIVE	OBJECTIVE
I	my, mine	me
we	our, ours	us
you	your, yours	you
he	his	him
she	her, hers	her
it	its	it
they	their, theirs	them

The proper form to employ is determined by the way the pronoun is used in the sentence (pronouns have the same uses as nouns; see Sec. 17).

41. A Nominative Case form (*I, we, you, he, she, it, they*) must be employed when the pronoun is used:

(1) As the subject of a verb.
He is coming.
They were in the city.

(2) As a predicate pronoun (the same construction as a predicate noun; see Sec. 19).
That man is *he.*
It is *I.*
It was *they.*

It is incorrect to use the objective case in these constructions. Do not say "That man is *him,*" or "It is *me.*"

(3) In apposition with the subject of a verb or with a predicate noun.
John Smith—*he* of whom I have already spoken—was the leader of the colonists.
The man was John Rolfe, *he* who later married Pocahontas.

(4) In the Nominative Absolute construction.
They having arrived at last, the conference was resumed.

(5) In direct address.
Now, *you* leaders, what is to be done?

42. An **Objective Case** form (*me, us, you, him, her, it, them*) must be employed when the pronoun is used:

(1) As the direct object of a verb.
The officer saw *us.*
A friend met *him.*

(2) As the indirect object of a verb.
The clerk gave *me* the book.
We sent *them* some flowers.

(3) As the object of a preposition.
I have a letter from *him.*
We waited for *them.*
They spoke to John and *me* (not *I*).

(4) In apposition with an object of a verb or of a preposition.
There they found Black Hawk—*him* and his band of Indians.

Note. Theoretically, a pronoun used as an objective complement would also be in the objective case, but in practice the objective complement is seldom a personal pronoun.

43. The **Possessive Case** of pronouns, like that of nouns, denotes possession.

The shorter possessive forms—*my, our, your, her,* and *their*—are used when a noun follows: as, "This is *my* book."

The longer forms—*mine, ours, yours, hers,* and *theirs*—are used when there is no noun following: as, "This book is *mine.*" (In older English and in poetry the longer forms also occur before nouns: as, "*Mine* eyes have seen the glory of the coming of the Lord.")

The possessive case of personal pronouns does not have an apostrophe: thus, *its, hers, theirs.* The form *it's* is not a possessive case, but is the contraction for *it is:* as, "*It's* a good book." Compare, "The company has lost *its* franchise" (possessive case).

44. **Case after "Than" and "As."** The case of the pronoun after *than* and *as* in comparisons requires especial attention. Shall we say, for example, "He is as strong as *I*," or "He is as strong as *me*"; "He is stronger than *I*," or "He is stronger than *me*"? These are elliptical constructions (see Chapter XII), and the proper form of the pronoun can be readily determined by expanding the sentence to its complete form. Thus the preceding sentences mean "He is as strong as *I* (am)," "He is stronger than *I* (am)." The form *I* is correct because it is the subject of the verb *am*.

Again, the sentence, "He visits John oftener than *me*," means "He visits John oftener than (he visits) *me*," in which *me* is correct because it is the object of the verb *visits*.

AGREEMENT BETWEEN PRONOUN AND ANTECEDENT

45. A pronoun must agree with its antecedent in person, number, and gender—but not in case.

This rule means, for example, that if the antecedent is in the third person, singular number, and feminine gender, the pronoun which refers to it must also be in the third person, singular number, feminine gender: thus, "The *girl* said that *she* had been studying *her* lesson." Compare, "The *boy* said that *he* had been studying *his* lesson" (third person, singular number, masculine gender).

Note the agreement in the following examples.

ANTECEDENT	PRONOUNS
girl	she, her, hers, herself
boy	he, his, him, himself
tree	it, its, itself
girls, boys, trees	they, their, theirs, them, themselves
(I—the speaker)	I, my, mine, me, myself
(you—the person spoken to)	you, your, yours, yourself, yourselves

46. The case of a pronoun is not influenced by the case of the antecedent: it is determined solely by the use of the pronoun in the sentence —as subject of a verb, object of a verb, etc. (see Secs. 41–43).

47. The antecedent of a personal pronoun may be in a sentence preceding the one in which the pronoun occurs: "The *boys* will come tomorrow. Be sure to wait for *them*."

Note. The pronouns *I* and *you* are regularly used without an expressed antecedent. *I* can refer only to the speaker, and *you* refers to the person who is addressed; hence a definite antecedent is not needed in the sentence. In conversation the other personal pronouns may also be used without an expressed antecedent, when the person or thing referred to is designated by a gesture, a look, or some other means: "Look at *him*." "Give the book to *her*."

COMPOUND PERSONAL PRONOUNS

48. The Compound Personal Pronouns are made by adding *-self* or *-selves* to the proper forms of the simple pronouns.

In the first and second persons the additions are made to the possessive case: *myself, ourselves, yourself, yourselves.* In the third person they are made to the objective case: *himself, herself, itself, themselves.* The forms *hisself* and *theirselves* are incorrect and illiterate.

Case

49. The case of the simple pronoun to which the suffix is added has nothing to do with the case of the completed compound pronoun.

Thus, although the suffix is added to the possessive case in the first and second persons, the resulting compound forms are never in the possessive case; they are either nominative or objective, depending upon their use in the sentence.

> I *myself* will bring the package (nominative—in apposition with the subject *I*).
> I deceived *myself* (objective—object of the verb).

Similarly, the third person forms, made from the objective case of the simple pronouns, may be either nominative or objective, depending upon their use in the sentence.

> He *himself* will go (nominative—in apposition with the subject).
> She saw the manager *himself* (objective—in apposition with the object, *manager*).

Uses of Compound Personal Pronouns

50. The compound personal pronouns have two uses.

51. Reflexive. In this use the action performed by the subject of the verb is *reflected* or comes back to the subject.

> He struck *himself* (direct object).
> They addressed the letters to *themselves* (object of a preposition).
> She bought *herself* some flowers (indirect object).

When a reflexive pronoun is the object of a verb, we have the only exception to the rule in Sec. 20: the reflexive pronoun, although it is the object of the verb, represents the same person as the subject. We know that it is the object because it names the receiver of the action.

Note. In older English and in colloquial modern English the simple pronouns are also used reflexively: as, "Now I lay *me* down to sleep." "I made *me* a sled." "He bought *him* an overcoat." "I looked about *me*." (In the last example, *me* is the regular form.)

52. Emphatic. In this use the compound pronoun adds emphasis to a pronoun or noun already named.

> I *myself* will go.
> They gave it to Henry *himself*.

These emphatic pronouns are in apposition with the preceding noun or pronoun.

(a) A somewhat different emphatic use is shown in the following sentences.

> This mistake, of *itself*, is not serious.
> He doesn't act like *himself*.
> They did the work by *themselves*.

Exercise 6

Give the case of each personal pronoun; and tell why that case is correct.

1. A jungle moon first showed me my beach. (William Beebe.) 2. Her loyalty made her an invaluable friend. 3. He, being the oldest of the group, was elected captain. 4. He being the oldest of the group, we elected him captain. 5. He might say something about it to her, hours later. (H. M. Tomlinson.) 6. Their servants were kept out, but they themselves were admitted. (Lytton Strachey.) 7. That is she sitting at the right of her father. 8. He asked me my opinion about them. (R. H. Dana.) 9. They have conferred with only two of their friends—you and me. 10. We wrapped ourselves in our blankets, and sat down by the fire. (F. Parkman.)

11. It was I who found it—not he. 12. You are at least two years older than she. 13. Have you heard the news about Harry and me? 14. John was surprised that the committee had selected Fred rather than him. 15. Every one of them talked about leaving the world a little better than he had found it. (Carl Van Doren.) 16. I sat me down and stared at the house of Shaws. (R. L. Stevenson.) 17. We sat rather silent through the meal—Mahon, the old couple, and I. (Joseph Conrad.) 18. Frank has as many friends as I. 19. If I were he, I would not go to the Convention. 20. The leaders themselves know that it is an impractical plan.

Exercise 7

Supply the proper case form of the pronoun; and tell why that case is correct.

1. Each problem was checked by the instructor and _____ (I, me).
2. The superintendent and _____ should have arranged for the meeting (she, her).
3. He will give it to either Fred or _____ (I, me).
4. The party consisted of _____ four and the guide (we, us).
5. No one was more surprised than _____ (I, me).
6. It surprised no one more than _____ (he, him).
7. They met Frank and _____ at the bank (I, me).
8. If you were _SHE_, where would you go? (she, her).
9. The choice lies between you and _____ (I, me).
10. This book has given my sister and _____ a great deal of pleasure (I, me).
11. It was _____ who gave us the invitation (they, them).
12. You can do it as well as _____ (he, him).
13. _____ girls were all invited to the party (we, us).
14. It was _____ girls who made the candy (we, us).
15. They will call for _____ girls at nine o'clock (we, us).
16. There were only two persons—Jack Arnold and _____ —in the room (I, me).
17. Who is there? It is _____ (I, me).
18. You had the same chance as _____ and _____ (he, him) (I, me).
19. It must have been _HE_, not _I_, whom they suspected (he, him) (I, me).
20. Habitual offenders such as _____ should not be paroled (they, them).
21. She seems much older than _____ (he, him).
22. I saw _____ and his brother going to work this morning (he, him).
23. Let's you and _____ go to the opera tonight (I, me). (See Sec. 330.)

Exercise 8

Give the person, number, and gender of each personal pronoun in Exercise 6.

RELATIVE PRONOUNS

53. A Relative Pronoun is both a connecting word and a reference word.

(1) As a **connective**, it introduces a clause—that is, a group of words having a subject and a verb—and connects that clause with the antecedent of the pronoun.

(2) As a **reference word,** a relative pronoun refers to and stands for

its antecedent, and thus makes the repetition of the antecedent unnecessary. The relative will therefore either be the subject of the verb in the clause which it introduces, or have one of the other uses of a noun in the clause.

Thus, in "John found the book *which* was lost," the relative pronoun *which* connects the clause *which was lost* with the antecedent *book,* and is used instead of *book* as the subject of the verb *was lost.* In the sentence, "This is the man *whom* you saw," the relative pronoun *whom* is both a connective and the object of the verb *saw.*

54. Notice that a relative pronoun is always accompanied by its own clause which has a subject and verb separate from the main subject and verb of the sentence.

For example, the sentence, "I bought the horse *which* you sold," contains the main subject and verb, *I bought,* and also another subject and verb, *you sold,* following the relative pronoun *which.*

55. Classes of Relative Pronouns. There are two classes of relative pronouns: Simple and Compound.

(1) The **Simple Relative Pronouns** are *who, which,* and *that.*

(2) The **Compound Relative Pronouns** are *what,* and combinations made by adding *-ever* and *-soever* to *who, which,* and *what:* thus, *whoever, whosoever; whosever, whosesoever; whomever, whomsoever; whichever, whichsoever; whatever, whatsoever.* In older English *whoso* was also commonly used as a compound relative pronoun.

Note. What is usually classed among the simple relative pronouns.*It has the form of a simple relative, but is like the compound relatives in that it does not have an expressed antecedent (see Sec. 68). Since the latter characteristic is more significant than the form, it seems advisable to include the word among the compound relatives.

SIMPLE RELATIVE PRONOUNS

Antecedent

56. The three simple relative pronouns, *who, which,* and *that,* regularly have an antecedent expressed in the sentence. This antecedent may be a noun or a pronoun.

> He *who* runs may read.
> The *lion which* escaped has been captured.

This man will accept *anything that* you give him.

Unlike personal pronouns (see Sec. 47), a relative pronoun is regularly in the same sentence with its antecedent, and the antecedent usually stands immediately before the pronoun.

Note. Which sometimes refers to a whole statement as an antecedent if the connection is clear: as, *"The night was dark, which* made the journey dangerous." This construction, though often condemned, is occasionally used by good writers. Frequently, in order to avoid this form, a noun which sums up the whole statement is inserted as the antecedent: "The night was dark, a *condition* which made the journey dangerous."

Person, Number, and Gender

57. A relative pronoun agrees with its antecedent in person, number, and gender. The form of the relative pronoun itself does not change for these different properties, and they are determined by referring to the antecedent. It is necessary, however, for a writer to know the person and number of each relative in order that he may use the correct form of the verb with it. The verb will be the same as would be used with the antecedent.

Take, for example, the sentences:
I who *am* here will do the work.
They who *are* here will do the work.

In the first sentence the antecedent is *I*, which is in the first person, singular number; the relative therefore has the same person and number, and requires the verb *am*. In the second, the antecedent *they* is in the third person, plural number, and the pronoun therefore requires the verb *are*.

Gender does not affect the use of the pronoun or the form of the verb; hence it needs no further discussion. There is, however, a suggestion of gender in the principles governing the use of *who, which,* and *that* (see Sec. 66).

Case and Use

58. The simple relative pronouns have the following case forms, which are the same for both singular and plural numbers.

Nominative	who	which	that
Possessive	whose	(of which) (whose)	——
Objective	whom	which	that

Who is the only one of these pronouns which changes its form for the different cases.

Which has the same form for the nominative and objective cases. It has no regular form for the possessive case, the phrase *of which* being used instead. Sometimes, however, *whose,* the possessive case of *who,* is borrowed and employed as the·corresponding form of *which.* Thus we may say either "A law the effects *of which* are so far-reaching should not be repealed," or "A law *whose* effects are so far-reaching should not be repealed."

Note that the possessive case is used more freely with pronouns than with nouns in referring to inanimate objects (see Sec. 16).

That does not change its form and is not used in the possessive case.

59. The case of a relative pronoun does not depend upon the case of the antecedent, but is determined entirely by the use of the pronoun in the clause which it introduces.

I met him *who* was here.
I met him *whom* you sent.
I met him of *whom* you spoke.
I met him *whose* house was burned.

In all these sentences *him,* the antecedent of the pronouns, is in the objective case because it is the object of the verb *met.* In the first sentence, however, the relative pronoun *who* is in the nominative case because it is the subject of the verb *was* in its own clause. In the second and third sentences *whom* is in the objective case because it is the object of the verb *sent* and the object of the preposition *of,* respectively. In the fourth sentence *whose* is in the possessive case because it indicates possession of *house,* a word in its own clause.

60. The **Nominative Case** is used with the subject of a verb.

This is the student *who* won the prize.
They recovered the purse *which* was lost.
The crew were rescued from the ship *that* was torpedoed.

61. The **Objective Case** is used:
(1) With the direct object of a verb.

He is the opponent *whom* you defeated.
He mailed the letter *which* he had written.
A man is judged by the books *that* he reads.

(2) With the object of a preposition.
> They met the agent from *whom* they bought the land.
> This is the letter to *which* you refer.
> He gets everything *that* he strives for.

62. The Possessive Case is used to denote possession.
> The enemy surrounded the company *whose* captain had been killed.

Note. Compound Relative Pronouns may also be used as predicate nouns (pronouns) in the nominative case: *"Whoever* the man was, he deserved a reward."

MISCELLANEOUS FEATURES

63. Determining the Use of a Relative Pronoun. It will be noticed that the relative pronoun—whatever its use may be—generally stands at the beginning of the clause which it introduces. The normal order of any sentence or clause is subject + verb + object + various other elements. Therefore, if the relative pronoun is the subject of the verb, it stands in the regular position for the subject—at the beginning of the clause—and its use is readily seen.

If the relative pronoun is not the subject, the student will find it helpful, in determining the use of the pronoun, to rearrange the clause so that the subject comes first, then the verb, then the rest of the clause, with the relative pronoun in its natural place.

For example, take the sentence, "This is the man *whom* you sent": rearranged, the clause becomes "you sent *whom*," in which *whom* is easily recognized as the object of the verb. Again, "This is the book *that* you sent for": rearranged, the clause becomes "you sent for *that*," in which *that* is clearly the object of the preposition *for*.

When a relative pronoun is the object of a preposition, the preposition is often placed at the beginning of the clause and before the pronoun: as, "He is the teacher *to whom* I referred." Rearranged, the clause would read, "I referred to *whom*."

64. Special attention should be given to the case of relative pronouns in clauses which contain parenthetical expressions like *we thought, they believed, she said.* Compare:
> He is the man *who* we thought should be censured.
> He is the man *whom* we thought you should censure.

In the first sentence *who* is the subject of the verb *should be censured,* and is therefore in the nominative case.

In the second sentence *whom* is the object of the verb *should censure,*
and the objective case form is therefore correct. The subject of the
verb is *you.*

65. Omission of the Relative Pronoun. Sometimes the relative pronoun is not expressed; it is then said to be "understood."

This is the book $\wedge$ you need (*that* is omitted before *you*).
He is a man $\wedge$ we all admire (*whom* is omitted).

66. Distinction in the use of "Who," "Which," and "That."
(1) *Who* is used with an antecedent denoting a person.
The general *who* was victorious.
The lawyer *whom* the prisoner selected.
(2) *Which* is used with an antecedent denoting anything except a
person.
The flower *which* is fragrant.
The rain *which* had fallen.
The horse *which* is lame.
The machine *which* is broken.
(3) *That* may be used with either persons or things.
The clerk *that* was late.
The water *that* flows by the mill.
See also Sec. 314.

COMPOUND RELATIVE PRONOUNS

67. The Compound Relative Pronouns are *what* (see Sec. 55, note),
whoever, whosoever (with their various case forms), *whichever, whichsoever, whatever,* and *whatsoever.*

ANTECEDENT

68. The Compound Relative Pronouns ordinarily have no antecedent
expressed in the sentence, but contain their own antecedents. Thus
what, whichever, and *whatever* (with corresponding forms in *-soever*)
are equivalent to *that which* (plural, *those which*): that is, they are
equivalent to the demonstrative pronoun *that* plus the relative pronoun
which, the former being the antecedent of the relative. Similarly, *whoever* is equivalent to *he who* (plural, *they who*)—the personal pronoun
he used as the antecedent, followed by the relative pronoun *who.*

For example, the sentence, "Tell me *what* you want," may be expressed as,

"Tell me *that which* you want." The sentence, "Take *whichever* is the best," may become "Take *that which* is the best." "*Whoever* wishes may go," is equivalent to "*He who* wishes may go."

Note. In some sentences the antecedent is expressed. Thus, in "*Whoever* brings the book, *he* will be paid," *he* is the antecedent of *whoever*. In these instances the antecedent frequently follows the pronoun.

Case and Use

69. *Whoever* and *whosoever* are the only compound relative pronouns that change their form for the different cases.

Nominative	whoever	whosoever
Possessive	whosever	whosesoever
Objective	whomever	whomsoever

What, whichever, whichsoever, whatever, and *whatsoever* have the same forms for the nominative and objective cases and have no possessive form.

70. The case of a compound relative pronoun, like that of a simple relative pronoun, is determined by the use of the pronoun in its own clause.

Tell it to *whoever* will listen.
Tell it to *whomever* you meet.
Give the book to *whomever* you wish.
I will help him, *whoever* he may be.

In the first sentence, *whoever* is in the nominative case because it is the subject of the verb *will listen.* It is not the object of the preposition *to.* The whole clause, *whoever will listen,* is the object of the preposition (see Sec. 227 (4)).

In the second sentence, *whomever* is in the objective case because it is the object of the verb *meet.* It is not the object of the preposition *to.*

In the third sentence, *whomever* is in the objective case because it is the object of a preposition *to* "understood," not the *to* expressed in the sentence: "Give the book to *whomever* you wish (to give the book *to*)."

In the last sentence, *whoever* is in the nominative case because it is a predicate pronoun after the verb *may be.* Note that here the predicate pronoun precedes the subject instead of following the verb.

Exercise 9

Give the case of each relative pronoun; and tell why it is in that case (find the clause which the relative introduces, and see how it is used in that clause). Point out the antecedents of the simple relative pronouns.

1. The lawyer who represented the defendant was reprimanded by the judge. 2. I spent the day with some of the crew whom I found quietly at work in the forecastle. (R. H. Dana.) 3. The house that he bought is on a dingy side street. 4. The man whom we honor today is your neighbor and mine. 5. The room in which the boys were fed was a large stone hall. (Charles Dickens.) 6. She did not volunteer the reason which he seemed to hope for, and he wished her good night. (Thomas Hardy.) 7. What they do will depend on future developments. 8. A reward will be given to whoever returns the purse. 9. Help is offered to whomever we consider worthy. 10. It is he who is to blame for the accident.

11. The six sonnets that accompany Longfellow's translation of Dante are all perfect. (John Macy.) 12. The evil that men do lives after them. 13. He is a man who we thought would make a good mayor. 14. One morning, however, he was disagreeably surprised by a visit from the professor, whom he had scarcely thought of for whole weeks. (Nathaniel Hawthorne.) 15. He suggested the name of a student whom he believed the committee had overlooked. 16. He is a man whose judgment is sound. 17. They left the hut for whoever might want it. (H. M. Tomlinson.) 18. Whoever they are, they must be found and notified. 19. Whatever she does, she does it well. 20. The men you move among will do that for you. (Rudyard Kipling.) 21. As he approached the village he met a number of people, but none whom he knew. (Washington Irving.) 22. The offense had been committed by a person whom he had considered a friend. 23. The shortest days they know are those they see when passing through the tropics. (*Scientific Monthly.*)

Exercise 10

Supply the proper case form of the relative pronoun; and tell why it is correct (because it is the subject of a verb, object of a verb, object of a preposition, etc.).

1. The candidate _____ the president endorsed was defeated (who, whom).
2. They recognized him as an opponent _____ they must reckon with sooner or later (who, whom).
3. A prospectus will be sent to anyone _____ asks for it (who, whom).
4. The party will accept _____ the leaders appoint (whoever, whomever).
5. The prisoner _____ we thought the governor had pardoned, was still in the penitentiary (who, whom).

6. The prime minister is the man ———— they believe is responsible for the treaty (who, whom).
7. The winner, ———— he may be, will then enter the national contest (whoever, whomever).
8. Give the letter to the girl ———— you see at the first desk (who, whom).
9. Their case was tried before a judge ———— they thought was prejudiced (who, whom).
10. Every person ———— they asked about has been identified (who, whom).
11. She had a number of friends in Chicago ———— she was visiting (who, whom).
12. Places will be reserved for ———— is invited (whoever, whomever).
13. Places will be reserved for ———— you invite (whoever, whomever).
14. The butler was a Russian ———— we were told had been a member of the nobility (who, whom).
15. ———— he was, he should be punished (whoever, whomever).
16. ———— they select, we must vote for him (whoever, whomever).
17. He is the sort of person ———— everybody thinks is honest (who, whom).
18. He is the sort of person ———— the newspapers call "Honest John" (who, whom).
19. The naturalist ———— the flower was named for was born in Sweden (who, whom).
20. The two men ———— we considered the most logical candidates were defeated (who, whom).

Exercise 11

Give the person, number, and gender of each relative pronoun in Exercise 9.

Exercise 12

Supply the proper relative pronoun, *who, which,* or *that* (see Sec. 66; also be sure to see Sec. 314).

1. The name ———— he gave is not in the directory.
2. Every person ———— believes in democracy should go to the polls and vote.
3. John Darrow, ———— invented the device, is the manager of the shoe factory.
4. To the west are the Rockies, ———— protect the valley from the ocean winds.

5. These are some of the words _____ you mispronounce.
6. The city _____ has the fewest accidents will be awarded the safety medal.
7. The official _____ you inquired about is not in the city.
8. We have found only a few voters _____ are in favor of the proposed ordinance.
9. His first novel, _____ was published in 1932, was a story about life in New Zealand.
10. The dinner was given in honor of President Allen, _____ was completing his twentieth year as head of the college.
11. The storm _____ swept the city yesterday was the cause of much suffering.

INTERROGATIVE PRONOUNS

71. The Interrogative Pronouns are used in asking questions. They are three in number: *who, which,* and *what.*

72. Antecedent. An interrogative pronoun does not have an antecedent expressed in the sentence.

73. Case. *Who* has the following case forms.

Nominative	who
Possessive	whose
Objective	whom

Which and *what* have the same form for the nominative and objective cases, and have no possessive form.

74. The case of an interrogative pronoun, like that of other pronouns, is determined by its use in the sentence—as subject, object of a verb, etc.

Who found the book? (nominative case—subject of the verb).
Who was John Smith? (nominative case—predicate pronoun).
Whose is that? (possessive case—denoting possession).
Whom do you want? (objective case—object of the verb).
Whom did you give it to? (objective case—object of the preposition).

75. Position in the Sentence. The interrogative pronoun is generally placed at the beginning of the sentence, even when it is a predicate pronoun or the object of the verb. When it is the object of a preposition, however, the preposition frequently precedes it: as, "From *whom* did you get the news?" (In conversation and informal writing a preposition is often placed at the end of a sentence.)

76. Interrogative Pronouns in Indirect Questions. Interrogative pronouns are used in indirect questions, as well as in direct questions: "Tell me *whom* you saw." "I asked him *what* he wanted." In an indirect question the thought of a direct question is expressed in a form somewhat different from that actually used by the speaker. It generally occurs after verbs like *ask, tell, wonder,* etc. Thus, "Tell me *whom* you saw" is the indirect form for the direct question, "*Whom* did you see?" The interrogation point is omitted after an indirect question.

77. Distinction between Relative and Interrogative Pronouns. *Who, which,* and *what* may be either relative or interrogative pronouns. In direct questions the interrogative pronoun is easily recognized. In indirect questions, also, the classification of *who* and *which* offers little difficulty, for as relatives these pronouns will have antecedents, as interrogatives they will not.

Give me the book *which* you selected (relative).

Tell me *which* you selected (interrogative).

Since *what* does not have an expressed antecedent either as a relative or as an interrogative, the classification will be determined by whether or not a question is implied.

I told you *what* he did (relative).

I asked you *what* he said (interrogative).

Exercise 13

Give the case of each interrogative pronoun, and tell why it is in that case (subject of a verb, etc.).

1. Whom did you ask for at the office? 2. Who was the last person that was in the room? 3. What were they doing when you saw them? 4. Whom can we select that will be acceptable to both factions? 5. Who won first prize in the Irish sweepstakes last month? 6. Whose book did you read first? 7. Whom did you say that you met in London? 8. They would not tell us whom they had seen entering the garage. 9. You must decide for yourself which is the better bargain. 10. Can you guess who the next president will be?

11. The debate will be on the question of what this country should do in case of war. 12. Who among all these candidates is best fitted for the posi-

tion? 13. Who did they think was coming? 14. Tell me who you think should be chosen. 15. Tell me whom you think you saw.

Exercise 14

Use the correct case form of the interrogative pronouns—*who* or *whom* —in the following sentences. Tell why the form that you use is correct.

1. _____ is he?
2. _____ did you find there?
3. _____ was it intended for?
4. _____ does he think it was?
5. _____ was responsible for the mistake?
6. _____ do you want?
7. _____ did she say was here?
8. _____ did she say she would invite?
9. _____ were you thinking about?
10. _____ has he selected for secretary?
11. _____ would you say made the best speech?
12. _____ should we have consulted about this matter?
13. _____ can I ask for help on this problem?
14. The judge asked them _____ their accomplices were.
15. Tell me _____ you are expecting.
16. There is some doubt as to _____ will be the Democratic nominee.
17. I was telling them _____ I thought were present last evening.
18. They would not tell me _____ they were visiting last evening.
19. The answer will depend upon _____ you ask.
20. The success of the plan will depend upon _____ the leader is.

DEMONSTRATIVE PRONOUNS

78. The Demonstrative Pronouns are *this* and *that,* with their plurals, *these* and *those.*

They are used to point out persons or things with especial emphasis or definiteness. (The word "demonstrative" comes from the same root as "demonstrate," meaning "to point out.")

79. Case. The demonstrative pronouns have the same form for the nominative and objective cases, and have no possessive form.

80. Antecedent. The antecedent of a demonstrative pronoun may be:
(1) A single noun: as, "I have been reading *Ivanhoe;* in my opinion *that* is the most interesting of Scott's novels."
(2) Two or more nouns, when the pronoun is plural: as, "I have been reading *Ivanhoe* and *Kenilworth;* in my opinion *these* are the most interesting of Scott's novels."
(3) A whole statement: as, "He is very proud, and *that* makes him unpopular." (This last construction should be avoided whenever there is any danger of ambiguity.)

81. The demonstrative pronoun frequently has no antecedent expressed. This is especially true in conversation, when the person or thing referred to can be indicated by a gesture or a glance. Thus a person seeing an accident might exclaim, "Look at *that!*" or, pointing to a book, might say, "Have you read *this?*"

82. *This* and *these* refer to things comparatively near; *that* and *those* to things comparatively remote: as, "Give me some of *this* and a little of *that.*" "I prefer *these* to *those.*"
This and *that* refer to a singular antecedent; *these* and *those* to a plural antecedent.

83. Distinction between Relative and Demonstrative Pronouns. *That* may be a relative pronoun or a demonstrative pronoun. Compare the following sentences:
He paid for the coat *that* he ordered (relative).
He objected to *that* for political reasons (demonstrative).
The demonstrative *that* points out something definitely, much as if one were to point his finger at the object; the relative *that* has none of this definite force. Again, the relative *that,* as a rule, is placed immediately after the antecedent, and introduces a separate or new clause which modifies the antecedent. The demonstrative *that* may be at a considerable distance from its antecedent, even in a following sentence, and it does not introduce a separate clause.

INDEFINITE PRONOUNS

84. The Indefinite Pronouns are so called because they do not refer to definite persons and things.

Compare *"Somebody* will do the work" (indefinite) with *"I* will do the work" (definite).

The indefinite pronouns include a rather large number of words which indicate varying degrees of indefiniteness. Some of the more common are:

>some, someone, somebody, something.
>any, anyone, anybody, anything.
>everyone, everybody, everything.
>one, none, nobody, nothing.
>other, another, either, neither, all, many, few, each, both.

85. Case and Number. The nominative and objective case forms are the same.

Some of the indefinite pronouns have a possessive case: as, *one's, other's, another's,* and the compounds of *one* and *body* (*anyone's, everybody's,* etc.).

Note. Both the forms *anybody else's* and *anybody's else* are correct. The former is more natural and is preferable.

One and *other* have plural forms: *ones* and *others:* as, "These are the *ones* I want." "The *others* will be here soon."

Exercise 15

Point out the demonstrative and indefinite pronouns, and tell how they are used (as subject of a verb, object of a verb, etc.).

1. Bring us some of this and a few of those. 2. At first one has eyes and thought for nothing but the landscape. (George Gissing.) 3. He had only a few friends, but these he knew intimately. 4. That was the message that someone had laid on his desk. 5. Each was envious of the other's success. 6. Southern enterprise and energy were all turned to planting. (Charles A. Beard.) 7. He fears nothing except his own conscience, and that he always obeys. 8. Something had happened to almost everything in the kitchen. (Frank Swinnerton.) 9. Each had a private feeling of bitterness about the other. (D. H. Lawrence.) 10. The face of another seemed to consist mainly of nose. (Washington Irving.)

11. These are the days when something is always happening to one or the other of them. 12. Soames was quite five or six years older than either of us. (Max Beerbohm.) 13. Many of them are wholly indifferent to the opinions of others. 14. Anyone's guess was as good as his own.

Exercise 16

Point out the pronouns; tell the class to which they belong (personal, demonstrative, etc.); give the case of each and tell how each pronoun is used (subject, object, etc.).

1. They brought us some of the reports that were in the files. 2. The world was new to me, and I had never seen anything like this at home. (Mark Twain.) 3. What is the nature of the luxury which enervates and destroys nations? (Henry Thoreau.) 4. The English writer whom you referred to is practically unknown to most of us in America. 5. Not many of those she looked at ever saw her again. (Joseph Conrad.) 6. He, whoever he was, was trying to call me by name, but his voice was no more than a husky whisper. (Rudyard Kipling.) 7. He boasted that nobody could tell him anything new about chess. 8. There is nothing like knowledge that one has picked up or reasoned out for oneself. (John Galsworthy.) 9. Which of the books do you consider the more interesting? 10. Unfortunately my father did not see me as I saw myself. (Hamlin Garland.)

11. She believed what they told her, for it agreed with her wish. (W. H. Hudson.) 12. He spoke to me of a daughter who lived with him. (Joseph Conrad.) 13. I found a long row of Carlyles, but he whom I sought was not among them. (John Burroughs.) 14. They, unlike me, were not merely listening—they were hearing something. (William Beebe.) 15. Whatever you do, it will be a credit to you. 16. Whom should we select for this work? 17. We ourselves have made this trip a number of times. 18. I found myself defending Jacob's unusual methods. (Joseph Conrad.) 19. Many were murmuring against the leader they had chosen. (Francis Parkman.) 20. Has a man gained anything who has received a hundred favors and rendered none? (R. W. Emerson.) 21. We have never given them money, for they are too proud to accept help of that sort. 22. That was the president himself whom you saw at the desk.

Chapter III   ADJECTIVES

86. An Adjective is a word that describes a noun or modifies its meaning.

An adjective may:

(1) Describe a noun: as, *brave* soldier; *bright* light; *torn* coat.

(2) Denote which member or members of a class of objects are designated by the noun: as, *this* book; *some* people; *every* man; *two* apples; *second* day.

Any word that thus describes or modifies a noun is an adjective. Thus, we ordinarily think of *Sunday* as a noun, but in the sentence, "I bought a *Sunday* paper," it is an adjective, because it modifies the noun *paper*.

The possessive case of a noun is, from this point of view, an adjective: as, *John's* book, the *girl's* bonnet (see Sec. 28 (2)).

PRONOMINAL ADJECTIVES

87. Various pronouns are frequently used to modify nouns; they then become adjectives (adjective-equivalents), and are called Pronominal Adjectives.

The following sentences show different classes of pronouns used as Pronominal Adjectives.

Personal Pronouns: "That is *my* book." "He lost *his* money."

Relative Pronouns: "The man *whose* name was called has arrived." "The shoes were sold for four dollars, *which* price allows the dealer only a small profit." "*Whichever* plan you choose, it will fail."

Interrogative Pronouns: "*Which* book do you want?" "*What* coat will he wear?"

Demonstrative Pronouns: "*That* boy is late." "*Those* plums are ripe."

Indefinite Pronouns: "*Any* title will do." "Bring me *some* bread." "The *other* clerk is more accommodating."

88. To determine whether a pronoun is used as a pronominal adjective or as a real pronoun, it is necessary only to see whether it *modifies* a noun or is *used as* a noun.

PRONOMINAL ADJECTIVE	PRONOUN
That man will succeed.	*That* is a good man.
Which answer is right?	*Which* is right?
The *other* rope is stronger.	The *other* is stronger.
It is *my* book.	This book is *mine*.

The shorter possessive forms of personal pronouns (*my, our, your, her, their,* as distinguished from *mine, ours, yours, hers, theirs*) are always pronominal adjectives, for they are used only as modifiers of nouns (see Sec. 43).

THE ARTICLES

89. The adjectives *a, an,* and *the* are called Articles.

A and *an* are known as Indefinite Articles; *the* is called a **Definite Article**. The significance of these names is shown in the following sentences.

Bring me *a* book (any book).

Bring me *the* book (a particular book).

The indefinite articles indicate some member of a class of objects without designating which member is meant; the definite article definitely specifies a particular member or members.

90. Uses of "A" and "An." (1) *A* is used before a word beginning with a consonant sound; *an* before a word beginning with a vowel sound: *a* man; *an* apple.

The vowels are *a, e, i, o, u,* and sometimes *y*. In English, an initial *y* is almost always a consonant (*yam, yellow*); in the middle of a word it is frequently a vowel (*analysis*).

(2) The letter *u* sometimes has a vowel sound, and sometimes a consonant sound. Before a word beginning with the former, *an* is used: as, *an* uncle; before one beginning with the latter, *a* is used: as, *a uniform* (pronounced as if it were spelled *yuniform*), *a use*.

(3) Before a word beginning with *h*, *an* is used if the *h* is silent; *a* if the *h* is sounded: thus, *an honest* man; *a home; a high* cliff.

This rule, however, is not universally followed; some writers use *a* before a word beginning with *h* when the first syllable of the word is accented, and *an* when it is unaccented: thus, *a* his'-tory; *an* his-tor'-ical fact.

Either rule may be followed, but the one first given is less likely to be abused, and, in general, is preferable.

For a further discussion of the Articles, see Secs. 365 ff

POSITION OF ADJECTIVES

91. An adjective usually precedes the noun which it modifies.

He was a *brave* man.

Occasionally, for special emphasis, and in some special constructions discussed below, it is placed after the noun.

He was a man, *brave* and *strong*.

92. Predicate Adjective. An adjective modifying the subject is frequently placed after the verb, which connects it with the subject; it is called a Predicate Adjective.

The boy is *small* (small boy).

This work will be *easy* (easy work).

The cloud looks *black*.

He seems *happy*.

The prisoner became *sullen*.

The predicate adjective is used with forms of the verb *be*, and verbs like *seen, appear, become, turn*, etc. (Compare the Predicate Noun—see Sec. 19.)

Occasionally, for special emphasis, the predicate adjective is placed before the verb, and the subject follows the verb.

Dark was the night.

93. Objective Complement. An adjective placed after the direct object of a verb is sometimes used both to modify the object and also to complete the meaning of the verb. This adjective is called an Objective Complement.

The apples made the boy *sick*.

Acid will turn the milk *sour*.

She found the patient *dead*.

The apples didn't make the *boy*—they made the *boy sick*. Compare this construction with the use of a noun as an objective complement (see Sec. 24). The test for an objective complement—either an adjective or a noun—is to see whether *to be* can be inserted between the direct object and the complement without changing the meaning of the sentence. Compare:

We made the stick (to be) *straight* (objective complement).
We found a stick *straight* as the shaft of an arrow (an ordinary adjective modifying the object).

COMPARISON OF ADJECTIVES

94. Adjectives have three degrees of Comparison—the Positive, Comparative, and Superlative.

(1) The **Positive Degree** is the simple form of the adjective used when no comparison is made between objects: *warm, large, beautiful.*

(2) The **Comparative Degree** is used in comparing one object with another one: that is, in comparing only two objects. The comparative degree is formed by adding *-er* to the simple form of the adjective, or by using *more* (sometimes *less*) before it: *warmer, larger, more beautiful (less beautiful).*

(3) The **Superlative Degree** is used in comparing three or more objects. The superlative degree is formed by adding *-est* to the simple form of the adjective, or by using *most* (sometimes *least*) before it: *warmest, largest, most beautiful (least beautiful).*

Thus we say:

My apple is *large* (positive degree).
My apple is *larger* than Harry's (comparative degree).
My apple is the *largest* of the three (superlative degree).
My plan is *practical.*
My plan is *more practical* than yours.
My plan is the *most practical* of all.

Sometimes the superlative degree indicates the greatest degree of a quality, without making a definite comparison of one object with other objects.

The audience listened with the *most intense* interest.
He was a *most loyal* servant.

95. No definite rule can be given for determining whether the forms in *-er, -est,* or those in *more, most,* are correct for any given adjective. The general tendency, however, is as follows:

With most adjectives of one syllable, and with some of two syllables, the suffixes *-er* and *-est* are preferable: *rich, richer, richest; thrifty, thriftier, thriftiest.*

With practically all adjectives of three or more syllables, and with many of two syllables, *more* and *most* are used: *beautiful, more beautiful, most beautiful; candid, more candid, most candid.*

With some adjectives, either *-er, -est,* or *more, most* may be used: *handsome, handsomer* or *more handsome, handsomest* or *most handsome.*

In case of doubt, the writer will have to be guided by the sound of the words, and choose the smoother combination.

96. Irregular Comparison. A few adjectives have irregular comparison.

POSITIVE	COMPARATIVE	SUPERLATIVE
good	better	best
bad, ill	worse	worst
much, many	more	most
little	less, lesser	least
far	farther, further	farthest, furthest
old	older, elder	oldest, eldest
late	later, latter	latest, last
————	inner	inmost, innermost
————	outer	outmost, outermost
————	utter	utmost, uttermost
————	upper	uppermost
top	————	topmost

Exercise 17

Point out the adjectives, and tell what noun each modifies; point out pronominal adjectives, predicate adjectives, and objective complements. Give the degree of comparison of each adjective.

1. Nature is good, but intellect is better. (R. W. Emerson.) 2. He was a very gentlemanly person, good natured and superior. (Joseph Conrad.) 3. Their long ride had made the passengers sleepy and irritable. 4. In its latest report the committee called attention to the urgent need for more members. 5. The general furniture was profuse, comfortless, antique and tattered. (E. A. Poe.) 6. The test made our class alert for errors in grammar. 7. The longest way proved to be the quickest way. 8. What book has been the best seller during the past decade? 9. It was a stiff oak branch, sound as iron. (Charles Reade.) 10. Meanwhile the lighthouse had been growing steadily larger. (Stephen Crane.)

11. I walked the streets, serene and happy. (Mark Twain.) 12. Each country will have its representatives at this conference. 13. The dense trees of the avenue rendered the road dark as a tunnel. (Thomas Hardy.) 14. The streets of toil stand shuttered and drab. (Thomas Burke.) 15. The solitary places do not seem quite lonely. (R. W. Emerson.) 16. Fine manners show themselves formidable to the uncultivated man. (R. W. Emerson.) 17. He is staying at which hotel? 18. My second mate was a round-cheeked, silent young man, grave beyond his years. (Joseph Conrad.) 19. The investigators found the boys happy and contented. 20. The night was cold and bleak, but full of stars. (H. G. Wells.)

21. Young as he was, he sensed the dramatic tenseness of the situation. 22. From these quiet windows the figures of passing travellers looked too remote and dim to disturb the sense of privacy. (Nathaniel Hawthorne.) 23. That made him angry, and he said that insular envy made me unresponsive. (Rudyard Kipling.) 24. Dear to me then was poverty. (George Gissing.) 25. After a time the house became quiet.

Exercise 18

Make sentences containing each of the adjectives *happy, sore, tired,* used as follows (a separate sentence for each adjective in each use).
1. An adjective placed before its noun.
2. An adjective following its noun.
3. A predicate adjective.
4. An objective complement.

Exercise 19

(A) Supply the proper form of the adjective—comparative or superlative.

1. Of all the rooms in the house the kitchen is the _____ (cooler, coolest).
2. Which of the two boys do you think is the _____ (older, oldest)?
3. I don't know whether your plan or mine is the _____ practical. (more, most).
4. From the list they selected the _____ appropriate title (more, most).
5. I could go by car or by train, but I preferred the _____ because it was the _____ (latter, last) (faster, fastest).
6. Who writes the _____ letters—John, Mary, or Helen (better, best)?

(B) Supply the form that seems preferable to you.

1. The result becomes _____ every day (doubtfuller, more doubtful).
2. She is _____ than her sister (prettier, more pretty).

3. He is the ———— man that I know (contrariest, most contrary).
4. This is the ———— thing that he ever did (foolishest, most foolish).
5. The heat is ———— today (intenser, more intense).
6. He is ———— than his colleagues (radicaller, more radical).
7. He should be ———— with the children (patienter, more patient).
8. This arrangement is the ———— for us (suitablest, most suitable).
9. The money is ———— in the bank (safer, more safe).

Chapter IV   VERBS

97. A Verb is a word that makes a statement about the subject.
In order to make a statement, two elements are necessary: something
to talk about, and something to say about that thing. The first element
is represented in a sentence by the noun or pronoun used as the subject;
the second element is represented by the verb.

98. A verb may express:
(1) Action: as, "I *walk.*" "He *ran.*" "They *are playing* ball."
(2) State or condition: as, "He *remained* silent." "He *rests* every afternoon." "We *are* at home."

Some verbs may express action in one sentence and state or condition
in another, depending upon their meaning.

He *turned* his head (action).
He *turned* pale (state or condition).

TRANSITIVE AND INTRANSITIVE VERBS

99. Verbs may be either Transitive or Intransitive.
(1) A **Transitive Verb** is one that takes an object.

We *saw* the *fire.*
The man *threw* the *ball.*
He *lifted* the *stone.*

(2) An **Intransitive Verb** is one that does not take an object.

The man *worked* rapidly.
He *is walking.*
Birds *fly.*

The word "transitive" has the same Latin root and prefix as "transit," and
means "going over" or "passing over." Thus with a transitive verb the action performed by the subject may be said to pass over the verb to the object, which receives the action.

48

100. A verb that is transitive in some cases may be intransitive in others.

TRANSITIVE	INTRANSITIVE
They *broke* the glass.	The rope *broke*.
He *dropped* the pencil.	The pear *dropped* to the ground.

LINKING VERBS

101. A Linking Verb is a verb that connects the subject with a predicate noun or a predicate adjective.

John *is* a soldier.

The boy *will be* brave.

A Linking Verb is also called a Copulative Verb.

102. The most common linking verb is *be* in its various forms: as, *am, is, was, were, will be, has been,* etc. Any verb, however, when used to connect the subject with a predicate noun or predicate adjective, is a linking verb: as, *seem, look, become, appear,* etc.

He *seems* honest.

They *looked* weary.

She *became* an artist.

It follows from what has been said that a linking verb never has an object.

The verb *be* in its various forms is not always a linking verb, for it may be an ordinary intransitive verb denoting *existence:* as, "God *is.*" "The boy *was* at home." It is a linking verb only when it is used as a connective in the manner described above.

HELPING (AUXILIARY VERBS)

103. An Auxiliary Verb is a verb which helps to make some form of another verb. (The word "auxiliary" means "helping.")

Thus, in *is going* the auxiliary verb *is* helps to make a form of the verb *go;* in *have found* and *will sing* the auxiliary verbs *have* and *will* help to make forms of *find* and *sing,* respectively.

104. The principal auxiliary verbs are *be, have, may, can, must, will, shall,* and *do,* together with their different forms *is, was, had, might, could, would, should, did,* etc.

Be, have, will, and *do* are not always auxiliary verbs; they may be complete verbs: as, "He *is* here." "I *have* the book." "I *will* it to be so." "I *do* the hard part of the work."

In making some forms of a verb two or more auxiliary verbs may be used: "He *has been* seen." "They *will have been* sent." "You *should have been* sleeping."

105. Sometimes intervening words are placed between the auxiliary verb and the part of the verb to which it belongs. In such cases the student, when naming the verb in the sentence, should be careful to include the separated auxiliary: as, "He *had* already *gone* home."

Exercise 20

Point out the transitive and intransitive verbs, linking verbs, and auxiliary verbs. Point out direct objects, predicate nouns, and predicate adjectives.

1. The wind had triumphed, and swept all the clouds from heaven. (R. L. Stevenson.) 2. Surely this was his native village which he had left but the day before. (Washington Irving.) 3. For nonconformity the world whips you with its displeasure. (R. W. Emerson.) 4. This may seem singular, but it has nearly always been my experience. (John Burroughs.) 5. Once a dripping servant brought him food, but he could not eat. (Rudyard Kipling.) 6. Then will justice reign and peace be in all the land. 7. Throughout the trial John remained a loyal friend of the prisoner. 8. He uncovered the vase, and threw the faded rose into the water which it contained. (Nathaniel Hawthorne.) 9. His loyalty I have never questioned, but his judgment is often faulty. 10. Those young men whom he knew seemed uneasy when he was in the room.

11. The accident might not have occurred if he had been watching the road. 12. At last my hand came in contact with the knocker and I lifted it. (Edith Wharton.) 13. Sweet are the fruits of victory. 14. Did you find the author's name in the card index? 15. A thin, gray fog hung over the city, and the streets were very cold; for summer was in England. (Rudyard Kipling.) 16. He appeared awkward and uncomfortable among these strangers. 17. He opened the volume, and took from its black letter pages a rose, or what was once a rose. (Nathaniel Hawthorne.) 18. Have you, by any chance, ever considered the cause for this social unrest? 19. Judge Watson's successor will be in the city tomorrow. 20. The train will probably be late tonight.

Exercise 21

(A) The following verbs may be either transitive or intransitive. Complete each sentence with a word or words that make the verb transitive. Then complete it with a word or words that make it intransitive. Mark each sentence *T* (transitive) or *I* (intransitive), thus: "He shot *a bear*." (T); "He shot *without taking aim*." (I).

1. The boy ran _fast_ (I) *The boy ran the 440 yd. dash.* (T.)
2. They stole _often_ (I) *They stole the car.* (T)
3. She turned _____.
4. We were singing _____.
5. He called _____.
6. The attendants rushed _____.
7. The guards fought _____.
8. The child can count _____.
9. He acts _____.

(B) Complete each of the following sentences so that the verb is (a) linking; (b) not linking. Mark each sentence *L* or *not L*, thus: "He is *a hero*." (L); "He is *at home*." (not L).

1. John has been _____.
2. The books were _____.
3. The author may be _____.
4. The fugitive looked _____.
5. We are _____.
6. The boy felt _____.
7. Both men appeared _____.

PERSON AND NUMBER

106. A verb must agree with its subject in Person and Number.
> I *am* in the city.
> He *is* in the city.
> We *are* in the city.

In the first sentence, the subject *I* is in the first person, singular number; hence the verb *am*, which is the form of the verb *be* in the first person, singular number, is used (see the table in Sec. 107). In the second sentence, the verb *is* agrees with the subject *he:* they are both in the third person, singular number. In the third example, the verb is *are*, agreeing with the subject *we*—first person, plural number.

CHANGES IN FORM TO INDICATE PERSON AND NUMBER

107. The Verb "Be." Throughout the discussion of verbs it will be noticed that the verb *be* is frequently referred to as having especially irregular forms and offering the most exceptions to general statements. The reason for this irregularity is that the modern forms of this verb are made up of the remains of three originally separate verbs.

In the present tense the verb *be* has distinct forms (*am* and *is*) for the first and third persons, respectively, in the singular number; the other forms in this tense are the same (*are*) for all persons. (For the meaning of *present tense* and *past tense,* see Sec. 114.)

The past tense has *was* in the first and third persons, singular number, and *were* in the other forms.

PRESENT TENSE

SINGULAR	PLURAL
1. I am.	1. We are.
2. You are.	2. You are.
3. He (she, it) is.	3. They are.

PAST TENSE

SINGULAR	PLURAL
1. I was.	1. We were.
2. You were.	2. You were.
3. He (she, it) was.	3. They were.

108. The Verb "Have." In the present tense the verb *have* takes the form *has* in the third person, singular number, and *have* in all the other forms.

SINGULAR	PLURAL
1. I have.	1. We have.
2. You have.	2. You have.
3. He (she, it) has.	3. They have.

109. All Other Verbs. In the present tense *all other verbs* add -*s* in the third person, singular number.

SINGULAR	PLURAL
1. I work.	1. We work.
2. You work.	2. You work.
3. He (she, it) works.	3. They work.

110. These are the only changes made in any verb to indicate person and number. In the other forms of verbs, the person and number are determined by referring to the subject.

111. The rule for person and number in verbs is therefore simple: In all verbs excepting *be* and *have* the only change in form to indicate person and number is made by adding *-s* in the third person, singular number, present tense.

Note. In the preceding discussion no account has been taken of the forms of the verb used with the second person, singular number pronoun *thou*, in the "solemn" style (see Sec. 34). This pronoun takes special forms of the verbs: thou *art*, thou *wast*, thou *hast been*, thou *walkest*, etc. These are now restricted almost entirely to prayer and poetry.

Note also that in the preceding sections and in those following (to Sec. 125) only the forms for the Indicative Mood are given. Additional changes in form to indicate Mood and Voice are discussed later.

Exercise 22

Give the person and number of each verb in Exercise 23.

TENSE

112. Tense is that property of a verb which indicates the time when an action takes place.

The word "tense" is derived from a French word meaning "time."

113. There are six tenses—three simple and three perfect tenses.

SIMPLE TENSES	PERFECT TENSES
Present	Present Perfect
Past	Past Perfect
Future	Future Perfect

The general uses of these tenses are shown in the following sections. In practice, however, some of the tenses are employed to indicate a variety of time relations. For these variations, see Secs. 385 ff.

SIMPLE TENSES

114. (1) The Present Tense regularly indicates that an action is going on at the present time: as, "He *hears* the bell now."

(2) The **Past Tense** regularly indicates that an action took place in past time: as, "He *heard* the bell yesterday."

(3) The **Future Tense** regularly indicates that an action will take place in future time: as, "He *will hear* the bell tomorrow."

PERFECT TENSES

115. The three simple tenses obviously cover all possible time: time *now*, time *gone by*, and time *to come;* and the perfect tenses, therefore, cannot indicate any time that is not included in the simple tenses. The perfect tenses are regularly used to call attention to the completion of an action; they set up a certain point of time and indicate that an action was completed before or by that time.

(1) The **Present Perfect Tense** regularly indicates that an action has been completed sometime before the present: as, "He *has finished* the work" (sometime before now).

This tense places the completion of the action at some *indefinite* time before the present. It never refers to a definite point of time in the past. Thus,

> I *have seen* him twice (correct).
> I *have seen* him last week (incorrect).

For reference to a definite point of time in the past, the past tense is used.

> I *saw* him last week.

(2) The **Past Perfect Tense** indicates that an action was completed before a certain time in the past: as, "He *had finished* the work before nine o'clock yesterday morning."

(3) The **Future Perfect Tense** indicates that an action will be completed before a certain time in the future: as, "He *will have finished* the work by next Saturday."

In Modern English the future perfect tense has been largely replaced by the simple future tense. Ordinarily a person would say, "He *will finish* the work by next Saturday," instead of "He *will have finished*."

FORMS OF THE TENSES

116. The forms for the different tenses are as follows.

(1) The **present tense** has the simplest form of the verb: *walk, know.*

(2) The **past tense** is regularly formed:

(a) by adding *-ed, -d,* or *-t* to the present tense form of the verb: *walk, walked; prove, proved; deal, dealt.*

(b) by changing the vowel in the present tense form, without adding a suffix: *know, knew; sing, sang; run, ran; find, found.* (For a more complete discussion of the past tense forms, and particularly for irregular forms, see Secs. 457 ff.)

✶(3) The **future tense** consists of the auxiliary verb *will* or *shall* combined with the simple form of the verb: *will walk; shall know.*

✶(4) The **present perfect tense** consists of the auxiliary verb *have* or *has* combined with the past participle: *have walked; has known.*

✶(5) The **past perfect tense** consists of the auxiliary verb *had* combined with the past participle: *had walked, had known.*

✶(6) The **future perfect tense** consists of the auxiliary verb *will have* or *shall have* combined with the past participle: *will have walked; shall have known.*

Note. For the past participle, see Sec. 162.

✶ **117. Principal Parts of a Verb.** Three forms or parts of a verb are especially important, and are therefore called the Principal Parts. They are the forms for the:

— 1. Present tense, singular number, first person.

— 2. Past tense.

— 3. Past participle.

• PRESENT	• PAST	• PAST PARTICIPLE
work	worked	worked
see	saw	seen
break	broke	broken
bring	brought	brought
steal	stole	stolen

118. These forms are important because every other verb form is made by combination with one of these three, and the combinations are the same in all verbs—except *be* and *have,* which are irregular.

The future tense adds *will* or *shall* to the simple present.

The perfect tenses add *have* or *has, had, will have* or *shall have* to the past participle.

The present participle adds *-ing* to the present form: *seeing, singing.*

The present infinitive adds *to* to the present form: *to see, to sing.*

119. Table of Forms. The following table gives the forms for the six tenses of the verbs *be, have,* and *work* in the different persons and numbers in the indicative mood, active voice.

The Verb "Be"

PRESENT TENSE

SINGULAR	PLURAL
1. I am.	1. We are.
2. You are.	2. You are.
3. He is.	3. They are.

PAST TENSE

1. I was.	1. We were.
2. You were.	2. You were.
3. He was.	3. They were.

FUTURE TENSE

1. I shall be.	1. We shall be.
2. You will be.	2. You will be.
3. He will be.	3. They will be.

PRESENT PERFECT TENSE

1. I have been.	1. We have been.
2. You have been.	2. You have been.
3. He has been.	3. They have been.

PAST PERFECT TENSE

1. I had been.	1. We had been.
2. You had been.	2. You had been.
3. He had been.	3. They had been.

FUTURE PERFECT TENSE

1. I shall have been.	1. We shall have been.
2. You will have been.	2. You will have been.
3. He will have been.	3. They will have been.

The Verb "Have"

PRESENT TENSE

1. I have.	1. We have.
2. You have.	2. You have.
3. He has.	3. They have.

PAST TENSE

1. I had.
2. You had.
3. He had.

1. We had.
2. You had.
3. They had.

FUTURE TENSE

1. I shall have.
2. You will have.
3. He will have.

1. We shall have.
2. You will have.
3. They will have.

PRESENT PERFECT TENSE

1. I have had.
2. You have had.
3. He has had.

1. We have had.
2. You have had.
3. They have had.

PAST PERFECT TENSE

1. I had had.
2. You had had.
3. He had had.

1. We had had.
2. You had had.
3. They had had.

FUTURE PERFECT TENSE

1. I shall have had.
2. You will have had.
3. He will have had.

1. We shall have had.
2. You will have had.
3. They will have had.

The Verb "Work"

PRESENT TENSE

1. I work.
2. You work.
3. He works.

1. We work.
2. You work.
3. They work.

PAST TENSE

1. I worked.
2. You worked.
3. He worked.

1. We worked.
2. You worked.
3. They worked.

FUTURE TENSE

1. I shall work.
2. You will work.
3. He will work.

1. We shall work.
2. You will work.
3. They will work.

PRESENT PERFECT TENSE

1. I have worked.
2. You have worked.
3. He has worked.

1. We have worked.
2. You have worked.
3. They have worked.

PAST PERFECT TENSE

1. I had worked.	1. We had worked.
2. You had worked.	2. You had worked.
3. He had worked.	3. They had worked.

FUTURE PERFECT TENSE

1. I shall have worked.	1. We shall have worked.
2. You will have worked.	2. You will have worked.
3. He will have worked.	3. They will have worked.

SIMPLE, PROGRESSIVE, AND EMPHATIC TENSE FORMS

120. Thus far we have considered only the commonest forms of the verb in the different tenses; there are, however, three forms for expressing the various tense relations: the Simple, Progressive, and Emphatic.

(1) The Simple forms are those just given in the tables: I *think*, I *thought*, I *shall think*, etc.

(2) The Progressive forms represent the action as going on, as being in progress, at the time indicated: I *am thinking*, I *was thinking*, I *shall be thinking*, etc.

In general, this form pictures the action more vividly than does the simple one. It consists of a form of the verb *be* used as an auxiliary verb, followed by the present participle of the main verb. (The present participle is the form of the verb ending with the suffix *-ing*.)

(3) The Emphatic forms are used to give emphasis to a statement: I *do think*, I *did think*.

Thus in answer to the question, "Why don't you think about what you are doing?" one might say, "I *think* about it," or "I *do think* about it." The latter is obviously the more emphatic answer. The emphatic form is made with the auxiliary verb *do* or *did*.

121. Table of Forms. The following table illustrates the three forms in the present and past tenses (the plural number is not included).

PRESENT TENSE

SIMPLE	PROGRESSIVE	EMPHATIC
1. I walk.	1. I am walking.	1. I do walk.
2. You walk.	2. You are walking.	2. You do walk.
3. He walks.	3. He is walking.	3. He does walk.

PAST TENSE

1. I walked.	**1.** I was walking.	**1.** I did walk.
2. You walked.	**2.** You were walking.	**2.** You did walk.
3. He walked.	**3.** He was walking.	**3.** He did walk.

The future tense and the perfect tenses have no emphatic form.

FUTURE TENSE

SIMPLE   **PROGRESSIVE**

1. I shall walk.	**1.** I shall be walking.
2. You will walk.	**2.** You will be walking.
3. He will walk.	**3.** He will be walking.

PRESENT PERFECT TENSE

1. I have walked.	**1.** I have been walking.
2. You have walked.	**2.** You have been walking.
3. He has walked.	**3.** He has been walking.

PAST PERFECT TENSE

1. I had walked.	**1.** I had been walking.
2. You had walked.	**2.** You had been walking.
3. He had walked.	**3.** He had been walking.

FUTURE PERFECT TENSE

1. I shall have walked.	**1.** I shall have been walking.
2. You will have walked.	**2.** You will have been walking.
3. He will have walked.	**3.** He will have been walking.

QUESTIONS AND NEGATIVE STATEMENTS

122. In questions and negative statements, the auxiliaries *do* and *did* are not devices for expressing emphasis. They are regularly supplied in these constructions when the corresponding affirmative statement is without an auxiliary.

I *like* the place (affirmative).
Do you *like* the place? (question).
I *do* not *like* the place (negative).

123. When there is an auxiliary in the affirmative statement, *do* or *did* is not required in questions and negative assertions.

He *will* come.
Will he come?
He *will* not *come*.

124. *Is, am, are, was,* and *were* do not require an auxiliary.

Is she at home?

They *were* not present.

Exercise 23

Name the tenses of the verbs; point out the progressive and emphatic forms.

1. We rode through the street between rows of deserted houses. 2. This bill provides for a sweeping reduction in duties on foreign books. 3. I had by that time heard a little more of him. (Joseph Conrad.) 4. The war has largely obliterated fine distinctions. (Thomas Burke.) 5. The paper did not give complete details of the accident, but it did show that the driver of the car had been negligent. 6. At present he is working in the copy room of the *Daily News.* 7. We shall begin our investigation on Monday and continue it throughout the week. 8. For months this country had known nothing but war and desolation. 9. The last of the leaves were falling, and snow filled the air. 10. In this instance we did feel that the penalty was too severe.

11. It has been months since we were in London. 12. You will find many things there, but few that will amuse and stimulate you. 13. Paul had slept very little, and he felt grimy and uncomfortable. (Willa Cather.) 14. They have been waiting at the station for the midnight train. 15. Justice and only justice shall always be our motto. (Woodrow Wilson.) 16. Some college students, you contend, do know how to spell. 17. When need arose, they did their duty fearlessly. 18. Nature has grown mellow under these humid skies. (John Burroughs.) 19. His mind hovered over the book that he had been reading that afternoon. (Hugh Walpole.) 20. By that time they will have forgotten the motive and forgiven the mistake.

21. Giant industry has this territory in thrall. (Thomas Burke.) 22. A red light burns far off upon the gloom of the land and the night is soft and warm. (Joseph Conrad.) 23. The tourists will be sailing for home in a few weeks. 24. They lay in the shade of the tree, waiting for the car to come. 25. He came in and laid his hat on the table. 26. Do you know the answer to this problem?

MOOD

125. Mood is that property of a verb which indicates the manner in which a statement is made.

The verb has three Moods: Indicative, Imperative, and Subjunctive.

126. The **Indicative Mood** is primarily used in making a positive statement of fact.

> I *came* at three o'clock.
> The house *is painted* white.
> They *are* loyal friends.

A verb in a direct question is also considered to be in the Indicative Mood, the reason being that the question anticipates a positive statement in answer.

> *Will* you *go* with me?
> *Has* the speaker *arrived?*

127. The **Imperative Mood** expresses a command or an entreaty.

> *Bring* me the book.
> *Be* sure to come early.
> *Let* us help you.
> *Let's* go early.

128. The **Subjunctive Mood** makes a conditional statement, expresses a wish, or indicates doubt and uncertainty.

> If he *were* at home, he would be contented.
> If that *be* the case, we must be careful.
> *Had* I *been* there, I would have objected.
> Oh, that John *were* here.
> I wish that he *were* stronger.

may or may not be true to fact

FORMS IN THE DIFFERENT MOODS

129. The **Indicative Mood** is used much more frequently than the others. The forms which we have studied under the subject of Tenses are all in the indicative mood (see Sec. 119).

130. The **Imperative Mood** takes the simplest form of the verb: as, *be* (Be still); *come* (Come at once); *think* (Think quickly).

(a) To make an emphatic command or a negative command, *do* is combined with the regular imperative form.

> *Do take* care of yourself.
> *Do* not *come* until tomorrow.

Note. The subject of a verb in the imperative mood is not usually expressed. A command is always addressed *to* a person, and the subject is therefore always *you*. Sometimes for special emphasis the subject is expressed: thus, "*You* come here" is more emphatic than the simple "Come here."

131. The **Subjunctive Mood** has the same forms as the indicative mood as given in the tables (see Sec. 119), with the following exceptions.

- SUBJUNCTIVE MOOD

The Verb "Be"

- PRESENT TENSE

SINGULAR	PLURAL
1. (If) I be.	1. (If) we be.
2. (If) you be.	2. (If) you be.
3. (If) he be.	3. (If) they be.

- PAST TENSE

1. (If) I were.	1. (If) we were.
2. (If) you were.	2. (If) you were.
3. (If) he were.	3. (If) they were.

The Verb "Have"

- PRESENT TENSE

1. (If) I have.	1. (If) we have.
2. (If) you have.	2. (If) you have.
3. (If) he have.	3. (If) they have.

All Other Verbs

- PRESENT TENSE

1. (If) I work.	1. (If) we work.
2. (If) you work.	2. (If) you work.
3. (If) he work.	3. (If) they work.

(*If* is not a part of the verb, but it is used in the foregoing tables because a group of words in which the subjunctive mood is employed, is most frequently introduced by *if*.)

132. Thus in the subjunctive mood the verb *be* has the form *be* throughout the different persons in both numbers of the present tense, and *were* throughout the past tense. Notice that *were* occurs in both the singular and the plural number.

Compare these forms with those of the indicative mood: I *am*, you *are*, he *is*, we *are*, you *are*, they *are* (present); I *was*, you *were*, he *was*, we *were*, you *were*, they *were* (past).

133. The verb *have* has only one form in the subjunctive mood different from the indicative: *have* instead of *has* in the third person, singular

elliptical construction

number, present tense—"If he *have* the time" (subjunctive). "He *has* the time" (indicative).

134. All other verbs show only one change: the *-s* which is the ending of the third person, singular number, present tense, in the indicative mood, is omitted in the subjunctive: "(If) he *work*" (subjunctive); "He *works*" (indicative).

In all verbs the present perfect tense—which is made by using some form of the verb *have* as an auxiliary verb—has a theoretical form with *have* instead of *has* in the third person, singular number, subjunctive mood: "(If) he *have* gone." In practice, however, this rarely occurs.

USES OF THE SUBJUNCTIVE MOOD

135. In earlier English the subjunctive mood was extensively used, and it is still frequently found in poetry. In ordinary prose it has been largely replaced by the indicative forms or by verb-phrases made with modal auxiliaries (see Sec. 443). The following are the most common uses of the subjunctive in modern prose.

136. Present Tense. The present tense forms of the subjunctive mood may be used:

(1) In expressing a condition that may or may not be true to fact (see Sec. 137). *Contrary to fact*
    If that *be* true, we must go at once.
    If this plan *fail*, there is no recourse.
    We shall go tomorrow, *rain* or *shine*. *an elliptical, if it rained, or if it shine*

Note 1. Rain or shine is an elliptical construction, equivalent to "if it *rain* or if it *shine*."

Note 2. In these conditional statements many writers prefer the indicative form *is* to the subjunctive form *be,* and most writers would use *fails* (indicative) instead of *fail* (subjunctive). Both usages are correct.

(2) In expressing a concession, after *though* or *although* (see Sec. 239).
    Even though that *be* the case, I will not go.

Note. The indicative mood (*is*) may also be used in this construction.

(3) In certain parliamentary expressions.
    I move that the nominations *be* closed.
    He moved that the report *be* accepted.

four express *concession*

(4) After verbs or adjectives expressing command, necessity, and the like.

> The tenant demands that the house *be* painted.
> The law requires that he *examine* the books monthly (not *examines*).
> The committee ordered that the case *be* continued.
> It is necessary that the papers *be* destroyed.

Note. Instead of the subjunctive forms in (4), a verb-phrase made with *shall* or *should* may be used: "The tenant demands that the house *shall be* painted." "The committee ordered that the case *should be* continued."

137. Past Tense. The past tense of the subjunctive mood should be used:

(1) In all clauses expressing a present condition which is *contrary to fact* (see Sec. 138).

> If he *were* here, he would consent (not *was*).
> If I *were* in his place, I should refuse (not *was*).
> Suppose she *were* at home—what could she do? (not *was*).
> If you *saw* him now, you wouldn't recognize him.
> If he *knew* the answer, he would tell you.

These conditions are *contrary to fact* because, in the first sentence, for example, he is *not* here; in the second, I am *not* in his place, etc. Compare these with "If he *was* at home, he must have been asleep when I called." This is not a condition contrary to fact, for he may, or may not, have been at home. Note that the indicative form *was* is used here instead of the subjunctive *were* (see Sec. 141, *note*).

(2) In wishes.

> I wish that he *were* stronger (not *was*).
> I wish that I *were* not so late (not *was*).

(3) After *as if* and *as though*.

> He looks as if he *were* very old (not *was*).
> She talked as though she *were* amused (not *was*).

138. The past tense in the subjunctive mood does not indicate actual past time—although the name seems to imply that it does. In modern English grammar the term *past tense* in the subjunctive mood serves chiefly as a label to designate the grammatical *form* of the verb: thus, *were* is the grammatical past subjunctive form of the verb *be*.

139. In conditional statements contrary to fact, the past subjunctive regularly refers to actual present time.

If he *were* here (now), he would consent.
If I *were* in his place (now), I should refuse.

In *wishes* and after *as if* or *as though,* the past subjunctive indicates the same time as that represented by the main verb in the sentence.

I wish (now) that he *were* stronger (now).
I wished (yesterday) that he *were* stronger (yesterday).
She acts (now) as if she *were* tired (now).
She acted (yesterday) as if she *were* tired (yesterday).

140. In the past tenses of all verbs, the only variation in form between the indicative and the subjunctive moods occurs in the first and third persons, singular number, of the verb *be*. Here the indicative has *was,* and the subjunctive has *were*. Especial care is therefore necessary in the use of the subjunctive *were*.

The other past tense forms of *be* and all the past tense forms of other verbs are identical in the two moods, and hence the mood in any particular sentence must be determined from the context. If the conditional statement refers to present time and is contrary to fact, the verb is in the subjunctive mood. If the conditional statement refers to past time and is *not* contrary to fact, the verb is in the indicative mood.

If he *knew* the reason, he would tell me (subjunctive—he does not know the reason).
If he *knew* the reason, he did not tell me (indicative—perhaps he knew the reason, perhaps not).

141. Past Perfect Tense. A condition *contrary to fact in past time* is expressed by the past perfect tense, subjunctive mood.

If I had been guilty, I would have confessed.
If he had gone, he would have enjoyed the play.
Had I seen him, I would have spoken.

Sentences of this sort, however, offer no opportunity for error, since the subjunctive and indicative forms of the past perfect tense are identical in *all* verbs.

Note. For conditions in past time which are *not* contrary to fact (that is, those which may or may not be true to fact) the *indicative mood* is used.

If he *was* here when we came, why did he refuse to see us? (perhaps he was here, perhaps not).
If he *was* responsible for the accident, he should have paid the damages.
If she *felt* the disgrace, she showed no signs of regret.
If he *has finished* the work, he will be here soon.

142. Summary. Modern usage prefers the indicative mood to the subjunctive everywhere except (a) in conditions contrary to fact, in wishes, and after *as if* and *as though* (Sec. 137); (b) in certain parliamentary expressions (Sec. 136 (3)). The subjunctive mood is required in (a), and is almost universally used in (b). The practical rule is this: In the constructions under (a) do not use *was* for *were;* in (b) use *be.*

Nevertheless, the writer may also, if he wishes, use the subjunctive mood in present conditions not contrary to fact, in concessions, and after words expressing command, etc. (Sec. 136 (1), (2), (4)).

Exercise 24

Give the mood of each verb. If the subjunctive mood is used, tell why.

1. When the storm broke, the canoes were a mile from shore. 2. If he were a year older, he would be eligible for membership. 3. If he was present, he knows what was said at the meeting. 4. When you have transcribed your notes, bring them to me. 5. I felt as though I were moving in the midst of a novel. (Rudyard Kipling.) 6. Many modifications of this plan are now on trial. (Carl Holliday.) 7. Let us hope that the prophecy will be amply fulfilled. (Mark Twain.) 8. The management requests that everyone be in his seat by eight o'clock. 9. Has he told you about his adventures in Brazil? 10. Make that child's food, clothing, and education your personal affair. (Thomas Burke.)

11. I wish that Jane were more interested in reading good books. 12. The evening meal was plain as the breakfast. (C. Gauss.) 13. If there be anything farcical in such a life, the blame is not mine: let it lie at fate's and nature's door. (R. W. Emerson.) 14. Another member moved that the amendment be referred to a committee for further study. 15. If he make ten voyages in succession—what then? (Mark Twain.) 16. Do tell us about your experiences in Russia. 17. The bride, if it was the bride, was a large doll with dark hypnotic eyes in a face of porcelain. (H. M. Tomlinson.) 18. The judge required that each witness sign his name in ink. 19. If he is ready, we can start at once. 20. After my bath, if breakfast be not ready, I sit down to my studies till I am called. (W. C. Bryant.)

Exercise 25

Tell the difference in meaning, and the time indicated in the following sentences. Point out the conditions contrary to fact.

1. If he is in trouble, he will write to you.
2. If he were in trouble, he would write to you.

3. If he was in trouble, he should have written to you.
4. If he had been in trouble, he would have written to you.
5. If that is true, you can go.
6. If that be true, you can go.
7. If that were true, you could go.
8. If that had been true, you could have gone.
9. If the day was clear, we could see the mountains forty miles away.
10. If the day were clear, we could see the mountains forty miles away.
11. If he has been there, he knows the story.
12. If he had been there, he would know the story.
13. If they were not at home, they were at school.
14. If they were not at home, they would be at school.

Exercise 26

Supply the proper form of the verb *be*—indicative or subjunctive—and tell why that form is correct.

1. If the road **WERE** not so winding, he would drive faster.
2. The rules require that each ticket **BE** individually signed.
3. If it _____ warmer this afternoon, we can go swimming.
4. If it _____ warmer, we could go swimming now.
5. Some members have asked that the minutes of the meeting _____ printed.
6. I wish that he _____ here this evening.
7. If that _____ true, he is responsible for the mistake.
8. It seemed as though the house _____ almost ready to collapse.
9. If the speaker _____ more prompt, the meeting would have begun on time.
10. If he _____ late for class today, he will be marked as absent.
11. He acts as if he _____ no longer interested.
12. If I _____ you, I would refuse the penalty.
13. If he _____ ready, he should have notified us.
14. If he _____ better prepared, he would have given a more interesting talk.

✴ MODAL AUXILIARIES

143. Various kinds of relations, such as permission, ability, possibility, obligation, necessity, and the like, are expressed by means of the Modal Auxiliaries.

144. The Modal Auxiliaries are *may, can, must, might, could, would,* and *should.* The following sentences show their use.

You *may* go home (permission).
They *may* be here tomorrow (possibility).
I *can* find the house (ability).
He *must* come at once (necessity).
They *might* be at home (possibility).
We *could* come at six o'clock (ability).
He *would* go without his overcoat (determination).
You *should* work the problems without help (obligation).

VERB-PHRASES MADE WITH THE MODAL AUXILIARIES

145. Verb-phrases made with the help of the Modal Auxiliaries have the following forms (there are no future tenses).

ACTIVE VOICE

PRESENT TENSE

SINGULAR	PLURAL
1. I may see.	1. We may see.
2. You may see.	2. You may see.
3. He may see.	3. They may see.

PAST TENSE

1. I might see.	1. We might see.
2. You might see.	2. You might see.
3. He might see.	3. They might see.

PRESENT PERFECT TENSE

1. I may have seen, etc.	1. We may have seen, etc.

PAST PERFECT TENSE

1. I might have seen, etc.	1. We might have seen, etc.

PASSIVE VOICE

Present Tense: I may be seen, etc.
Past Tense: I might be seen, etc.
Present Perfect Tense: I may have been seen, etc.
Past Perfect Tense: I might have been seen, etc.

For a discussion of the passive voice, see Secs. 148–151.
For verb forms made with the other auxiliaries, substitute in the preceding table *can* or *must* for *may* (*can see, must see*); *could, would,* or *should* for *might* (*could see, would have seen,* etc.).

It will be noticed that *might* and *could* are the past tense forms for *may* and *can*. *Should* and *would* are the past tenses of *shall* and *will*, but the latter (*shall* and *will*) are not included in the Modal Auxiliaries.

Although *might, could, would,* and *should* are classified as past tense forms, they are often used in connection with actual present, or even future, time.

They *might* be ready now.
We *could* go tomorrow.

146. **Progressive Forms.** There are also progressive forms for the different tenses in the active voice: I *may be seeing*, etc.; I *might be seeing*, etc.; I *may have been seeing*, etc.; I *might have been seeing*, etc. For a further discussion of Modal Auxiliaries, see Secs. 438 ff.

VOICE

147. Voice is that property of a verb which indicates whether the subject of the verb is performing or receiving an action.

148. There are two voices: Active and Passive.

(1) A verb in the **Active Voice** represents the subject as acting.

He *wrote* the letter.
They *are working* in the city.
We *have seen* the president.

(2) A verb in the **Passive Voice** represents the subject as receiving the action.

The soldier *was wounded* by a shell.
We *were impressed* by the beauty of the performance.

149. When a transitive verb is in the active voice, the *direct object* names the receiver of the action (see Sec. 20); when it is in the passive voice, the *subject* names the receiver. Hence any sentence containing a transitive verb in the active voice can be changed into one having a verb in the passive voice by using the object of the original verb as the subject of the new verb.

For instance, the sentence "The boy lost a *dollar*" (active) would become "A *dollar* was lost by the boy" (passive). In this change, the original subject usually becomes the object of a preposition: thus in the example just given, the original subject, *boy*, is the object of the preposition *by* in the new sentence.

(a) When the original sentence contains a noun used as an objective complement this noun is generally retained in the new sentence as a predicate noun.

The society elected Harry *president* (active).

Harry was elected *president* by the society (passive).

(b) When the active verb has both a direct and an indirect object, either of these may become the subject of the verb in the passive voice.

The committee gave *John* a *prize* (active).

John was given a *prize* by the committee (passive).

A *prize* was given to *John* by the committee (passive).

(c) Occasionally the object of a preposition occurring after an intransitive verb is made the subject of the verb in the passive voice, the preposition remaining as an adverb (see Sec. 183).

The audience jeered at the *speaker* (active).

The *speaker* was jeered at by the audience (passive).

FORMS OF THE PASSIVE VOICE

For the forms of the active voice, see Secs. 119, 131.

150. The passive voice of any verb is made by adding the past participle of that verb to the proper form of the verb *be* in the various tenses and moods. Some form of the verb *be* is therefore always used as the auxiliary verb in making the passive voice.

151. The following table shows the passive voice of the verb *know* in the different tenses.

INDICATIVE MOOD

PRESENT TENSE

SINGULAR	PLURAL
1. I am known.	1. We are known.
2. You are known.	2. You are known.
3. He is known.	3. They are known.

PAST TENSE

1. I was known	1. We were known.
2. You were known.	2. You were known.
3. He was known.	3. They were known.

FUTURE TENSE

1. I shall be known.	1. We shall be known.
2. You will be known.	2. You will be known.
3. He will be known.	3. They will be known.

PRESENT PERFECT TENSE

1. I have been known.
2. You have been known.
3. He has been known.

1. We have been known.
2. You have been known.
3. They have been known.

PAST PERFECT TENSE

1. I had been known.
2. You had been known.
3. He had been known.

1. We had been known.
2. You had been known.
3. They had been known.

FUTURE PERFECT TENSE

1. I shall have been known.
2. You will have been known.
3. He will have been known.

1. We shall have been known.
2. You will have been known.
3. They will have been known.

SUBJUNCTIVE MOOD

PRESENT TENSE

SINGULAR

1. (If) I be known.
2. (If) you be known.
3. (If) he be known.

PLURAL

1. (If) we be known.
2. (If) you be known.
3. (If) they be known.

PAST TENSE

1. (If) I were known.
2. (If) you were known.
3. (If) he were known.

1. (If) we were known.
2. (If) you were known.
3. (If) they were known.

The other tenses have the same forms as those in the indicative mood, with the exception of the theoretical form (*If*) *he have been known*, instead of *He has been known*, in the present perfect, third person, singular number (see Sec. 134).

Exercise 27

Give the voice of each verb.

1. A hurried survey revealed the wretched conditions under which the employees were working. 2. The low white tents of the hospital were grouped around an old school-house. (Stephen Crane.) 3. This is the eternal question which confronts the artist and the thinker. (John Galsworthy.) 4. They are living in a house which was built by their great-grandfather. 5. But the evil has come with the good, and much fine gold has been corroded. (Woodrow Wilson.) 6. Titles distinguish the mediocre, embarrass the superior, and are disgraced by the inferior. (G. B. Shaw.) 7. Such a policy

could not very well be advertised from the house-tops. (G. T. Garratt.) 8. The ships were already crowded with refugees who were seeking a new home in a new land. 9. Does any sensible person believe that legislation will curb this abuse? 10. Here and there a soldier fell in the ranks, and the gap was filled in silence. (Francis Parkman.)

11. Meantime food would be sent daily in a boat under an armed escort. (Rudyard Kipling.) 12. For years he had been earnestly advocating these reforms. 13. The paper had been sealed in several places with a thimble by way of seal. (Robert L. Stevenson.) 14. I shall call at his office tomorrow morning.

Exercise 28

Restate the following sentences, changing the verbs in the active voice to the passive voice—and changing the verbs in the passive voice to the active voice.

1. Scientists had been investigating these phenomena for many years.
2. The walls of the room were almost covered with priceless engravings.
3. A trade agreement with Canada has been approved by the Senate.
4. The natives brought the travelers gifts of gold and ivory.
5. This book was written by Dickens in his later years.
6. In the distance one could see the summit of Mt. Shasta.
7. Most of their spare time was spent on their farm.
8. A new president will soon be selected by the directors.

INFINITIVES

152. An infinitive is a form of a verb introduced normally by the sign *to,* and used as a noun, an adjective, or an adverb: as, *to see, to think, to run, to find, to write.*

The infinitive, consisting of *to* followed by a verb, must not be confused with a phrase consisting of the preposition *to* followed by a noun used as its object: compare *to bring, to feel* (infinitives) with *to Europe, to the city* (prepositional phrases). The *to* used in the infinitive was originally a preposition, but in modern English it is better to regard it as simply the *sign* of the infinitive, not as a preposition.

Uses of the Infinitive

153. An infinitive is never used *by itself* as a verb: that is, it cannot be used alone with a subject to make a complete statement. For example, the phrases, "a plan *to submit* for your approval" or "they *to bring* a package," do not make a statement. A complete sentence must have a verb in addition to the infinitive: "I *have* a plan to submit for your approval." "They *are* to bring a package."

154. An infinitive may be used as a noun, an adjective, or an adverb modifying an adjective, adverb, or verb.

(1) As a Noun.

To run is healthful (subject of the verb).

I want *to go* (object of the verb—answers the question, *What?*).

To see is *to believe* (subject of the verb and predicate noun).

(2) As an Adjective.

Here is water *to drink* (modifies *water*).

He has a task *to perform* (modifies *task*).

(3) As an Adverb, modifying an adjective, verb, or another adverb.

We are glad *to come* (modifies the adjective *glad*).

The ship was ready *to sail* (modifies the adjective *ready*).

He went *to buy* a paper (modifies the verb *went*).

We came *to see* the manager (modifies the verb *came*).

It is too early *to go* (modifies the adverb *too*).

Note 1. Historically, words like *go, see,* and *find* in *can go, will see,* and *must find* are infinitives.

Note 2. Notice that an infinitive used as the object of a verb answers the question *what?* (see Sec. 20); infinitives used as adverbs answer the questions *where, when, how, how much, why,* etc. (see Secs. 231 ff.).

155. Since infinitives are verb forms, they may be modified by adverbs and have direct or indirect objects, even though the infinitives themselves are used as nouns or adjectives or adverbs.

They want to come *early* (adverb modifying *to come*).

To get *there early* was their intention (two adverbial modifiers).

He asked to see the *manager* (direct object of *to see*).

He promised to give the *boy* a *dollar* (indirect object and direct object).

FORMS OF THE INFINITIVE

156. The various forms of the infinitive are shown in the following table.

ACTIVE VOICE

	PRESENT TENSE	PERFECT TENSE
Simple	to see	to have seen
Progressive	to be seeing	to have been seeing

PASSIVE VOICE

Simple	to be seen	to have been seen

157. Tenses and Voice. The infinitive has two tenses: the present and the perfect (called Present Infinitive and Perfect Infinitive).

(1) In the **Active Voice,** the simple form of the present infinitive is made by prefixing *to* to the root form of the verb (*to turn*); the progressive form, by prefixing *to be* to the present participle (*to be turning*).

The simple form of the perfect infinitive is made by prefixing *to have* to the past participle (*to have turned*); the progressive form, by prefixing *to have been* to the present participle (*to have been turning*).

(2) In the **Passive Voice,** the present infinitive is made by prefixing *to be* to the past participle (*to be turned*); and the perfect infinitive by prefixing *to have been* to the past participle (*to have been turned*). There are no passive progressive forms.

158. Infinitives with the Sign "to" Omitted. The infinitive normally has the sign *to,* but after certain verbs this sign is regularly omitted.

They dare not *go* (to go).
I dare *say* (to say).
You need not *come* so early (to come).
They heard him *scream* (to scream).
I saw him *run* (to run).
They felt the house *shake* (to shake).
We let him *talk* (to talk).

Notice that in the last sentence, if *allowed* is substituted for *let,* the *to* is not omitted: "We allowed him *to talk.*" Also in the third sentence, if the auxiliary *do* is used before *need,* the *to* is not omitted: "You do not need *to come* so early."

Exercise 29

Point out the infinitives, and tell how each is used (as subject of a verb, predicate noun, object of a verb, adjective, adverb, etc.).

1. To grant this claim would be a mistake. 2. The committee refused to comment on the court's decision. 3. He turned to walk home, meditating. (Rudyard Kipling.) 4. To have been called his friend would have been honor enough. 5. His dominant trait was to take all things into earnest consideration. (Joseph Conrad.) 6. Many strangers came in the summertime to view the battlefield. (Nathaniel Hawthorne.) 7. Not for some minutes did we have a chance to scrutinize our surroundings. (Christopher Morley.) 8. The first problem to be solved is a difficult one. 9. With a great deal of trouble we managed to get them down to the boat with us. (R. H. Dana.) 10. Their chief concern was to find the missing will.

11. He has no desire to be known as a philanthropist. 12. The effort to establish a European standard of living in the wilderness was too great. (James T. Adams.) 13. City folks generally want to get the unemployed out of sight and out of mind. (Stuart Chase.) 14. To have many of these is to be spiritually rich. (R. L. Stevenson.) 15. Here we found our companions who had refused to go to ride with us. (R. H. Dana.) 16. You need not stop before six o'clock. 17. These berries are not good to eat. 18. The day was too warm to be pleasant.

Exercise 30

(A) In the following sentences supply the form of the infinitive as indicated. Tell how the infinitive is used (as object of a verb, adjective, etc.).

1. _____ him was a real honor. (Use (a) present active infinitive of *know;* (b) perfect active infinitive of *know*.)
2. He is pleased _____ for the presidency. (Use (a) present passive infinitive of *consider;* (b) perfect passive infinitive of *consider*.)
3. They want _____ early. (Use (a) present active infinitive of *go;* (b) present passive infinitive of *call*.)
4. The city is said _____. (Use (a) present active progressive infinitive of *burn;* (b) perfect passive infinitive of *destroy*.)
5. Her ambition is _____ Queen of the Carnival. (Use (a) present active infinitive of *be;* (b) present passive infinitive of *choose*.)
6. I am sorry _____ so much trouble. (Use the perfect active progressive infinitive of *cause*.)

(B) Use the following infinitives as indicated (a separate sentence for each use).

1. *To work* for the government—as (a) direct object of a verb; (b) predicate noun; (c) adjective.

2. *To travel* in Europe—as (a) subject of a verb; (b) an adverb; (c) an adjective.

3. *To mail* the letter—as (a) subject of a verb; (b) predicate noun; (c) direct object of a verb; (d) adjective; (e) adverb modifying a verb; (f) adverb modifying an adjective.

PARTICIPLES

159. A Participle is a verbal adjective: that is, it is a form of a verb used as an adjective to modify a noun or a pronoun.

FORMS OF THE PARTICIPLE

160. The Participle has three principal forms: the Present Participle, the Past Participle, and the Perfect Participle.

PRESENT PARTICIPLE	PAST PARTICIPLE	PERFECT PARTICIPLE
turning	turned	having turned
looking	looked	having looked
sinking	sunk	having sunk
breaking	broken	having broken
catching	caught	having caught
writing	written	having written

In the passive voice the Participle also has the following forms.
   Present Passive Participle: as, *being seen, being heard.*
   Perfect Passive Participle: as, *having been seen.*
In the active voice the Participle also has the following form.
   Perfect Active Progressive Participle: as, *having been seeing.*

161. The **Present Participle** always ends in *-ing,* and is made by adding *-ing* to the simple form of the verb: as, *being, finding, coming.* (When the simple form of the verb ends in *-e,* that letter is generally dropped when *-ing* is added: *bake, baking.*)

162. The **Past Participle** is usually made by adding *-ed, -d, -t, -en,* or *-n* to the simple form of the verb: as, *walked, placed, slept, fallen, driven;* or by changing the vowel, with or without the addition of a suffix: as, *sung*—for the verb *sing; found*—for the verb *find; spoken*—for the verb *speak.* (For a more complete list, see Sec. 462.)

163. The **Perfect Participle** consists of more than one word, and is made by prefixing *having* to the past participle: as, *having found, having walked, having fallen.*

164. A participle is used to modify a noun or pronoun, and is therefore an adjective.

The *running* water undermined the bank.

The book *lying* on the table is a volume of plays.

The man *struck* by the automobile will recover.

In the first sentence, *running* describes *water;* in the second and third, *lying* and *struck* tell which book and which man, respectively, are referred to.

165. The participle has four specific uses.

(1) As a Predicate Adjective (see Sec. 92).

This work is *interesting.*

The coat was *torn* and *faded.*

(2) As an Objective Complement (see Sec. 93).

This incident made the trip *exciting.*

They found all the prisoners *gone.*

(3) In the Nominative Absolute construction (see Sec. 25).

The train *having arrived,* we bade farewell to our friends.

The work *being finished,* we went home.

He rose quickly, his lips *trembling.*

He stood motionless, his eyes *fixed* on his opponent.

It was dark, the sun *having set* an hour before.

(4) As part of a verb.

The girl *is singing.*

The man *was injured.*

Although a participle is a form of a verb, it is never used *by itself* as a verb. When it is combined with an auxiliary verb, however, the resulting combination makes a verb: *is singing, will be coming, has been working* (auxiliary verb with a present participle); *have walked, had come, will have seen; was hurt, will be taken* (auxiliary verb with a past participle).

In constructions having *be* as an auxiliary, the participle has some of the force of a predicate adjective following a linking verb (see Sec. 101). For example, in the sentence, "The girl is *singing,*" the participle *singing* describes the subject *girl* (the singing girl) somewhat as in the sentence, "The girl is *small,*" the adjective *small* describes the subject (the small girl). However, in these verb-phrases the participle is much more than a predicate adjective, for it is the participle, and not the auxiliary, that names the action which is taking place. Hence the entire verb-phrase, such as *is singing,* is the verb in the sentence.

From what has been said, it follows that a participle used as a predicate adjective (see (1) above) should be carefully distinguished from a participle used as a part of a verb.

The work is *interesting* (predicate adjective).

The agent *is interesting* the farmers in tractors (part of a verb).

166. Since participles are derived from verbs, they may be modified by adverbs and may have objects.

Turning *quickly,* he faced his accusers (adverb modifying *turning*).

The man standing *there* is the mayor.

The chair facing the *window* is more comfortable (direct object *of facing*).

Giving the *teacher* a blank *look,* the boy sat down (indirect object and direct object).

THE GERUND, OR VERBAL NOUN IN "-ING"

167. The student must guard against the common misconception that every "verb + *ing*" is a participle.

A "verb + ing" is a Participle only when it is used as an adjective; it is a Gerund or Verbal Noun when it is used as a noun: that is, as the subject of a verb, object of a verb, etc.

Compare the following sentences:

The boy *swimming* in the lake was drowned (participle—modifies *boy*).

Swimming in the lake is good exercise (verbal noun—subject of the verb).

The boy enjoys *swimming* in the lake (verbal noun—object of the verb).

The best exercise is *swimming* (verbal noun—used as a predicate noun).

He was arrested for *swimming* in the lake (object of the preposition *for*).

168. A verbal noun may have a direct object, or both a direct and an indirect object.

Giving the *employees* a just *wage* will satisfy them.

Exercise 31

Point out the participles and gerunds, and tell how each is used (adjective, subject of a verb, object of a preposition, etc.).

1. It is a small country abounding in mineral resources. 2. Driving in the crowded city was a new and absorbing experience for him. 3. The forest behind the house needed cutting back. (John Masefield.) 4. Frequently he must content himself with devouring his evening meal uncooked. (Francis Parkman.) 5. Every voter living in the precinct should register on Tuesday. 6. This does not mean refraining from doing what we want to do. (Norman Angell.) 7. A letter mailed in the morning will be received the following day. 8. The long, low clouds seemed rather threatening. (R. H. Dana.) 9. Preparing for the bar examination meant spending long hours in the library. 10. The Earl was surrounded by his shouting and gesticulating followers. (Lytton Strachey.)

11. He had not thought of being stranded without money in an almost deserted city. 12. Coal and iron beds lay unopened. (Charles A. Beard.) 13. In place of the burning plains we were now passing among hills crowned with a dreary growth of pine. (Francis Parkman.) 14. Do you mind my giving you a little advice? (Rudyard Kipling.) 15. We heard a man calling for help. 16. He lay in the shade, his head pillowed on a smooth rock. 17. The coming of darkness prevented us from finishing the work. 18. Rising with the sun and snatching a hasty breakfast did not seem inviting to him. 19. His father having disowned him, young Calvert was now engaged in looking for work. 20. They liked being interviewed, and being asked to comment on current plays. 21. All the world being thus given me for a stage, my abilities appeared to me no bigger than a pinhead. (Joseph Conrad.) 22. We waited until we saw the money counted and locked in the vault.

Exercise 32

Write sentences containing participles and gerunds as indicated.

1. Use *encouraging*—as (a) regular adjective; (b) predicate adjective; (c) part of a verb.
2. Use *broken*—as (a) regular adjective; (b) predicate adjective; (c) part of a verb.
3. Use the following participles in nominative absolute constructions: *having come; being; being broken; having been sold.*

4. Use *working*—as (a) subject of a verb; (b) direct object of a verb; (c) predicate noun; (d) object of a preposition.

5. Use the participles *interesting* and *interested* as objective complements.

STRONG AND WEAK VERBS

169. Verbs are divided into two classes—Strong Verbs and Weak Verbs—according to the method of forming their past tenses and past participles.

170. A Strong Verb is one which forms its past tense by changing its vowel, without the addition of an ending; and its past participle either by changing its vowel, by adding *-en* or *-n*, or by both methods.

PRESENT TENSE	PAST TENSE	PAST PARTICIPLE
sing	sang	sung
find	found	found
rise	rose	risen
forget	forgot	forgotten

171. A Weak Verb is one which regularly forms its past tense and past participle by adding *-ed, -d,* or *-t,* to the form of the present tense.

PRESENT TENSE	PAST TENSE	PAST PARTICIPLE
walk	walked	walked
plan	planned	planned
wave	waved	waved
deal	dealt	dealt
mean	meant	meant

For irregular forms of verbs, see Secs. 458–462.

DEFECTIVE VERBS

172. A Defective Verb is one in which some of the forms are lacking. The Defective Verbs are *may, can, will, shall, must,* and *ought.* *May, can, will,* and *shall* have a past tense—*might, could, would,* and *should*—in addition to the present tense, but have no future and perfect tenses, infinitive, or participle. *Must* and *ought* have only the one form. Members of this group are primarily used as auxiliary verbs (*re* Sec. 103).

Chapter V   ADVERBS

173. An Adverb is a word used to modify a verb, adjective, or another adverb.

He ran *swiftly* (modifies the verb *ran*).

She was *nearly* frantic (modifies the adjective *frantic*).

He speaks *very fluently* (*very* modifies the adverb *fluently*, which in turn modifies the verb *speaks*).

CLASSES OF ADVERBS

174. The main classes of adverbs are:

1. Adverbs of Manner: "She reads *distinctly*." "He works *faithfully*." Adverbs of manner answer the question *how?* For example, "She reads *how?*" Answer, *distinctly*.

2. Adverbs of Place: "They live *here*." "I went *home*." "She is traveling *abroad*."

Adverbs of place answer the question *where?*

3. Adverbs of Time: "John will come *soon*." "My father went *yesterday*." "I will write *frequently*."

Adverbs of time answer the question *when?*

4. Adverbs of Degree: "He was *very* tall." "She spoke *most* earnestly." "They were *completely* exhausted."

Adverbs of degree approximately answer the question *how much?* or *how little?* Sometimes they seem to answer the question *how?* but with a meaning different from that expressed by adverbs of manner. In adverbs of degree there is always present the idea of *amount, extent,* or *degree*

The negative adverb *not* is an adverb of degree expressing the greatest possible degree of restriction—the entire absence of a given quality.

Note. The four classes just given cover most of the uses of *single words* as adverbs; some other adverbial relations, however, are expressed by *groups of words* (phrases and clauses)—see Secs. 198, 229 ff.

FORMS OF ADVERBS

175. Many adverbs are made by adding *-ly* to the adjective form: as, *poorly, rapidly, surely,* from the adjectives *poor, rapid,* and *sure.* Thus we say, "He is a *poor* boy" (adjective); but "He dresses *poorly"* (adverb).

Not all adverbs, however, end in *-ly:* for example, *very, almost, fast, late, hard, little, here, there,* and *often.* When an adverb of this sort has a corresponding adjective, the two are identical in form and are distinguished only by their use in the sentence: thus, "This is a *fast* train" (adjective) and "The horse ran *fast"* (adverb).

On the other hand, a word ending in *-ly* is not always an adverb; it may, for example, be an adjective: as, a *princely* gift, a *lovely* rose, a *likely* candidate, a *comely* woman.

(a) Nouns are frequently used as adverbs, especially to indicate *time* or *place* (see Sec. 28).

> They arrived last *Monday.*
> He went *home.*

176. Comparison of Adverbs. Adverbs, like adjectives, have three degrees of comparison: the Positive, Comparative, and Superlative.

A few adverbs make their comparative and superlative degrees by adding *-er* and *-est,* respectively, to the positive form: as, *late, later, latest; often, oftener, oftenest; soon, sooner, soonest.*

Most adverbs, however, form their comparative and superlative degrees by using *more* and *most,* or *less* and *least:* as, *beautifully, more beautifully, most beautifully; finely, more finely, most finely; rapidly, less rapidly, least rapidly.*

With some adverbs, both methods of comparison may be used: as, *often; oftener* or *more often; oftenest* or *most often.*

177. The following adverbs have an irregular comparison.

POSITIVE	COMPARATIVE	SUPERLATIVE
far	farther, further	farthest, furthest
near	nearer	nearest, next
well	better	best
little	less	least
much	more	most
ill, badly	worse	worst
late	later	latest, last

Some adverbs, such as *now, then, there, hitherto,* etc., cannot be compared.

For a further discussion of adverbs, see Chapter XVI.

Exercise 33

Point out the adverbs; give the class to which each belongs (time, place, etc.); and tell what word it modifies. Name the degree—positive, comparative, or superlative.

1. The audience were now listening more intently. 2. He laughs best who laughs last. 3. The wind slowly died away. (Stephen Crane.) 4. I shortly heard the raindrops falling on deck thick and fast. (R. H. Dana.) 5. Not many persons were immediately aware of the severity of the storm. 6. Then he sat down in the sun at one of the windows and silently smoked. (R. L. Stevenson.) 7. His rage had ebbed away now altogether. (H. G. Wells.) 8. They decided each spring that they had planted too many onions. 9. One of the islands formerly called the Two Sisters is gone entirely. (Mark Twain.) 10. Spring usually comes somewhat later here in this northern country.

11. The young man felt suddenly quite homesick. (John Galsworthy.) 12. We do not expect them to be here tomorrow. 13. I had never seen him so completely bewildered as he was today. 14. On these occasions we moved from our chairs, not gently but discourteously. (Rudyard Kipling.) 15. Living conditions were undoubtedly more comfortable in western Spain. (G. T. Garratt.) 16. They searched far and wide for a more promising candidate. 17. He was now idly reading a copy of the local paper, and was hardly conscious of her entry. (Thomas Hardy.) 18. The storm broke sooner than we had expected. 19. Visitors never spoke loudly there in that room of horrors. 20. Soon we came to a trail which seemed to meander idly through the forest. 21. It was already late in the day, and the sun had almost disappeared. 22. They crept forward slowly, thinking that they could no longer be seen by the campers. 23. Go now, and come back early.

178. A Preposition is a connecting word which shows the relation of a noun or pronoun to some other word in the sentence.

Thus in the sentence, "John came *from* the city," the preposition *from* shows the relation of the noun *city* to the verb *came*—John came *from,* not *to,* the city.

Many prepositions indicate direction or position: as, *over, behind, from, to, above, below, out, in, around, through, beyond, across, beside,* etc.

Other prepositions represent various kinds of relations: as, *of, except, for, besides,* etc.

179. Object of a Preposition. A preposition is regularly followed by a noun or pronoun which is called the object of the preposition (see Sec. 22).

> They work at *home.*
> Here is a letter from *her.*

180. In a few idiomatic expressions, an adverb or an adjective is used as the object, and thus becomes a noun-equivalent.

(1) Adverb.

> I did not know until *now.*
> He had come before *then.*
> They will go from *there.*
> I can see it from *here.*

(2) Adjective.

> We worked in *vain.*
> They looked on *high* for help.

181. The object is occasionally placed before the preposition.

> They searched the world *over* (*over* the world).
> He looked the house *through* (*through* the house).

182. Groups of Words Used as Prepositions. Sometimes two or more words are used together to form, in effect, a single preposition: as, *in spite of, on account of, out of, instead of, according to,* etc.

They will go *in spite of* the rain.

The building was constructed *according to* specifications.

These groups are usually parsed as single prepositions.

183. Words Used as Prepositions and as Adverbs. Some words which are generally thought of as prepositions may also be used as adverbs. They are prepositions when they have an object expressed, and adverbs when they are without an object.

PREPOSITIONS	ADVERBS
They came *in* a carriage.	Come *in!*
He fell *down* the embankment.	He fell *down*.
She walked *on* the grass.	She walked *on*.
He ran *around* the house.	He turned *around*.

Exercise 34

Point out the prepositions and name their objects.

1. The cable-cars glided to all points of the compass. (Rudyard Kipling.) 2. They walked down the main street and across the park to their hotel. 3. Without exception all the windows were wide open and filled with spectators. (Arnold Bennett.) 4. The coach started early on account of the muddy roads. 5. From now until the end of March they will be in Atlanta. 6. In spite of himself, the captain could not regain his neutrality of feeling toward his orderly. (D. H. Lawrence.) 7. The smoke kept coming out through imperceptible crevices. (Joseph Conrad.) 8. One by one they came in and took their seats in the gallery. 9. The sight of that plain sheet of paper had recalled the past with a painful vividness. (William McFee.) 10. Because of his preoccupation, he did not notice the interruption.

11. Against the blackness of the pines the windows of the old office above the express office stood out strongly bright. (Bret Harte.) 12. The period was one of suffering and anxiety to the colonists. (Francis Parkman.) 13. The same conditions exist the world over. 14. There was not another building within several leagues of the place. (Mark Twain.) 15. It is at least as far as from here to Chicago.

Exercise 35

Use the following words in sentences as (a) prepositions; (b) adverbs.

before	over	down
by	off	in
through	behind	along
up		

Chapter VII CONJUNCTIONS

184. A Conjunction is a connecting word used to join words or groups of words in a sentence.

John *and* James came today (*and* connects the nouns *John, James*).

The waves rose *and* fell (*and* connects the verbs *rose, fell*).

He must go to church *or* to school (*or* connects the groups *to church, to school*).

The sun was shining, *but* the wind was cold (*but* connects the groups *the sun was shining, the wind was cold*).

They came *when* they were invited (*when* connects the groups *they came, they were invited*).

He will come *if* he is asked.

185. There are two classes of Conjunctions—Co-ordinate and Sub-ordinate.

186. A Co-ordinate Conjunction connects things of equal rank, as nouns with nouns, verbs with verbs, adjectives with adjectives, phrases with phrases, clauses with clauses of equal rank, etc.

It was a black *and* white dog (*and* connects the adjectives *black* and *white*).

He can play the piano *or* the guitar (*or* connects the nouns *piano, guitar*).

He went *but* I stayed (*but* connects the two main clauses *he went, I stayed*).

The first three sentences given above in Sec. 184 show the use of co-ordinate conjunctions to connect nouns, verbs, and phrases.

Note. A phrase is a group of words without a subject and a verb. A clause is a group of words having a subject and a verb.

The principal Co-ordinate Conjunctions are *and, but, or,* and *nor.*

187. These Conjunctions in combination with other words form **Correlative Conjunctions:** as, *both—and, not only—but (also), either—or, neither—nor.*

Both the brother *and* the sister were present.

Neither the window *nor* the door was open.

188. A Subordinate Conjunction connects a subordinate clause with a word or another clause on which it depends.

He worked *while* it was raining.
They will go *if* you wish.
He refused *because* he was timid.

A subordinate clause may be placed at the beginning of a sentence. Thus the second sentence given above might be written, "*If* you wish, they will go." From a logical and grammatical point of view, the subordinate conjunction in such instances still connects the two clauses, although it does not actually stand between them.

Some of the more common subordinate conjunctions are: *if, although, though, when, while, until, as, since, that, because.*

189. Distinguishing between Prepositions and Conjunctions. Some rough rules may be given for distinguishing between prepositions and conjunctions—both of which are connecting words.

(1) *And, but, or,* and *nor,* together with the correlatives formed from them, are almost always conjunctions. An exception occurs in the use of *but* in the sense of *except,* as in "All were there *but* (except) my father," in which case *but* is a preposition (followed by an object).

(2) Most of the other conjunctions are used to introduce clauses: that is, they will be followed by a subject and a verb; whereas prepositions are followed by an object—a noun or a pronoun—and not by a subject and verb.

Note. These rules are intended as an aid to the student in his present stage of progress. A better idea of conjunctions will be obtained in the later study of clauses.

190. Words Used as Prepositions or as Conjunctions. Some connectives may be either prepositions or conjunctions, depending upon their use in a sentence (see Sec. 189).

PREPOSITIONS (FOLLOWED BY AN OBJECT)	CONJUNCTIONS (FOLLOWED BY A SUBJECT AND A VERB)
He went *after* dinner.	He went *after* dinner had been served.
He came *before* noon.	He came *before* the clock had struck twelve.

191. Groups of Words Used as Conjunctions. Sometimes a group of two or more words is used as a conjunction: *in order that, as if, as* *though, as well as,* etc.: "He worked rapidly, *in order that* he might finish early."

Exercise 36

Point out the co-ordinate, subordinate, and correlative conjunctions, and tell what words or groups of words they connect.

1. The room was large and neatly furnished, but not homelike. 2. They cut down the old oak tree, because it shut off their view of the mountain. 3. It seemed as though we had been forgotten by the world. (Joseph Conrad.) 4. There is no fire in the forecastle, and we cannot dry clothes at the galley. (R. H. Dana.) 5. His father, as well as an uncle and the paternal grandfather, were teachers of private schools. (Will Durant.) 6. Before he left that evening, Spode made an alarming discovery. (Aldous Huxley.) 7. You must start at once, or you will be late for work. 8. We found that someone had destroyed both the original and the copy of the letter. 9. All this the young man noticed, but it neither quickened his pulse nor hastened his hand. (James F. Cooper.) 10. It was years since he himself had coasted the China seas. (H. M. Tomlinson.)

11. If you are tired, you should either take a nap or go for a walk. 12. The copy should be in on Thursday in order that we may finish the printing by Saturday.

Exercise 37

Point out the prepositions and conjunctions. Name the objects of the prepositions. Tell what words or groups of words the conjunctions connect.

1. The steamer disappeared around a bend in the river, and we were alone. 2. He leaned over the bulwarks and stared at the broad stream and the steamer. (William McFee.) 3. They walked on until they came to a lone farmhouse beside a small lake. 4. The sun was shining, but the wind was cold and damp. 5. To my surprise, he lit no candle or lamp, but set forth into the dark passage. (R. L. Stevenson.) 6. The captain waited anxiously for the signal, for he knew that he was in dangerous waters. 7. No one knew anything about her, because there was nothing to know. (Arnold Bennett.) 8. We took two or three blankets for protection against frosty weather in the mountains. (Mark Twain.) 9. When he died, in 1903, he had come to think that his work had been done in vain. (Will Durant.) 10. He led her to a door, and down three steps. (Frank Swinnerton.)

11. He rose up and went on tiptoe to the cabin door. (William McFee.) 12. They would not return before evening, unless they caught a fast train. 13. She would not go back, she said, before the last of the soldiers had left Scutari. (Lytton Strachey.) 14. I beheld no sun either then or at any moment during the rest of the day. (George Gissing.) 15. If I did anything that he liked, I could count upon him for cordial recognition. (W. D. Howells.)

Exercise 38

Complete the following sentences, using the italicized words (a) as prepositions; (b) as conjunctions.

1. They will be here immediately *after* _____
2. They were late *for* _____.
3. We had known these people *before* _____.
4. He cannot go *until* _____.
5. They have been studying *since* _____

Chapter VIII   PHRASES

In the preceding chapters we have been dealing with the eight parts of speech. In the present section and the one that follows we pass to the discussion of groups of words, made up of various combinations of the parts of speech. These groups are Phrases and Clauses.

192. A Phrase is a group of related words without a subject and a verb.

Broadly speaking, the term "phrase" includes any group of related words without a subject and a verb: as, *a red book, running very rapidly*. In practice, however, it is usually restricted to certain groups having a formal introductory word (see below).

FORMS OF PHRASES

193. Phrases may be divided, according to the nature of their introductory words, into four classes.

(1) Prepositional Phrases: "He lives *at home*."
(2) Infinitive Phrases: "He went *to buy a hat*."
(3) Participial Phrases: "They arrested the man *driving the car*."
(4) Gerundive Phrases: "*Playing the piano* is his favorite amusement."
These are introduced by prepositions, infinitives, participles, and gerunds, respectively.

194. Prepositional Phrases. A prepositional phrase consists of a preposition and its object, together with any modifiers that may be present. Thus the phrase, *on an extremely hot afternoon*, consists of the preposition *on*, the object *afternoon*, the article *an* and the adjective *hot* modifying *afternoon*, and the adverb *extremely* modifying *hot*.

195. Infinitive, Participial, and Gerundive Phrases. Infinitive, participial, and gerundive phrases consist respectively of an infinitive, participle, or gerund, followed by an object or by other adjuncts (see the next section). To take only one example, the infinitive phrase, *to understand clearly the exact plans*, consists of the infinitive *to understand*, its object *plans,* the adverb *clearly* modifying the infinitive, the article *the* and the adjective *exact* modifying the noun *plans.*

ADJUNCTS USED IN FORMING PHRASES

196. Infinitives, participles, and gerunds are derived from verbs, and because they retain some of the characteristics of the original verbs, they may have any of the verbal adjuncts, such as an object or an adverb.

For example, a gerund is used as a noun, and ordinary nouns do not take adjuncts of this sort. These are possible because of the verbal element that has been retained. On the other hand, a gerund, because of the noun element present in it, may be modified by an adjective.

197. Table of Adjuncts. The principal adjuncts used with infinitives, participles, and gerunds to form phrases are as follows (the phrases are set off by vertical lines; the adjuncts are indicated by italics).

(1) Direct Object.

He wanted | to borrow a *dollar.*
The man | carrying the *parcel* | was arrested.
Reading the *reports* | occupied most of the day.

(2) Indirect Object.

To send the *commander* this reply | required considerable courage.
The man | bringing *us* the book | is the chief clerk.
Buying his *mother* a present | was a pleasant duty.

(3) Predicate Adjective.

To be *honest* | is his desire.
Being *ill,* | I postponed the trip.
Being *wealthy* | does not always mean | being *happy.*

(4) Predicate Noun.

He wanted | to be a *sailor.*
Being an *invalid,* | he does not attend school.
Being a *soldier* | requires self-sacrifice.

(5) Adverb.

He expects | to go *immediately.*
Turning *quickly,* | he opened the door.
Swimming *rapidly* | is good exercise.

(6) Adjective.

Careful planning | will prevent mistakes.

(7) Phrase.

He told me | to wait *at the station.*

The man | sitting *at the desk* | is the manager.

Walking *in the park* | is his favorite amusement.

(In these constructions we have a phrase within another phrase.)

(8) Clause.

To study *when the brain is weary* | means inefficient work.

(In these cases we have, not a pure phrase, but a mixed phrase and clause.)

Note. Adjectives and nouns occurring after infinitives, participles, and gerunds derived from verbs like *be, seem,* and *appear* are predicate adjectives and predicate nouns. In many cases there is no subject to which they belong, but their nature may be seen by making the following test: For the infinitive, participle, or gerund, substitute a simple form of the corresponding verb (for instance, substitute *is* for *being*); place a subject, such as *he* or any other suitable noun or pronoun, before the verb; then after the verb place the adjective or noun that is being tested. Thus in the sentence, "Being an invalid, he does not attend school," change *"being* an invalid" to *"he is* an invalid," and it is obvious that *invalid* is a predicate noun. It is therefore called a predicate noun after the participle.

USES OF PHRASES

198. Phrases are used as single parts of speech: as nouns, adjectives, or adverbs.

(1) As a Noun.

Subject of a Verb:

To read the report was the work of a moment.

Swimming the river was a difficult task.

Predicate Noun:

His object is *to defeat the enemy.*

The most difficult process is *making the cylinder.*

Direct Object of a Verb:

He hopes *to find the money.*

He enjoys *playing chess.*

Object of a Preposition:

He persisted in *beating the drum.*

In Apposition:

Her avowed purpose—*to help mankind*—was only a pretense.

His chief ambition—*making a large fortune*—has been realized.

(2) As an Adjective.
>   The man *from home* has arrived.
>   They gave us permission *to buy candy.*
>   The man *writing the letter* is the secretary.

(3) As an Adverb.
>   He came *in the morning.*
>   He went *to see the parade.*
>   The boy, *hearing the noise,* went to the window.

Adverbial phrases, like adverbial clauses, express time, place, manner, degree, cause, purpose, condition, and concession. For a discussion of these classes, see Secs. 229 ff.

199. The **Infinitive Phrase** is the only type of phrase that regularly performs the functions of all the three parts of speech. A gerundive phrase is used as a noun; a participial phrase as an adjective or as an adverb in a dual relation (see Sec. 200); and a prepositional phrase chiefly as an adjective or as an adverb.

200. Some **Participial Phrases** have a peculiar **dual function:** the participle which introduces the phrase is an adjective modifying a noun, but the whole phrase is an adverb modifying a verb. For example, in the sentence, "Harry, *seeing the danger,* shouted a warning," the participle *seeing* modifies *Harry,* but the whole phrase modifies *shouted*—that is, it is an adverb telling *why* he shouted.

A participial phrase is not used as an adverb except in this dual relation; the noun to which the participle belongs should always be in the sentence.

201. A **Gerundive Phrase** is the same in *appearance* as a participial phrase; the two are distinguished by their use—the former as a noun and the latter as an adjective or as an adverb in a dual relation, respectively.

SPECIAL TYPES OF PHRASES

202. There remain three types of phrases which are different, in general structure, from those previously discussed.

203. Verb-Phrase. The term *Verb-Phrase* is a convenient expression t use in designating those forms of a verb which are made with a auxiliary—that is, those forms which consist of more than one word: as, *will be, could go, had found, is walking, have been searching.*

204. Nominative Absolute Phrase. This construction consists of a noun and a participle used as follows (see Sec. 25).

> *The sun having set,* darkness slowly descended.
> *Our baggage having been found,* we boarded the train.
> *Dinner being over,* we assembled in the drawing room.
> *His mind failing,* he was sent to a sanitarium.
> *All things considered,* the decision was just.

(a) The Nominative Absolute Phrase generally stands at the beginning of the sentence, but it may be placed elsewhere.

> The train was late, *the bridges having been swept away by the flood.*
> He sat quietly, *his face buried in his hands.*

(b) The Nominative Absolute Phrase is regularly used as an adverb. It usually indicates reason or time, but sometimes condition, concession, or manner (for the different adverbial relations, see under Clauses, Secs. 230 ff.).

(c) Occasionally the participle is omitted in the absolute phrase, when it can be easily supplied by the reader.

> *Dinner over,* we assembled in the parlor (dinner *being* over).

205. Infinitive Phrase with a Subject. An infinitive is sometimes used with a noun or pronoun which stands in much the same relation to the infinitive as the subject of an ordinary verb bears to that verb.

> We knew *them to be friendly.*
> We believed *him to be a deserter.*
> They expected *the messenger to return at once.*

In these sentences the infinitive phrase with a subject is the object of the verb, and is equivalent to a noun clause (see Sec. 227 (3)). Thus "We knew *them to be friendly*" is equivalent to "We knew *that they were friendly.*" In the phrase, the infinitive *to be* takes the place of the verb *were,* and *them* stands for *they,* the subject of *were. Them* is called the subject of the infinitive.

(a) Sometimes *to,* the sign of the infinitive, is omitted (see Sec. 158)

> I heard him *speak* last evening.

206. A somewhat different type of infinitive with a subject is illustrated in the following sentences.

> They told *us to speak quickly.*
> He commanded *me to open the door.*

In these sentences, the simple infinitive might be regarded as the direct object of the verb and the noun or pronoun as the indirect object. Thus, in "They told *us to speak quickly,*" the infinitive *to speak quickly* tells *what* they said (direct object) and *us* shows *to whom* they said it (indirect object). However, at this stage of our study, it is simpler to regard the entire phrase—the infinitive with its subject—as the direct object of the verb.

207. An infinitive with a subject is sometimes used as the object of the preposition *for,* and the prepositional-infinitive phrase thus formed may be the subject of a verb, a predicate noun, or the object of a verb.

For him to falter would be dangerous (subject).
The best plan is *for Henry to write a personal letter* (predicate noun).
I did not intend *for you to leave so early* (object).

208. The Subject of an Infinitive is in the *objective* case—in direct contrast to the *subject of a verb,* which is always in the nominative case.

The committee considered *him* to be trustworthy.
The jury found *him* to be insane.

209. A Predicate Noun or Pronoun after an infinitive having a subject in the objective case, is in the same case, to agree with the subject.

We thought her to be *him.*
We believed these men to be *them.*

Notice that if the infinitive is changed into an ordinary verb, both the subject and the predicate pronoun are in the nominative case: "We thought that *she* was *he.*"

Exercise 39

Point out the prepositional, infinitive, participial, and gerundive phrases; tell how they are used (as nouns, adjectives, or adverbs).

1. At the table sat a wizened little man playing solitaire. 2. I had felt the need of asserting myself without loss of time. (Joseph Conrad.) 3. Then lifting the tent door, he emerged into the open air. (Thomas Hardy.) 4. The bridge spanning the creek had been washed away by the flood. 5. A desire to see his old friends had brought him back to the village. 6. It was nine o'clock, and the adverse armies stood motionless, each gazing at the other. (Francis Parkman.) 7. A hillside rising above the water promised a clear view. (Christopher Morley.) 8. The consul advised us to report at once to the British embassy. 9. Having money does not always result in

having friends. 10. The treasurer promised to submit some plan for correcting these abuses.

11. He retired to his room to soothe himself for a night's rest by perusing his account-books. (Joseph Conrad.) 12. It was a riot of twisted vines, interlacing the trees and bushes. (Theodore Roosevelt.) 13. We saw them stop before the village inn. 14. To relax for a moment was to lose all the advantage that he had gained. 15. The travelers, having eaten nothing for seven hours, decided to have lunch at the little inn. 16. Dick looked down the long, lightless streets and at the appalling rush of traffic. (Rudyard Kipling.) 17. Two weeks having passed without a letter, they sent a cablegram to New York. 18. Hence he reached the church without observation, and the door being only latched, he entered. (Thomas Hardy.) 19. Their latest proposal is for us to meet them in Washington. 20. Then we struck into the forest, and in an instant the sun was shut from sight by a thick screen of wet foliage. (Theodore Roosevelt.) 21. The neighbors believed him to be insane. 22. For him to do that would be dishonorable. 23. He enjoys reading detective stories and books of travel.

Exercise 40

Use the following prepositional phrases as (a) adjectives; (b) adverbs (a separate sentence for each use).

on a farm	in a democracy
from his home	toward the setting sun
with a foreign accent	on the manager's desk
beside a lake	through the dense forest

Exercise 41

In the following sentences, change the adverbs and adjectives to equivalent prepositional phrases.

1. He spoke *quietly* to one of the ushers.
2. A *New York* firm has been given the contract.
3. John was *then* a stamp collector.
4. He did the work *neatly* and *quickly*.
5. This law is *important* for *home* owners.
6. It is a *large* book with *colored* illustrations.

Exercise 42

Use the following phrases as indicated (a separate sentence for each use).

1. *Writing the letter*—as (a) adjective; (b) gerund—subject of a verb; (c) gerund—direct object of a verb; (d) gerund—predicate noun.
2. *Sowing the wheat*—as (a) direct object of a verb; (b) object of a preposition.
3. *Renting the farm*—as object of the prepositions *from, about,* and *on account of.*
4. *To get the money*—as (a) subject of a verb; (b) predicate noun; (c) direct object of a verb.
5. *To see the city*—as (a) adjective; (b) adverb.

Exercise 43

Change the infinitive phrases to gerundive phrases.

1. He likes to read good books.
2. To find the answer was his first task.
3. One of his jobs was to deliver the evening paper.
4. The best time to catch fish is early in the morning.
5. They have found a way to eliminate this expense.

Chapter IX CLAUSES

210. A Clause is a group of words forming a part of a sentence, and containing a subject and a verb.

The chief distinction between a clause and a phrase is that the former has a subject and a verb, whereas the latter is without these two elements.

211. Main Clauses and Subordinate Clauses. There are two classes of clauses: Main Clauses and Subordinate Clauses. The former are sometimes called Independent or Co-ordinate Clauses; the latter are also known as Dependent Clauses.

(1) A **Main Clause**, as its name implies, is the principal part of the sentence, the part which normally makes the most important statement. Without it, the sentence would be incomplete.

(2) A **Subordinate Clause** is a clause which is dependent upon the main clause, and which is used as a single part of speech in the sentence—that is, as a noun, adjective, or adverb.

Thus in the sentence, "He came home when I called," the main clause, *he came home,* makes the principal statement, and the subordinate clause, *when I called,* is used as an adverb to modify the verb *came—* it tells *when* he came.

MAIN CLAUSES

212. A Main Clause is the clause which makes the principal statement in a sentence.

In the simplest form of sentence (containing only one group of words having a subject and a verb—for example, "They will arrive at noon") it is not customary to call the group a clause, that term being reserved for *a part of a sentence.* In effect, however, this group is equivalent to a main clause.

In any sentence made up of two or more clauses, *one of them at least must be a main clause.* The others may be subordinate, or there may be one or more additional main clauses. The various combinations of clauses will be discussed in the next chapter, on Sentences.

213. **Relationship between Main Clauses.** When there are two or more main clauses in a sentence, the statements which they make must have a definite logical relationship with each other. The four principal relations are:

1. Harmony or Agreement in Thought.
2. Contrast or Opposition in Thought.
3. Alternation or Choice.
4. Consequence or Inference.

The typical conjunctions for these four classes are *and, but, or,* and *therefore,* respectively.

1. HARMONY OR AGREEMENT IN THOUGHT

214. In this group the second clause may add another statement that naturally follows and carries forward the thought of the first clause, may set forth another step in a series of incidents, or may give another item of detail in a description.

> The owner died, *and* the property passed into the hands of strangers.
> We went to the door, *and* there we found a messenger with a telegram.
> He had never paid the fine; *furthermore,* he had no intention of paying it.
> The house is modern; *moreover,* it is conveniently located.

The principal conjunctions for this group are *and, likewise, moreover, furthermore, in like manner,* and *besides.*

This general class includes two special classes.

215. **General Statement and Specific Example.** The second clause gives an example illustrating the general statement in the first clause.

> There are a number of mistakes in the article: *for example,* in the first paragraph the writer twice uses the word "effect" for "affect."
> In many respects the witness was unsatisfactory: *for instance,* he evaded pertinent questions and forgot certain essential details.

The principal conjunctions are *for example, for instance,* and *thus.*

216. **General Statement and Specific Explanation.** The second clause explains—sometimes practically repeats—the thought of the first clause in more specific terms.

He is a very wealthy man: his property is conservatively valued at twenty million dollars.

She practised the golden rule: *that is*, she treated others as she would have them treat her.

Clauses in this relation are frequently not connected by conjunctions; sometimes *that is, in other words*, and similar connectives are employed. Note the use of the colon with the clauses in Secs. 215 and 216.

2. CONTRAST OR OPPOSITION IN THOUGHT

217. The thought in the second clause is in contrast to that in the first clause.

Harry is intelligent, *but* he lacks initiative.

The president spoke eloquently in favor of the amendment; *nevertheless*, the members refused to adopt it.

The society is only four years old; *however*, it has already effected a number of reforms.

The principal conjunctions for this group are *but, nevertheless, however, yet, on the other hand*, and *on the contrary*.

3. ALTERNATION OR CHOICE

218. The second clause presents an alternative to the statement in the first one.

You must bring your ticket, *or* you will not be admitted.

Either the train is late, *or* my watch is fast.

You must go now; *otherwise* you will be late.

The principal conjunctions are *or, nor, either—or, neither—nor, otherwise*, and sometimes *else*.

4. CONSEQUENCE OR INFERENCE

219. The fact stated in the second clause is a consequence of that in the first clause, or is an inference from it.

He had made a thorough study of the subject; *consequently* he was able to answer all the questions.

The boy was small for his age and somewhat frail; *hence* he was unable to do any of the heavy work.

The books have been missing for a year; *therefore* they have probably been stolen.

In each of the first two sentences the second clause states a fact which is a direct consequence of what was said in the first clause. In the last sentence the second clause contains an inference made from the preceding statement.

The principal conjunctions are *therefore, consequently, hence, accordingly, so, thus, as a result*, and *for this reason;* sometimes *so that.*

CO-ORDINATE CONJUNCTIONS

220. The principal co-ordinate conjunctions have already been cited under the different classes of relations.

And, but, or, and *therefore*—the typical or "key" conjunctions for the four classes—are the ones most frequently employed. The others are used for the sake of variety or occasionally for greater emphasis.

221. Sometimes a "key" conjunction is combined with another connective belonging to its group.

> *and likewise, and furthermore, and moreover,* etc.; *but nevertheless but yet,* etc. (rarely, if ever, *but however*); *or else* (rarely, *or otherwise*).

And is also frequently combined with the regular conjunctions expressing consequence: *and therefore, and consequently, and so,* etc. *And* alone should not be used with this class.

222. Position of the Conjunctions. *And, but, or,* and *nor* stand at the beginning of the clause. The other conjunctions may be placed at the beginning of the clause, or within it.

> He was angry, *and* he could not conceal the fact.
>
> He was angry; *furthermore,* he could not conceal the fact.
>
> He was angry; *and furthermore,* he could not conceal the fact.
>
> He was angry, *and* it was apparent, *moreover,* that he could not conceal the fact.
>
> He had many friends in the county; his election, *therefore,* seemed assured.

223. Omission of the Conjunction. The conjunction is sometimes omitted if it is easily understood by the reader and the resulting connection is smooth.

> His father is the president of the company; ∧ his uncle was formerly the secretary (*and* is omitted).
>
> Poor boys have often risen to positions of honor: ∧ Abraham Lincoln was born in poverty and became president of the United States (*for example* is omitted).

His enemies call him a traitor; ∧ his friends say that he is merely a victim of circumstances (*but* is omitted).

224. When there are three or more main clauses in a sentence, the conjunctions are usually omitted between all the clauses except the last two.

Our plans were complete, the contracts were signed, *and* we were waiting for the contractor to begin work.

(a) Occasionally, however, conjunctions are placed between all the clauses.

The rain descended, *and* the floods came, *and* the winds blew and beat upon that house, *and* it fell not, for it was founded upon a rock.

Exercise 44

Point out the main clauses, and indicate the type of relationship existing between those in each sentence. Also name the co-ordinate conjunctions.

1. It was a dark, rainy evening, and there was no sound in the house. (James Joyce.) 2. There were many curious volumes in the library, but I had not time to look at them. (Nathaniel Hawthorne.) 3. He had no money; therefore he did not eat. 4. My native country was full of youthful promise; Europe was rich in the accumulated treasures of age. (Washington Irving.) 5. She was undeniably tired; yet she had merely loitered away the day. (William McFee.) 6. On Sundays we climbed the steep mountain trails, or we visited our friends in the valley below. 7. There were two other routes from Fort Laramie; but both of these were less interesting, and neither was free from danger. (Francis Parkman.) 8. Only one caution is necessary: that is, all holders of reserved tickets should be in their seats by eight o'clock. 9. We could not see those on deck; nor could we imagine what had caused the delay. (Joseph Conrad.) 10. There might be some difficulty at first; nevertheless, he felt sure of winning his case.

11. All the installments have been paid; moreover, they have been paid on time. 12. Franklin was a man of many interests: he was printer, publisher, author, diplomat, and philosopher. 13. The planters still offered only food, clothing, and shelter; the freedmen gave their labor in return. (Charles A. Beard.) 14. The band now struck up another melody, and by the time it was ended the dinner was over, and speeches began to be made. (Thomas Hardy.)

Exercise 45

Complete each of the following sentences by adding a main clause showing the relationship indicated. Use a different conjunction in each sentence.

1. There was a disturbance in the street _____ (clause showing harmony or agreement in thought).
2. He had lost his money during the depression _____ (harmony or agreement).
3. For a year the police had searched for the missing man _____ (contrast or opposition).
4. This candidate had the backing of the local machine _____ (contrast or opposition).
5. He had studied for three years in a German university _____ (consequence or inference).
6. There was only one reasonable way to settle the dispute _____ (specific explanation).
7. A number of improvements have been made in the apartment _____ (specific example).
8. We must have rain soon _____ (alternation or choice).
9. The road was narrow and winding _____ (a) consequence; (b) harmony or agreement; (c) contrast or opposition. (Make a separate sentence for each.)

SUBORDINATE CLAUSES

225. A Subordinate Clause is a group of words containing a subject and a verb, and used as a single part of speech in a sentence.

226. Subordinate Clauses are used as Nouns, Adjectives, or Adverbs, and are then called respectively, Noun Clauses, Adjective Clauses, and Adverbial Clauses.

Uses of Noun Clauses

227. The principal uses of Noun Clauses are:
(1) As the Subject of a Verb.
That he will succeed is evident.
Whatever you do will be satisfactory.
What you say is true.
(2) As a Predicate Noun.
The truth is *that the army was not prepared.*
(3) As the Direct Object of a Verb.
He said *that he was a lawyer.*
They know *where the gold is hidden.*

(4) As the Object of a Preposition.

I was frightened by *what he said.*

Give it to *whoever comes first.*

(5) In Apposition with a Noun.

The statement *that all men are created equal* must not be taken too literally.

(6) As an Objective Complement.

We will make the price *whatever you think is reasonable.* (Compare, "We will make the price *fifty dollars.*")

(7) In Direct Address.

Whoever did that, stand up.

(8) As the Indirect Object of a Verb.

They gave *whoever came* a present (better, "They gave a present to *whoever came*").

(9) In the Nominative Absolute Construction.

That the plan was successful having been admitted, payment should be made at once (better, "*The success of the plan having been admitted,* payment should be made at once").

Note. Uses (8) and (9) are permissible, but these constructions are often awkward and should be used with caution.

Exercise 46

Point out the noun clauses, and tell how each one is used.

1. That the report of the flood was exaggerated is now generally admitted.
2. That patent monopoly has occasionally been used to the detriment of society, few would deny. (*Time.*) 3. Your life is what you make it. 4. This venture had made him what he most wanted to be—a leader in Wall Street. 5. The fact that Pontiac was born the son of a chief would in no degree account for the extent of his power. (Francis Parkman.) 6. You could see distinctly where it ended and where the sky began. (John Burroughs.) 7. The obvious answer is that the firm was already insolvent. 8. I had lived near what was called the Jersey Market. (Benjamin Franklin.) 9. The settlers took comfort in the thought that winter would soon be past. 10. It is not a question of what we can do, but of when we can do it.

11. At sunset the second mate said that he saw land on the starboard bow. (R. H. Dana.) 12. The general impression was that everybody was rapidly taking leave of his senses. (William McFee.) 13. Yesterday one might have asked whether the democratic states would be obliged to follow this lead. (New York *Times.*) 14. What they all want most is economic security. 15. Whoever finds the money will receive a reward.

Exercise 47

Use the following noun clauses as indicated:

1. *That business will improve*—as (a) subject of a verb; (b) object of a verb; (c) predicate noun.
2. *What the result will be*—as (a) object of a preposition; (b) object of a verb.
3. *Whether democracy will survive*—as (a) subject of a verb; (b) object of a preposition; (c) predicate noun.
4. *Where he can borrow the money*—as (a) object of a verb; (b) object of a preposition.
5. *That the earth is round*—(a) in apposition with a noun; (b) as predicate noun.

USES OF ADJECTIVE CLAUSES

228. Adjective Clauses modify nouns or pronouns.

He lost the watch *which you gave him.*
The men *who work in the factory* are well paid.
He did not know the hour *when we arrived.*
The house *where Shakespeare lived* is now a museum.

The majority of adjective clauses are introduced by relative pronouns, but some have other introductory words, as in the last two of the preceding examples. Sometimes the connective is omitted.

An adjective clause regularly follows the noun which it modifies

Exercise 48

Point out the adjective clauses, and tell what nouns they modify.

1. All the villagers whom we met seemed prosperous and contented. 2. Then I went down into the streets, which are long and flat and without end. (Rudyard Kipling.) 3. The days that make us happy make us wise. (John Masefield.) 4. At present it is the farmer who pays most dearly for the luxury of high prices. (Rudyard Kipling.) 5. Places where people work are particularly fascinating after the bustle is over. (Christopher Morley.) 6. He was a man I had known years before in San Francisco. 7. This is the book to which the speaker referred in his lecture. 8. The old sexton, whom I frequently saw in the churchyard, lives in the Carlyle house. (John Burroughs.) 9. Like all people whose minds are very active, Gissing hated to attend to little details like this. (Christopher Morley.) 10. They chose an hour when the streets were almost deserted.

11. This place is the first American city I have visited. (Rudyard Kipling.)
12. Other men are lenses through which we read our own minds. (R. W. Emerson.) 13. All men are afraid of books, who have not handled them from infancy. (Oliver Wendell Holmes.)

Exercise 49

Change the adjective clauses—(a) to phrases; then (b) to single adjectives—having the same or nearly the same meaning as the clauses.

1. A friend who lives in Canada wrote to us.
2. A man who is wealthy has many responsibilities.
3. A wind which was blowing from the north drove us into the house.
4. People who have a friendly disposition make friends easily.

Exercise 50

Indicate with an *A* or an *N* the clauses which are used as adjectives or as nouns, respectively.

1. The statement that he made was false.
2. The statement that the bank had failed was false.
3. They could not discover where the gold was buried.
4. He had never revisited the town where he was born.
5. Columbus was firm in his belief that the world was round.
6. The critics cannot agree on which is the better play.
7. They did not know which they should select.
8. We have not found the passage which he quoted.

Uses of Adverbial Clauses

229. Adverbial Clauses usually modify verbs, sometimes adjectives or adverbs.

230. Adverbial clauses are divided into nine general classes, depending upon the kind of relationship which they express.

231. Clauses of Time.

Bryant wrote this poem *when he was eighteen years old.*
They arrived *before the arrangements had been completed.*
Whenever you come, you will find someone at home.
Adverbial Clauses of Time answer the question, *When?*

232. Clauses of Place.

They will be standing *where you can see them.*
Wherever he goes, he makes himself agreeable.

Adverbial Clauses of Place answer the question, *Where?*

233. Clauses of Manner.

The president acted *as if he were bored.*
They did the work *as they were directed.*

Adverbial Clauses of Manner answer the question, *How?*

234. Clauses of Degree.

They have more money *than they need.*
He is older *than his appearance indicates.*
A man is as old *as he feels.*
a They work as hard *as you do.*
He ran more swiftly *than his companion did.*
b She has so far recovered *that she can walk downstairs.*
The wound was so serious *that an operation was necessary.*

Adverbial Clauses of Degree answer the question, *How much? How little? How far?* etc.

235. Under clauses of degree are included clauses which also express the idea of: (a) *Comparison,* illustrated by the fourth and fifth sentences above; and (b) *Result,* illustrated by the last two.

For example, in the fourth sentence a comparison is made between how *they* work and how *you* work; in the last sentence the result of the serious character of the wound was *that an operation was necessary.* These clauses, however, also indicate degree, and for convenience may be classified under this heading.

236. Clauses of Cause or Reason.

They came *because they were invited.*
As he was very feeble, we objected to his going alone.
This candidate should be elected, *for he is honest and sincere.*

Adverbial Clauses of Cause or Reason answer the question, *Why?*

237. Clauses of Purpose.

They live frugally *in order that they may save money.*
They marked the trail *so that the rest of the party might find it easily.*
Men work *that they may eat.*

Adverbial Clauses of Purpose—like clauses expressing cause or reason

—answer the question, *Why?* The distinguishing feature between the two classes is that a purpose clause carries the idea that the action was *definitely planned beforehand* with a particular end in view.

238. Clauses of Condition.

The work can be finished *if each man will do his part.*
Should it be necessary to change your plans, please write to us at once.
He will not come *unless he is invited.*

Adverbial Clauses of Condition are introduced by *if* or by some equivalent word. *Should it be* is equivalent to *if it should be; unless* means *if —not. Provided* and *provided that* are other equivalents.

These clauses state the circumstances or condition under which a certain thing will be done, or is possible.

239. Clauses of Concession.

Although it was only nine o'clock, the streets were deserted.
They were not disheartened, *though the first attempt had failed.*
The plan was a good one, *even though it was not successful.*

An Adverbial Clause of Concession is introduced by *although* or some equivalent conjunction. It concedes or admits that the statement which it contains is opposed to the statement made in the main clause, but asserts that *in spite of* this opposing factor the main statement is true.

(a) The compound relative pronouns *whatever, whichever, whoever,* and expressions like *however much, no matter what,* etc., are sometimes used as equivalents of *although* at the beginning of clauses of concession.

Whatever the provocation may have been, the attack was unjustifiable.
However much we try, we cannot make any progress.
No matter what plans you make, you must be ready to adapt them to new conditions.

The first sentence, for example, is equivalent to "Although the provocation may have been great, the attack was unjustifiable."

240. Complementary Clauses Modifying Adjectives.

He was sorry *that he came.*
I am sure *that you will agree.*
We are confident *that he is the right man.*
He was careful *that we should not see him.*

This group consists of clauses used after certain adjectives, such as *sorry, glad, sure, afraid, confident,* etc., to complete the meaning of the adjectives. A few of them approximate in meaning some of the eight classes named above. For instance, in the sentence, "He was sorry *that he came,*" the subordinate clause has a meaning somewhat, although not exactly, like that of the clause in "He was sorry *because he came*" (clause of reason). Others, such as "I am sure *that you will agree,*" do not fall into any of the preceding classes. In parsing the clauses of the present group, it is sufficient to call them Complementary Adverbial Clauses Modifying Adjectives, without regard to their affiliation with any of the eight previous groups.

POSITION OF ADVERBIAL CLAUSES

241. Adverbial clauses may:
(1) Follow the main clause: "He will go *when you are ready.*"
(2) Precede the main clause: "*While you were in the city,* two men came to the house."
(3) Stand between the subject and the verb of the main clause: "This plan, *if it is successful,* will make him wealthy."

Exercise 51

Point out the adverbial clauses, and tell the kind of relation that they indicate.

1. Geography would be more interesting if it were taught with the help of lantern slides. 2. Although some repairs have been made, the property is still in bad condition. 3. The Captain turned on the electric stove in his cabin, for the night was cold. (Christopher Morley.) 4. The deck looked as though no man had been on it for years. (H. M. Tomlinson.) 5. The clouds now covered the whole sky so that one could see nothing on the forecastle-head. (William McFee.) 6. She can type a letter as fast as he can dictate. 7. He was glad that the work was finished. 8. If nature had been comfortable, man would never have invented architecture. (Oscar Wilde.) 9. When closed motor cars were first coming in, it took seventeen days to paint a car. (C. F. Kettering.) 10. The characters in the story are convincing, because they are the people we meet and talk to every day.

11. As soon as their war of prices began, everybody was interested, and some few guessed the end. (Thomas Hardy.) 12. He was a man who talked as if he had seen life and found it a tragedy. 13. He slept through the early gray of morning until the direct rays of the sun smote his closed eyelids. (Jack London.) 14. The reader, if he likes, may supply further details of the sordid picture. 15. While he was looking after the animals, I sat by

the fire engaged in the novel task of baking bread. (Francis Parkman.) 16. Thus the average contemporary American novel, though it is workmanlike and well mannered, fails to achieve its first business. (H. L. Mencken.) 17. She was sure that the money would be found. 18. They cannot finish the work by Friday even if they hire more help. 19. Wherever he goes, he is a welcome guest, for he is always an interesting companion. 20. The house, when it is finished, will be more homelike than it was before the remodeling was begun. 21. I am glad that you called on Mrs. Wright while you were in the city.

Exercise 52

Complete the following sentences, using adverbial clauses as indicated. Make a separate sentence for each use.

1. He paid his bills promptly _____. (a) clause of reason; (b) clause of time; (c) clause of condition; (d) clause of concession; (e) clause of manner.
2. _____, we shall have to hurry. (a) clause of condition; (b) clause of reason.
3. They found the purse _____. (a) clause of time; (b) clause of place; (c) clause of concession.
4. The door had been left unlocked _____. (a) clause of purpose; (b) clause of reason; (c) clause of time.
5. The firm has made more money this year _____. (a) clause of degree; (b) clause of reason; (c) clause of concession.

Exercise 53

Place the adverbial elements in as many legitimate positions as possible in the following sentences.

1. The troops paraded through the streets lined with cheering spectators. (Use *slowly*.)
2. Many of the workers asked for government aid. (Use *when they were in dire need*.)
3. The other plan would have been preferable. (Use *in some respects*.)

SUBORDINATE CONNECTIVES

242. A Subordinate Clause is introduced by (a) a Subordinate Conjunction, (b) a Conjunctive Adverb, or (c) a Relative or an Interrogative Pronoun.

243. A Subordinate Conjunction is purely an introductory or connecting word. It introduces the subordinate clause, at the same time connecting the latter with the main clause, and it has none of the functions of the other parts of speech.

> She succeeded *because* she worked hard.
>
> He will come *if* he is able.

(a) When an adverbial clause precedes the main clause, the conjunction is a connecting word even though it does not actually stand between the clauses.

(b) In some instances, such as noun clauses used as subjects of verbs, the conjunction is chiefly an introductory word, having little if any of the function of a connective: thus, "*That* he will come is certain."

244. A Conjunctive Adverb combines the functions of both a connective and an adverb: as a connective it joins the subordinate clause with the main clause; as an adverb it modifies the verb in the subordinate clause. Thus in the sentence, "He told me *where I could find the manager,*" the conjunctive adverb *where* connects the two clauses and also serves as an adverb of place modifying the verb *could find.*

245. A Relative or an Interrogative Pronoun combines the functions of both a connective and a noun: it connects the subordinate clause with the main clause, and also serves in the subordinate clause as the subject or as the object of the verb, as the object of a preposition, or as a predicate noun (see Secs. 60–62).

A relative pronoun used as a pronominal adjective, is both a connective and an adjective: as, "I know *which* apple is the best."

246. Groups of Words Used as Connectives. Frequently a group of two or more words is used as a connective. In such instances the group is treated as if it were a single word. Examples are: *as if, as though, even if, so that, in order that.*

247. Correlative Subordinate Connectives. Sometimes in addition to the connective introducing the subordinate clause another one is placed before the main clause to emphasize the relation. These two words form a Correlative Connective. Examples are: *although—nevertheless; when—then; where—there; as—therefore.*

> *Although* he is a small boy, *nevertheless* he is very strong.
>
> *When* the president signs the bill, *then* it will become a law.
>
> *Where* the soldier fell, *there* he lay motionless.

248. The Same Connective in Different Kinds of Clauses. Some connectives may introduce different kinds of clauses: noun, adjective, or adverbial. The connective is therefore not always a safe guide as to the kind of clause which follows it; that must be determined by the way in which the clause is used in the sentence. For example:

Where:

I know *where* the book belongs (noun clause—I know *what?*).

This is the town *where* he was born (adjective clause—*which* town?).

He goes *where* he pleases (adverbial clause—He goes *where?*).

That:

They said *that* they were satisfied (noun clause).

Here is the book *that* you wanted (adjective clause).

We were sorry *that* you were absent (adverbial clause).

Men study *that* they may know the truth (adverbial clause).

Note. In the second sentence *that* is a relative pronoun. In the others it is a conjunction.

249. The connectives *how* and *why* deserve special attention. We have seen that an adverbial clause of manner answers the question, *How?* and an adverbial clause of reason or purpose answers the question, *Why?* Yet these two words, *as connectives,* are commonly used to introduce noun clauses, *not* adverbial clauses. They themselves are adverbs in relation to the verbs of their own clauses.

I know *how* you feel (I know *what?*).

He asked *why* you came (He asked *what?*).

Why sometimes introduces an adjective clause.

He suspected the reason *why* you left so early.

250. The Same Connective Expressing Different Adverbial Relations. Sometimes a connective is used to express different adverbial relations.

Since:

He has lived here *since* the war ended (time).

He must go, *since* the general commands it (reason).

As:

The work was done *as* you directed (manner).

I saw him *as* I was crossing the street (time).

He defied the law, *as* he believed it to be wrong (reason).

251. Connective Omitted before Subordinate Clauses. Sometimes the connective is omitted before a subordinate clause, when the omitted

word may be easily understood or supplied by the reader or hearer. This
practice is more common in speaking than in writing.

He said ∧ they would be late (*that* omitted).

This is the coat ∧ you selected (*which* or *that* omitted).

Be it ever so humble, there's no place like home (*though* omitted—
"*Though* it be ever so humble").

Chapter X   SENTENCES

252. A sentence is a group of words expressing a complete thought.

253. The elements that have been previously studied—parts of speech, phrases, and clauses—are only *parts of sentences*. When used by themselves, they do not express a complete thought, they do not make a statement. In order to do this, they must be combined according to definite grammatical principles, and the resulting combination is a sentence.

254. Sentences are divided, according to their construction, into three classes: (1) Simple Sentences, (2) Complex Sentences, (3) Compound Sentences. This classification is based on the number and character of the clauses contained in the sentence.

SIMPLE SENTENCES

255. A Simple Sentence is a sentence which contains only one group of words having a subject and a predicate.
The simple sentence, therefore, has only one subject and one predicate. The subject and the predicate may be simple, or either or both of them may be compound (see Secs. 275–6; 280–1).

> *John went* to the office (simple subject, simple predicate).
> The *guests came* early and *stayed* late (simple subject and compound predicate).
> The *boy* and his *sister are* in town (compound subject, simple predicate).
> *Harry* and *James went* to the factory and *asked* for work (compound subject, compound predicate).

The subject may therefore contain two or more nouns, and the predicate two or more verbs; but the nouns will form one connected group, and the verbs a connected group. In complex and compound sentences, which have more than one clause, there will be a separate subject group and a separate predicate group in each of the clauses.

COMPLEX SENTENCES

256. A Complex Sentence is a sentence which contains one main clause and one or more subordinate clauses.

The manager believed *that his decision was just.*

This book, *which was written by an eye-witness,* is authoritative.

Although he was wounded, he remained in the trenches.

257. Sentences having a noun clause as the subject of the main clause show a variation from the usual form of the complex sentence. They do not have two *separate, complete* clauses, for the noun clause is a part of the main clause, the latter being co-extensive with the entire sentence. They are, however, classed as complex sentences.

That he should fail seemed incredible.

Whatever you do will be satisfactory.

COMPOUND SENTENCES

258. A Compound Sentence is a sentence which contains two or more main clauses.

The signal was given, | and | *the steamer moved slowly from the dock.*

The tents were pitched, | *a fire was started,* | and | *our dinner was soon ready.*

259. A compound sentence may also contain one or more subordinate clauses, in addition to the main clauses.

The traveler registered *when he arrived at the hotel,* and then he was taken to his room, *which was on the fourth floor.*

Structurally, therefore, a compound sentence consists of two or more simple or complex sentences combined to form a single sentence.

VARIOUS COMBINATIONS OF CLAUSES

260. Thus far, only the simpler forms of complex and compound sentences have been discussed. Those described below show different combinations of clauses.

261. A series of two or more subordinate clauses is sometimes used in the same construction in a sentence.

The foreman reported *that* the necessary supplies had been procured, *that* the required number of workmen had been hired, and *that* work on the foundation would begin on the following day. (Three noun clauses—all objects of the verb *reported.*)

A man *who* is trustworthy and *who* has the proper training will advance rapidly in this firm. (Two adjective clauses modifying the same noun *man.*)

262. A compound sentence may contain three main clauses which fall into two groups: one group consisting of two clauses strictly co-ordinate with each other; and the other having a single clause co-ordinate with the combined group rather than with each of the two clauses separately.

The weather was cold *and* a heavy snow was falling; *therefore* we postponed our journey. (The first two clauses are co-ordinate; the result is co-ordinate with the combined two.)

Our journey was interesting enough at first; *but* the scenery soon became monotonous *and* the torrid heat irritated us almost beyond endurance.

263. The following sentences show miscellaneous combinations of clauses.

(a) While I was waiting at the station, a man who had been talking with the agent told me that the train had been delayed by a wreck.

A man told me is the main clause.

While I was waiting at the station is an adverbial clause modifying the verb *told.*

Who had been talking with the agent is an adjective clause modifying the subject *man.*

That the train had been delayed by a wreck is a noun clause used as the direct object of the verb *told.*

(b) The fire which destroyed the building is said to have been set by a discharged employee while the watchman was absent from his post; but if this is the case, the officials who are investigating the affair cannot understand why the man did not select a more valuable part of the factory as the object of his revenge.

The fire is said to have been set by a discharged employee is the first main clause.

The officials cannot understand is the second main clause.

Which destroyed the building is an adjective clause modifying the noun *fire.*

While the watchman was absent from his post is an adverbial clause modifying the infinitive *to have been set.*

If this is the case is an adverbial clause modifying the verb *cannot understand*.

Who are investigating the affair is an adjective clause modifying the noun *officials*.

Why the man did not select a more valuable part of the factory as the object of his revenge is a noun clause used as the object of the verb *cannot understand*.

(Notice that the conjunction *but* does not connect the two adverbial clauses *while the watchman . . .* and *if this . . .* ; it connects the two main clauses, *the fire is said to have been set by a discharged employee* and *the officials cannot understand*.)

DECLARATIVE, INTERROGATIVE, IMPERATIVE, AND EXCLAMATORY SENTENCES

264. Sentences may be divided into four classes according to the manner in which the thought is expressed: (1) Declarative Sentences, (2) Interrogative Sentences, (3) Imperative Sentences, (4) Exclamatory Sentences.

265. A **Declarative Sentence** is one which states something as a fact. It is punctuated with a period.

The message was written last Monday.

He hopes to be here for the meeting.

266. An **Interrogative Sentence** is one which asks a question. It is punctuated with an interrogation point (question mark).

Will you see him today?

Can you go with us?

267. An **Imperative Sentence** is one which expresses a command or an entreaty. It is punctuated with a period.

Come at six o'clock.

Let us start immediately.

268. An **Exclamatory Sentence** is one which expresses strong feeling or emotion, as delight, fear, or surprise. It is punctuated with an exclamation point.

How beautiful the evening is!

What a time we had!

269. Variations in Form. The examples just given show the typical forms of sentences used in stating a fact, asking a question, giving a command, and expressing strong emotion, respectively. There are, however, a number of variations from these forms.

270. A question may be asked in a sentence having the form or word order of a declarative sentence, the interrogative meaning being indicated by an interrogation point.

> You believe this report? (instead of "Do you believe this report?").
> The note was forged, you say?

271. A command may be expressed:

(1) In the form of a question.

> Will you please send your check at once.

Sentences of this sort obviously express a command or positive request, and not a mere inquiry. The interrogation point is sometimes used at the end, but the period is often preferable.

(2) In the form of a declarative sentence.

> You will please report for duty on Tuesday.

(3) In the form of a combined command and question.

> Come at once, won't you?

These forms are used when a writer or speaker wishes to soften a command or express it more politely than the usual type of imperative sentence permits.

272. An exclamation may be expressed:

(1) In the form of a question.

> Who would have thought it possible!

(2) In the form of a declarative sentence.

> The idea is simply preposterous!

(3) In the form of a command.

> Don't hesitate! Go at once!

In these sentences the strong feeling is indicated by the exclamation point in writing, and by stress of voice in speaking.

Exercise 54

Tell whether the following sentences are simple, complex, or compound. Point out the main and subordinate clauses. Name the relationship existing between the main clauses, and tell how the subordinate clauses are used.

1. In spite of all our anxiety, we enjoyed this search for work. (Hamlin Garland.) 2. The night was dark, and a stiff wind was blowing from the north, as we neared the mouth of the harbor. 3. Liberty may be an un-

comfortable blessing unless you know what to do with it. (Walter Lippmann.) 4. Character is what we are; reputation is what men say we are. 5. He had two alternatives: he could take the evening train, or he could go by plane the next morning. 6. He had seen thatched and timbered cottages, and half-a-dozen inns with creaking signs. (H. G. Wells.) 7. This was the first blow that I had seen which could be called a gale. (R. H. Dana.) 8. He liked the other employees, he was interested in the work, but sometimes he felt the futility of it all. 9. He was well connected; yet there was something wrong with his luck, and he never got on. (Joseph Conrad.) 10. He was a man now; therefore he must do man's work.

11. Knowing the captain's fondness for this dish, the cook had prepared a steaming steak and kidney pie. 12. About an hour before sundown, having stowed our water-casks, we commenced getting under way. (R. H. Dana.) 13. They rounded another corner, and still more steeply the hill rose before them. (H. G. Wells.) 14. You may think from all this that I am a confirmed reactionary who deprecates experiment. (John Galsworthy.) 15. He has twice been in prison for forgery; moreover, he is now under indictment for smuggling. 16. Even after they were safely settled on this side of the water, immigrants had to work many months before they could harvest a crop of grain for their bread. (Charles H. Beard.) 17. And he knew that the day had come again, when he must go on with his round. (D. H. Lawrence.) 18. Democracy is on its trial, and no one knows how it will stand the ordeal. (William James.) 19. This was natural, for if Miller was a spy he was probably a clever person who knew what he wanted. 20. A few in the ward could read, but more could not; and almost without exception they spoke that peculiar dialect which is the curious inheritance of the Londoners. (A. E. Newton.) 21. The men in the boat continued to stare at the place where their boat had been, as though they still saw her. (H. M. Tomlinson.) 22. Yet the scene is tame in one sense: there is no hint of the wild and the savage. (John Burroughs.)

Exercise 55

Change the following compound sentences to complex and, if possible, to simple sentences. Try to give two or three different versions that express practically the same thought as the original sentence.

1. The work was hard, but we enjoyed doing it.
2. Dinner was finished, and we went downtown to the opera.
3. Mayor Gifford had the support of the machine, and he was re-elected by a large majority.
4. He had no ticket, and therefore he was not admitted.

5. There was no moon, but we had little difficulty in keeping to the trail.
6. He has been working on the problem for over a year, and during that time he has made some striking discoveries.
7. Men were gathered in groups on the avenue, and they seemed excited over something.
8. You must return the book, or you will have to pay a fine.
9. Give them three days more, and they will have the house ready for you.
10. I met a friend at the club, and he invited me to play a game of golf with him.
11. He wants to keep his credit clear; consequently he always pays his bills promptly.
12. Monday was a holiday, and the banks were closed.
13. We liked the characters in the novel, but we did not approve of the plot.
14. There were few people on the street at that hour of the night, and they looked forbidding.
15. The roads were muddy, and we made slow progress that day.
16. He is taller than John, but John is heavier.
17. I was in Springfield yesterday, and I met the Governor.

Chapter XI   SUBJECT AND PREDICATE

273. In order to make an assertion two elements are necessary: something to talk about, and something to say about that thing. In a sentence the first element is represented by the subject, the second one by the predicate. Every complete sentence, therefore, must have a subject and a predicate.

THE SUBJECT

274. The subject of a sentence may be Simple or Compound.

275. Simple Subject. The Simple Subject consists of a single noun or noun-equivalent without modifiers or other adjuncts.

Thus in the sentence, *"Dogs* are faithful animals," the simple subject is *dogs;* in the sentence, "The first *visitor* from Boston has arrived," the simple subject is *visitor.*

Instead of an ordinary noun or pronoun, any of the following constructions may be used as the simple subject.

(1) An Adjective: "The *poor* are always with us."
(2) A Gerund: *"Skating* is healthful and pleasant exercise."
(3) An Infinitive: *"To err* is human."
(4) A Phrase: *"Writing letters* will require some time."
(5) A Clause: *"That he will go* is certain."
(6) Any part of speech when it is spoken of as a *word,* not as the name of something: *"Was* is a verb."

Note. The bare skeleton of a phrase or clause, without any modifiers, is the simple subject: as, *"To find* the best *methods* of doing the work | is their problem." *"That some* of us *will go* after dinner | is certain." (The simple subjects are indicated by italics.)

276. Compound Subject. A Compound Subject consists of two or more simple subjects. These simple subjects are usually, but not necessarily, connected by conjunctions.

Thus in the sentence, "The *horses* and the *sheep* were sold," the compound subject is *horses* and *sheep*.

277. Complete Subject. The simple or the compound subject may be modified or amplified by various adjuncts. The combined group is called the **Complete Subject.**

The honest man who does his work well will succeed.

278. The principal adjuncts which are thus used are:

(1) An Adjective: "The *beautiful* flowers | have faded."
(2) A Noun in Apposition: "My dog, *Rover,* | is lost."
(3) A Noun in the Possessive Case: *"John's* book | is the best."
(4) A Phrase: "The sleeve *of the coat* | is torn." "The man *crossing the street* | is the judge." "His desire *to own the horse* | was obvious."
(5) A Clause: "The official *who is responsible* | will be indicted."
(6) Any adjunct belonging to the preceding classes of adjuncts.

For instance, an adjective modifying the simple subject may in turn be modified by an adverb—"An *exceedingly* severe storm had risen"; a participle modifying the simple subject may be modified by an adverbial phrase or clause—"A man living *where the winters are long* becomes accustomed to the cold weather"; or a noun used as the adjunct of the simple subject may have any of the ordinary adjuncts of a noun.

Exercise 56

Point out the simple or compound subject, and the complete subject; then name the adjuncts which help to form the complete subject, and give their use.

1. Citizens of a free country are indeed fortunate. 2. The freshness of the summer morning inspired and braced him as he stood. (Thomas Hardy.) 3. Watching a coast as it slips by the ship is like thinking about an enigma. (Joseph Conrad.) 4. After many experiments, peaches, oranges, grapes, and other fruits were found to grow luxuriantly. 5. The sealed and sullen sunset behind the dark dome of St. Paul's had in it smoky and sinister colours. (G. K. Chesterton.) 6. Captain Rossiter, the explorer, who was to have been the chief speaker, was unable to come to the meeting. 7. The day and the hour came; but a drizzling rain fell. 8. A huge mist, capped with black clouds, came driving towards us. (R. H. Dana.) 9. To visit this primitive wilderness had been a cherished dream. (W. H. Hudson.) 10. A half-starved dog that looked like Wolf, was skulking about it. (Washington Irving.)

THE PREDICATE

279. The main word, or nucleus, of the predicate is a verb. The predicate may be either Simple or Compound.

280. Simple Predicate. The Simple Predicate consists of a single verb, like *walk*, or a single verb-phrase, like *have walked*.

I *walk*.
We *have walked* to town.

281. Compound Predicate. The Compound Predicate consists of two or more simple predicates, usually connected by conjunctions.

The girls *read* and *knit*.
He *went* to the office and *wrote* some letters.

282. Complete Predicate. The simple or compound predicate may be modified or amplified by various adjuncts. The combined group is called the **Complete Predicate.**

283. The principal adjuncts which may be thus used are:

(1) A Predicate Noun or Adjective: "The man | is a *lawyer*." "His father | is *wealthy*."

Note. A predicate noun or a predicate adjective actually belongs to the subject, but since its position is after the verb, in the *predicate,* it is regarded as an adjunct of the verb.

(2) A Noun or Pronoun used as a Direct Object: "The clerk | submitted his *report*."

(3) A Noun or Pronoun used as an Indirect Object: "They | gave the *officer* a medal."

(4) An Objective Complement—either a noun or an adjective: "We | made him a *major*." "They | painted the house *white*."

(5) A Noun in Apposition: "We | met General Pershing, the *commander* of the army."

(6) An Adverb: "He | worked *silently*."

(7) An Adverbial or Noun Phrase: "They | came *from California*." "John | went *to buy a book*." "I | expect *to send a telegram*."

(8) An Adverbial or Noun Clause: "The regiment | surrendered *because it was outnumbered*." "He | said *that he would go*."

(9) Any adjunct of any of the preceding adjuncts. These may include practically any part of speech.

Exercise 57

Point out the simple, compound, and complete predicates; then name the adjuncts used in the complete predicates and tell how each is used.

1. His dream had now become a reality. 2. The ringing of the telephone aroused him from his reverie. 3. Activity is the only road to knowledge. (G. B. Shaw.) 4. A few ragged crows flapped by over the naked fields. (Ellen Glasgow.) 5. The captain spun around on his heel and fronted us. (Robert L. Stevenson.) 6. As he watched the shadows among the trees, a strange feeling of unreality came over him. 7. Then I unhooked and closed the door, and even pushed the bolt. (Joseph Conrad.) 8. The two men carrying heavy oak staves advanced cautiously, for they knew that the guards were armed. 9. Elizabeth, that silent, observing woman, had long noted how he was rising in favour among the towns-people. (Thomas Hardy.) 10. The party of explorers had for some hours been following a well defined trail through the jungle.

11. He shrugged his shoulders, shook his head, cast up his eyes, but said nothing. (Washington Irving.) 12. Had he no friends possessed of even slight intelligence? (Booth Tarkington.) 13. Through a clearing in the forest, we could see a lone cabin.

POSITION OF THE SUBJECT AND PREDICATE

284. Normal Position. In the normal arrangement of a sentence, the subject with its adjuncts is placed first and the verb or predicate with its adjuncts follows it. With this arrangement a line drawn between them will make two separate and complete groups. For example:

> The building which we finally decided to lease | had been built for use as a hotel during the World's Fair.

285. Variations from the Normal Arrangement. Frequently—for emphasis, variety in structure, or other reasons—this normal arrangement is changed, either by reversing the order of the groups as a whole, or by giving a special position to some of the adjuncts.

(1) The predicate and all its adjuncts may precede the subject
> *Here comes* the officer!
> *Swiftly and smoothly flows* the river.

(2) The object may precede the subject.
> *These mistakes* you must avoid.
> *What his ambition is,* everybody in the city knows.

(3) An adverbial element modifying the verb may be placed at the beginning of the sentence; this element may be a single adverb, a phrase, or a clause.

Silently they laid him to rest.

At ten o'clock the president and his cabinet entered the room.

When we arrived at the hotel, our party, consisting of ten people, found that no accommodations were available.

Note. In questions the verb or part of the verb-phrase regularly precedes the subject (see Secs. 122 ff.).

Can you *come?*

286. Introductory "It" and "There." Sometimes a special type of arrangement is secured by the use of an introductory *it* or *there.*

It was true *that he had failed.*

It is gratifying *to see so many people here.*

There are two *men* in the room.

There will be a noted *speaker* at the meeting.

The subjects of the verbs are the italicized expressions, as may be seen from the following rearrangement of the sentences, in which the *it* and *there* have been omitted without making any change in the meaning.

That he had failed was true.

To see so many people here is gratifying.

Two *men* are in the room.

A noted *speaker* will be at the meeting.

287. In the original sentences, the "it" and "there" are rhetorical devices used to allow the subjects to be placed after the verbs; in parsing they are to be called merely "introductory words" or "expletives" (the word "expletive" means a "filler").

Note 1. In sentences of this type beginning with *it,* the *it* is in an appositive relation with the phrase or clause which follows the verb: for example, *"It* (namely, *that he had failed)* is true." *It* might, therefore, be regarded as the subject; but since this introductory word is colorless by itself, and gets its meaning from the phrase or clause, the latter is more properly called the subject.

There, on the other hand, has none of the nature of a subject; it is purely an introductory word.

Note 2. In some instances it is not possible to omit the *it* or *there* and rearrange the rest of the sentence so as to make a good grammatical construction. Thus, the sentence, "There will be a place for everyone," cannot be changed to read, "A place for everyone will be," or "A place will be for everyone." The introductory word is necessary in a case of this sort, but it is not the subject: that follows the verb just as it does in the sentences previously given.

Note 3. It always requires a singular verb. *There* may be followed by a singular or a plural verb: singular if the subject is singular; plural if the subject is plural.

It *is* certain *that the criminal will be arrested* (single clause as subject).
It *is* true *that his condition is serious and that some remedy must be found at once* (two clauses as subject).
There *is* one *book* on the table (singular subject).
There *are* two *books* on the table (plural subject).

Exercise 58

Point out the subjects and predicates—simple, compound, and complete; name the adjuncts in each complete subject and predicate.

1. The smoke of the invisible fire was coming up again. (Joseph Conrad.) 2. Precautions have already been taken to prevent a repetition of the accident. 3. From a single chimney smoke rose in columns. (Ellen Glasgow.) 4. Never did mortal suffer what this man suffered. (Nathaniel Hawthorne.) 5. To get the money from the bank was their next step. 6. Now they lived a very simple life, he and his mother. 7. Down the stairs and into the courtyard streamed the frenzied mob. (Lytton Strachey.) 8. Mr. Allison, the purser of the steamer *Amazon,* which was lying at anchor in the harbor, was the only witness of the accident. 9. It was not easy to state the argument simply, although he knew the subject thoroughly. 10. History and exact science he must learn by laborious reading. (R. W. Emerson.)

11. The quiet good humour of his manner left his two opponents helpless. (G. K. Chesterton.) 12. There were a good many passengers, but I had very little to say to them. (Mark Twain.) 13. When the old patriarch went home that evening, he was almost reconciled to death. (Will Durant.) 14. Having sufficiently rested, they proceeded on their way at evenfall. (Thomas Hardy.) 15. Just then a distant whistle sounded, and there was a shuffling of feet on the platform. (Willa Cather.) 16. Scattered in the ranks of the volunteers are a fair number of old soldiers. (Rudyard Kipling.) 17. It is almost certain that the Senate will accept the president's recommendation. 18. Feeling that he was trespassing, he walked to the western side of the house, climbed the stone steps, and rang the bell, which gave forth a jangle far away to

the left. (John Masefield.) 19. Whatever we do about it will probably be futile. 20. Behind their backs was a small window, with a wheel ventilator in one of the panes, which would suddenly start off spinning. (Thomas Hardy.)

Chapter XII

SOME IRREGULAR
CONSTRUCTIONS

ELLIPTICAL SENTENCES

288. An Elliptical Sentence is one which is incomplete because of the
omission of some part or parts.

This type of sentence is used under certain circumstances when the
omitted part may be readily supplied from the context.

As the result of ellipsis, a sentence may be without an expressed subject or verb, and often a short phrase or even a single word may stand
for a complete statement.

289. Ellipsis may occur in a simple sentence, in a main or subordinate
clause, or in a phrase. The following examples are typical.

290. Simple Sentences.

(1) Exclamations.

Shame on you! (May shame be on you!)
Welcome to our city! (You are welcome to our city.)
Success to you! (I wish success to you.)
Away with your foolishness! (Go away with your foolishness.)
Nonsense! (That is nonsense.)

(2) Commands or Requests.

Come here. (You come here.)
Less noise, please. (Let us have less noise, please.)
Some more coffee, please. (Give me some more coffee, please.)

(3) Questions.

All ready? (Are you all ready?)
Why such haste? (Why are you in such haste?)
Why write at all? (Why do you write at all?)
You here so late? (Are you here so late?)
Well, what of that? (Well, what is the significance of that?)
He will not come. *Why?* (Why will he not come?)
Did you see that man? *Which one?* (Which one do you mean?)

(4) Statements in Answer to a Question.

Who brought the message? *John*. (John brought the message.)
When did you come? *Yesterday*. (I came yesterday.)
Did you find it? *Of course*. (Of course, I found it.)

291. Main Clauses in Compound and Complex Sentences.

A few more days, and the convention will close (a few more days will pass).
Mr. Smith is a lawyer; *his son, a physician* (his son is a physician).
What if they refuse? (What will you do if they refuse?)
If he would only come! (If he would only come, I should be content.)

292. Subordinate Clauses.

If necessary, we can go at once (if it is necessary).
When last seen, John wore a gray hat (when he was last seen).
While fighting in France, he was seriously wounded (while he was fighting in France).
The book is interesting, *though rather brief* (though it is rather brief).
He worked harder *than usual* (than it was usual for him to work).
He is as old *as Harry* (as Harry is old).
They like him better *than her* (than they like her).
You may give it to *whomever you wish* (whomever you wish to give it to).
The game will be played, *rain or shine* (if it rain or if it shine—subjunctive forms of the verbs—see Sec. 134).
He thought you would be there (the conjunction *that* is omitted).
This is the boy they sent (the relative pronoun *whom* (or *that*) is omitted).

293. Phrases.

(1) The participle is sometimes omitted in Nominative Absolute Constructions.

Breakfast over, we hurried to the station (breakfast being over).

(2) The preposition is sometimes omitted.

He sat quietly, *every sense alert for danger* (with every sense alert for danger).

Note. This sentence may be regarded as showing the omission of a participle instead of a preposition: "*keeping* every sense alert for danger."

(3) The object of a preposition is sometimes omitted after a noun or pronoun in the possessive case.

He is living *at his brother's* (at his brother's house).
I traded my book *for his* (for his book).

Note. A similar omission of a noun after a possessive case occurs also in other constructions: *"His* is the best book" (His book is the best book).

INDEPENDENT ELEMENTS

294. An Independent Element is one which is without grammatical connection with the rest of the sentence.

These elements are related in *thought,* but they are not connected with the context in accordance with the principles of *grammatical* relation which govern the use of other constructions in the sentence.

295. The chief forms of Independent Elements are Interjections, Parenthetical Expressions, and Independent Adverbs.

296. Interjections. These usually express surprise, or some other emotion.

> *Oh,* I have been in the office all day.
> *Ah,* is that so?
> *Oh yes!* that is the usual answer.
> His father, *alas,* is no better.
> *There!* that finishes my part of the work.
> *Why!* I didn't know that he had gone.
> *Nonsense!* he won't hurt you.
> *Handsome!* you surely don't consider him handsome!

297. Parenthetical Expressions. These range in nature from short phrases which have a comparatively close connection in thought with the rest of the sentence, to complete statements thrown into the sentence as "asides" or afterthoughts.

> This book, *in my opinion,* is the best of his works.
> *To be perfectly frank,* I do not approve of his methods.
> His name, *by the way,* is the same as yours.
> Their opinion, *it seems to me,* is not worth consideration.
> A considerable number of signatures—*say fifty*—must first be secured.
> That man—*I hope that you will tell him what I say*—is a scoundrel.

298. Independent Adverbs. These adverbs modify the thought of an entire sentence, rather than any single word in it, and also serve as a sort of connective with the preceding sentence.

> *Fortunately,* we were able to secure a week's supply of food.
> This decision, *unfortunately,* was made too late.

Certainly, I shall be glad to go.
Happily, no one was injured.

Exercise 59

Point out the elliptical constructions, and expand them into their full form.

1. Books are the best of things, well-used; abused, among the worst. (R. W. Emerson.) 2. Millions for defense, but not one cent for tribute. 3. That done, he was ready for the next task. 4. He was a failing man, no doubt of that. (E. L. Masters.) 5. Nine o'clock at last, and the drudging toil of the day was ended. (O. Henry.) 6. Colet moved as if to ask the critic a question. (H. M. Tomlinson.) 7. Well, what if he did say it? 8. Strange to say, his fame vanished almost as quickly as it came. (Will Durant.) 9. "What sort of job?" asked her father suspiciously. "Shorthand." "In the city?" "Yes." (William McFee.) 10. We had to hold on while on deck, and cling to our bunks when below. (Joseph Conrad.)

11. Why go today when you are so busy? 12. The boy was twelve years old; the girl, only ten. 13. A few minutes later, and the train drew up at the grimy little station. (Hamlin Garland.) 14. You will find him at the dentist's. 15. He was sixty, if a day, a little man with a broad, not very straight back. (Joseph Conrad.) 16. For all this loss and scorn, what offset? (R. W. Emerson.) 17. When you left the Bishop's Hotel, what then? (E. A. Poe.) 18. Every excess causes a defect; every defect an excess. (R. W. Emerson.) 19. The sooner I drive him away, the better. (Nathaniel Hawthorne.) 20. It became almost as dark as night. (R. H. Dana.)

21. Though tired and discouraged, he pushed onward through mist and mud. 22. A gray-haired woman was sitting in a rocking-chair, her hands in her lap. (Hamlin Garland.) 23. Good! But a little more slowly, please. 24. The story, if true, is an amazing revelation of political corruption. 25. So far, so good.

PART TWO

Chapter XIII NOUNS AND PRONOUNS

USES

299. The principal uses of nouns and pronouns are (see Secs. 17 ff.):

Subject of a Verb	Objective Complement
Predicate Noun	Direct Address
Direct Object of a Verb	Nominative Absolute
Indirect Object of a Verb	Apposition
Object of a Preposition	

Some special uses are also to be noted.

COGNATE OBJECT

300. Some verbs which are ordinarily intransitive may take what is known as a Cognate Object, which expresses an idea similar to that of the verb.

They died a horrible *death*.
She lived a *life* of ease.
He smiled a happy *smile*.

RETAINED OBJECT

301. A verb in the passive voice may be followed by what is known as a Retained Object.

He was granted a *furlough* by his superior.
The buyer was allowed a *discount* of two per cent.

302. Either a direct or an indirect object of a verb in the active voice may remain as the retained object when the verb is changed to the passive voice. Thus the sentence, "The citizens gave the *soldiers* a hearty *welcome*," which has the verb in the active voice, may be expressed in the passive voice as follows.

The soldiers were given a hearty *welcome* by the citizens. (The direct object remains as the retained object.)
A hearty welcome was given the *soldiers* by the citizens. (The indirect object remains as the retained object.)

303. A clause or an infinitive phrase may be used as a retained object.

They were told *that the letter had arrived.*

He was commanded *to appear in court.*

With the verbs in the active voice, these sentences would read:

We told *them that the letter had arrived.*

The judge commanded *him to appear in court.*

Reciprocal Pronouns

304. *Each other* and *one another* are called Reciprocal Pronouns. They represent two or more persons or things as interacting.

They admired *each other.*

They saw *one another* frequently.

In these constructions a peculiar combination of subject and object exists. Thus, in the first sentence, *they* appears to be the subject of the verb, and *each other* appears to be the direct object. Actually, however, *they* includes both *each* and *other; each* is the logical subject; *other* is the logical object; and *they* is a sort of expletive or "filler." Reconstructed from this point of view, the sentence would read, "*Each* admired the *other.*"

Special Forms of Apposition

For the ordinary forms, see Sec. 23.

305. Introduced by "Namely," etc. A noun in apposition may be introduced by *that is, namely, or, for example,* and *such as.*

The chief magistrate, *that is, the president,* will not be present.

Two officials—*namely, the president and the secretary*—have been indicted.

A small quantity of sodium chloride, *or common salt,* should then be added.

Some nations—*for example, France*—have become republics.

Certain commodities, *such as flour and sugar,* have become cheaper.

A noun introduced by *for example* and *such as* is not a complete appositive, for it represents only a part of the idea expressed by the preceding noun: thus, in the next to the last sentence, *France* is only one of the *nations.*

306. Introduced by "As." *As* may be used to introduce a certain sort of appositive which also has some adverbial meaning.

I have never thought much of him *as a writer.*

Algebra, *as a study,* is very interesting.

You, *as a stockholder*, must do your part.

In the first sentence, *writer* is in a sort of apposition with *him*, but *as a writer* also performs some of the function of an adverb: it indicates in what manner or in what respect I think of him. In the third sentence, *as a stockholder* carries some of the idea of reason that is conveyed by "You must do your part *because you are a stockholder.*"

(a) A peculiar variant of this construction has the second noun in apposition with another noun or pronoun in the possessive case.

John's record as a *soldier* was excellent.

Two nouns in apposition are regularly in the same case; hence a more regular construction would be "the record of John as a soldier." However, the form given above is a recognized idiom.

Note. In expressions like "his *sister Mary's* hat," which have different case forms for the nouns in apposition, the two nouns may be regarded as forming a single name, with the sign of the possessive added to the second part.

307. Introduced by "Of." Certain nouns form an appositive by means of the preposition *of*, the appositive being the object of the preposition.

Examples: City of Chicago, state of Illinois, county of Cook, republic of France, the play of *Macbeth*, the title of president, the firm of Jones & Smith.

308. A Clause or a Phrase. (1) A noun may be used in apposition with a clause.

The building was dingy and dilapidated, a *condition* which made a thorough overhauling necessary.

Here the general idea of the main clause is summed up in a single noun, which furnishes a definite antecedent for the following relative pronoun. This construction is used to avoid a loose reference between a relative pronoun and a clause-antecedent (see Sec. 56, *note*).

(2) A noun clause or phrase may be used in apposition with a noun.

The statement *that the city was destroyed* proved to be false.

The first proposal, *to send the canoe by freight,* was accepted.

He enjoys his work, *selling bonds.*

309. Separated from Its Noun. A noun in apposition is not always placed immediately after the noun with which it belongs.

The *castle* stood on a high cliff, a crumbling *relic* of former grandeur (*relic* is in apposition with *castle*).

He sat at the head of the table, a well-preserved *man* of eighty years.

OBJECTIVE COMPLEMENT

For a preliminary discussion, see Sec. 24.

For adjectives used as objective complements, see Sec. 93.

310. A pronoun may be used as an objective complement.
> He did call me *that*.
> You named him *what?*

311. A phrase or a clause may be used as an objective complement.
> They took him *for a gentleman*.
> You may call me *what you will*.

312. An objective complement is sometimes introduced by *as*.
> They selected him *as captain*.
> They elected me *as their secretary*.
> He chose a lawyer *as his representative*.

In these constructions *as* seems to be little more than an introductory word whose main function is to make a smooth transition to the objective complement. It is used especially when the complement is preceded by a modifier: "They elected me as *their* secretary." Compare this sentence with "They elected me secretary," in which there is no modifier and *as* is omitted.

313. An objective complement with the introductory *as* is sometimes related in meaning to an adverbial element.
> They regarded him *as* an honest *man*.

In this sentence, the expression, *as an honest man,* has some of the meaning of an adverb of manner, showing *how* they regarded him; but if we compare it with "They *considered* him *an honest man*," we see its relation to an objective complement.

Note. In "We considered him *to be an honest man*," the infinitive phrase is equivalent to an objective complement introduced by *to be*. It may be classified as such, or the whole expression "him to be an honest man" may be regarded as an infinitive phrase with a subject, used as the direct object of the verb (see Sec. 205). With the regular objective complement the *to be,* which serves as a test for the construction (see Sec. 24), is not expressed.

"THAT," "WHICH," AND "WHO"

For the use of these three relative pronouns with personal or non-personal antecedents, see Sec. 66. The following distinction should also be noted.

314. *That* is used only in restrictive relative clauses; *who* and *which* may be used in either restrictive or non-restrictive clauses.

> The man *that* (or *who*) received the most votes was ineligible (restrictive).
>
> Any house *that* (or *which*) is burned will be rebuilt.
>
> Chicago, *which* (not *that*) is the metropolis of the Middle West, is a great industrial center (non-restrictive).
>
> My father, *who* (not *that*) was president of the company, met us at the office.

A restrictive clause is one which points out what person or thing is meant: that is, it restricts the statement to that person or thing. It cannot be omitted without changing the meaning of the sentence (see the first two sentences above).

A non-restrictive clause is descriptive or explanatory, and can be omitted without changing the essential meaning. The person or thing that is spoken of is definitely indicated without the clause (see the last two sentences).

Note. A restrictive clause is not punctuated; a non-restrictive clause is set off with commas.

Nouns Used as Adjectives and as Adverbs

315. A noun, equivalent to a prepositional phrase, may serve as an adjective in certain idiomatic expressions.

> The shoes are a *size* too large (of a size).
>
> The rope is just the right *length* (of just the right length).
>
> Her cheeks are the *color* of roses.

These are elliptical constructions in which the preposition is omitted. They should be used with discretion, for they are sometimes awkward and ambiguous. For example, a sentence like "The frame is *wood;* the cylinder is *steel*" should be avoided. It should read, "The frame is *of wood;* the cylinder is *of steel.*" Ordinarily, when a noun follows a form of *be,* it is a predicate noun ("The man is a soldier"); hence the writer should be careful not to omit *of* if its object might be mistaken for a predicate noun.

For common uses of nouns and pronouns as adjectives, see Secs. 86, 87.

316. A noun used as an adverb (see Sec. 28 (1)) may modify a real adverb or an adjective.

> He ran a *mile* farther (modifies the adverb *farther*).
>
> They left *two weeks* earlier.
>
> It weighed *five pounds* more.

These shoes are worth *six dollars* (*worth* is an adjective).
It is a *foot* longer.
He appeared to be *several pounds* heavier.

Exercise 60

Point out cognate objects, retained objects, reciprocal pronouns, special forms of apposition, objective complements, and nouns used as adverbs and adjectives.

1. Scientific inventions succeeded one another. (J. T. Adams.) 2. Each of the crew was allotted his share of the booty. 3. A country lawyer by the name of Lincoln was making himself a leader in the anti-slavery campaign. 4. For it all came to this: I was nearly thirty-three years of age. (Edgar Lee Masters.) 5. Then first did I know myself for a sun-worshipper. (George Gissing.) 6. The prime minister was given a vote of confidence by the House. 7. It revelled all through my head till sunrise again, a frantic and tireless nightmare. (Mark Twain.) 8. The continent, however, was not so limited. It stretched nearly three thousand miles farther. (J. T. Adams.) 9. The importance of Milton as a writer of prose is overshadowed by his fame as a poet. 10. These people pronounced me an authority, and I speedily accepted myself as an authority. (Arnold Bennett.)

11. But he was exhausted now; he had run his race and fought his fight. (Will Durant.) 12. My comrades accepted me without hesitation for a person of their own character and experience. (R. L. Stevenson.) 13. The firm of Staley and Son is our representative in the state of Texas. 14. Otherwise there is no sunshine, summer or winter. (Stuart Chase.) 15. Occasionally there were wanderers like himself on the other side of the way, figures with no character, in no hurry. (H. M. Tomlinson.) 16. He was asked what was his trade, and replied that he was a *tapper*. (R. L. Stevenson.) 17. They disliked each other heartily, but without any definite reason. 18. The valley was heaped with great blocks of granite—a feature which has interest for the geologist. (George Gissing.) 19. The lone button was the size of a half-dollar. (O. Henry.) 20. He had what they all dreamed of having—fame, wealth, and the respect of his fellows.

21. He has various hobbies, such as collecting stamps and playing the piccolo. 22. Everywhere we find them (monasteries) as centers of light spreading useful arts. (H. G. Wells.) 23. The third procedure—that is, unloading in Floyd Bennett harbor—would be the last resort. (Richard Byrd.) 24. They were no longer enemies, but they liked each other less than ever. (William D. Howells.)

CONSTRUCTIONS USED AS NOUNS OR PRONOUNS

317. Various constructions are commonly used in place of regular nouns and pronouns. These substitutes are called noun-equivalents.

1. Gerund and Gerundive Phrase (see Secs. 167, 201): "He enjoys *swimming*." "He objected to *writing the letter*."
2. Infinitive and Infinitive Phrase (see Secs. 154, 198): "They promised *to come*." "*To work the problem* will require an hour."
3. Clause (see Sec. 227): "*What you say* may be true." "I know *that he will go*." "He objected to *what we said*."
4. Adjective (see Sec. 180): "The *weakest* are sometimes the *strongest*."
5. Adverb (see Sec. 180): "Where do we go from *here?*"
6. Any word used as the name of a word, not as the name of an object (see Sec. 27): "*From* is a preposition."

318. "As." *As* may be used as a relative pronoun after *such* and *same*.

> Such of the neighbors *as* were invited came early. (Cf. "Those of the neighbors *who* were invited.")
> Such funds *as* are needed will be provided.
> Such a record *as* this (is) should not be forgotten.
> We gave the same answer *as* you gave.

319. After *same*, the relative pronoun *that* is sometimes used instead of *as*.

> We followed the same trail *that* the Indians formerly used.
> He has the same position *that* he had last year. (Cf. "He has the same position *as* he had last year.")

320. A special use of *as* as a relative pronoun is shown in the following sentences. In some cases the relative clause is so common and colorless that it might be classified as a parenthetical expression (see Sec. 297).

> The plan was impractical, *as the speaker proceeded to demonstrate*.
> He was, *as you know*, a companion of the prince.
> However, he was right, *as later developments proved*.
> *As is well known*, this is an age of opportunity.
> *As has already been stated*, his return was the signal for a revolt.
> *As predicted*, the parade was a success (elliptical—"as was predicted").

In constructions such as these, *as* generally refers to a whole statement instead of to a definite word antecedent, just as *which* is used by some writers to refer to a whole clause (see Sec. 56, *note*). Thus the first sentence given above is equivalent to "The plan was impractical, *which* (*a fact which*) the speaker proceeded to demonstrate." The second sentence means "He was a companion of the prince, *which* (*a fact which*) you know."

321. "But." *But*, when used as in the following sentence, is sometimes regarded as a relative pronoun, equivalent to *that—not, which—not*, or *who—not.*

There is not a city *but* is affected by this law (*that* is *not* affected).

Some grammarians call *but* in this construction a conjunction introducing a clause whose subject is not expressed: thus, "There is not a city *but* (it) is affected by this law."

322. "How" Plus an Infinitive. *How, when, where, whether, what*, or *who*, followed by an infinitive, is used as a noun-equivalent (see Sec. 432).

He did not know *how to write his name* (object of the verb).

We have not decided *whether to go or stay*.

The problem of *how to get food* was a serious one (object of *of*).

Where to go was the next question (subject of the verb).

323. "For" Plus an Infinitive. A construction consisting of the preposition *for* followed by an infinitive with a subject may be used as a noun-equivalent (see Sec. 207).

For him to do that was foolish (subject of the verb).

He said *for you to bring the book* (object of the verb).

Exercise 61

Point out the less common words, phrases, and clauses used as nouns or pronouns (ordinary nouns and pronouns may be omitted).

1. In those early days crossing the Great American Desert was a long and arduous undertaking. 2. We took only such articles as could be packed in a handbag. 3. They told us that our best plan now was to keep to the northward. (Francis Parkman.) 4. This afternoon Hannibal was fortunate in having an end seat. (William McFee.) 5. To read well, that is, to read true books in a true spirit, is a noble exercise. (Henry Thoreau.) 6. It seems he knows how to speak to his contemporaries. (R. W. Emerson.) 7. For him to handle all this detail without help is manifestly impossible. 8. Instead of writing a letter to the auditors, he sent a cablegram asking them to meet him in New York. 9. But otherwise he was very restless, except when he

was with Marcia. (W. D. Howells.) 10. People always went crazy before whatever they worshipped. (H. M. Tomlinson.)

11. "Come out of there, whoever you are." (Rudyard Kipling.) 12. He asked for me to send him the paper. 13. Besides this, he knows very well how to handle a rifle and picket a horse. (Francis Parkman.) 14. The best plan is for us to spend the winter in Florida. 15. If the scrub was on fire, as he supposed, he would have difficulty in escaping. 16. My precious letters of introduction immediately caused me to be under suspicion. (Carveth Wells.) 17. The best is none too good for her. 18. He has the same name as his father.   19. You have in England only one art of any consequence —that is, iron-working. (John Ruskin.) 20. He was, as we later learned, the representative of a London firm.

GENDER

For a previous discussion of Gender, see Secs. 7, 8.

324. The Masculine and Feminine Genders are distinguished:
(1) By the use of different words: as, *king, queen; gentleman, lady; boy, girl; uncle, aunt.*
(2) By the use of suffixes.
(a) The more common suffixes added to the masculine form to make a feminine form are *-ess, -ix, -ine:* as, *host, hostess; count, countess; lion, lioness; actor, actress; executor, executrix; hero, heroine.*
(b) In the group *widow, widower,* the suffix *-er* is added to the feminine noun to make the masculine form.
(c) Some words borrowed from foreign languages retain their original suffixes denoting the masculine and feminine genders: as, *alumnus, alumna* (plural, *alumni, alumnæ*); *Augustus, Augusta; Julius, Julia, fiancé, fiancée.*
(3) By the placing of a distinguishing word (masculine or feminine) either before or after another word: as, *man-servant, maid-servant; he-goat, she-goat; billy-goat, nanny-goat; foreman, forewoman; landlord, landlady.*

325. With some words, the masculine form is used, like the common gender, for both masculine and feminine nouns: thus *alumni* (strictly a masculine form) may mean both men and women graduates; *poet* and *editor* are preferred to *poetess* and *editress.*

FORMS FOR THE PLURAL NUMBER

See also Sec. ·6

326. The plural number of most nouns is formed by adding *-s* or *-es* to the singular: as, *park, parks; book, books; porch, porches.*

(1) Some nouns ending in *f* or *fe* in the singular change the *f* to *v* before adding *-es* or *-s*: as, *loaf, loaves; calf, calves; life, lives.* Not all nouns ending in *f* or *fe,* however, do this: as, *brief, briefs; roof, roofs.*

(2) Most nouns ending in *y,* preceded by a consonant, change the *y* to *i* before adding *-es:* as, *lady, ladies; pony, ponies; penny, pennies.* (The *y* is not changed to *i* after a vowel: as, *valleys, moneys.*)

Proper names usually retain the *y:* the *Harrys,* the *Derbys,* the *Marys.*

327. Other methods of forming the plural are:

(1) By adding *-en:* as, *ox, oxen; child, children; brother, brethren* (more commonly *brothers*). Sometimes the vowel is also changed.

(2) By changing the vowel, without adding anything to the singular: as, *man, men; goose, geese; mouse, mice.*

(3) Some foreign nouns taken over into English retain their original foreign plurals: as, *memorandum, memoranda; phenomenon, phenomena; alumnus, alumni; formula, formulæ; vortex, vortices.* In some instances nouns of this class also have a plural in *-s:* as, *memorandums, formulas.*

(4) In compound nouns the sign of the plural may be given to the last or to the first member; sometimes to both: as, *spoonfuls, forget-me-nots; editors-in-chief; brothers-in-law; menservants; Knights Templars.*

(5) The plurals of letters, signs, and names of words add *'s:* as, "There are two *t's* in the word." "Your + *'s* are too small." "Find all the *that's* in the sentence."

Exercise 62

Give the plural form for the following nouns. If necessary, consult the dictionary.

self, wharf, gulf, knife, wife, staff, thief, chief, calf, cliff, leaf, scarf, fife.
echo, banjo, piano, volcano, solo, dynamo, lily, buffalo, monkey, enemy, body, alley, potato, Henry, Lily.
foot, woman, louse, 8, and, w, two.
erratum, curriculum, stratum, focus, radius, terminus, fungus.

alumna, nebula, vertebra, larva.

thesis, axis, crisis, basis, analysis, parenthesis, synopsis, species, index, appendix.

CASE

328. The principal regular uses of cases with nouns and pronouns are as follows.

(1) The **Nominative Case** is used in the Subject of a Verb, a Predicate Noun, a word in Direct Address, and a noun in the Nominative Absolute construction (see Sec. 41).

(2) The **Objective Case** is used in the Direct Object of a Verb, the Indirect Object of a Verb, the Object of a Preposition, and a noun employed as an Objective Complement (see Sec. 42).

(3) A noun in Apposition has the same case as the noun with which it is used.

(4) The **Possessive Case** denotes possession (see Secs. 13 f. and 43).

Special or exceptional uses of cases are given below.

329. Subject of an Infinitive. The subject of an infinitive is in the objective case (see Sec. 208).

> I believe *them* to be trustworthy.
>
> I saw *him* fall.
>
> Let *me* go.

After some verbs, as in the last two examples, the *to* of the infinitive is not expressed. These sentences are equivalent to "I saw him (*to*) fall," "Let me (*to*) go." With the last one compare "Allow me *to* go."

330. The colloquial *let's* in expressions like *"Let's do it now,"* is a contraction of *let us,* in which *us* is the subject of the following infinitive. In *"Let's you and me* do it," *you* and *me* are in apposition with *us* ("Let *us, you and me,* do it."). They are in the objective case to agree with the case of *us;* hence the form "Let's you and *I* do it," which is frequently heard, is incorrect.

331. Predicate Noun after an Infinitive. A predicate noun is in the objective case after an infinitive which has a subject in the objective case (see Sec. 209).

> I took him to be *her.*
>
> We believed the traveler to be *him.*

332. In Exclamations. The nominative, objective, and possessive cases are all used in exclamations.

> *I!* I don't care!
> Dear *me!*
> *My!* What a large hat!

333. Elliptical Constructions. The possessive case of a noun or pronoun sometimes appears to be used—instead of the nominative or objective case—for the subject of a verb, a predicate noun, an object of a verb, or an object of a preposition.

> *Harry's* is the better coat (Harry's coat is the better coat).
> That book is my *father's* (my father's book).
> I lost my hat, but John gave me *his* (his hat).
> Come to the *photographer's* at noon (photographer's studio).
> You can buy it at your *grocer's* (grocer's store).

These are elliptical constructions. The real subjects, predicate nouns, and objects are the nouns which have been omitted after the possessives.

334. The following sentences show not only ellipsis, as described above, but also the substitution of one form of the pronoun for another.

> *Mine* is the larger apple.
> Give him *yours.*

Thus the first sentence is equivalent to *"My apple* is the larger apple." The subject *apple* has been omitted, and for *my* has been substituted the form *mine,* which is the one regularly used when the possessive case is not followed by a noun (see Sec. 43).

335. The Double Possessive. In the so-called Double Possessive the idea of possession is expressed both by the preposition *of* and by a noun or pronoun in the possessive case used as the object of the preposition.

> He is a friend of *mine.*
> This is a favorite horse of my *father's.*

This construction, as well as those in the preceding sections, is a well-established idiom.

Exercise 63

Explain the special or irregular case forms of the nouns and pronouns.

1. The lotion is on sale at your druggist's. 2. He will send you some of his. 3. Let's tell them the whole story. 4. We found him to be a staunch supporter of the cause. 5. No discontent would be theirs. (Frank Swinnerton.) 6. Let him pay for it himself. 7. The world is his who can see through its

pretensions. (R. W. Emerson.) 8. We believed the stranger to be her. 9. Oh my! I didn't mean to do that. 10. He had blue eyes in that old face of his which were amazingly like a boy's. (Joseph Conrad.)

11. Dear me! What shall we do about it? 12. I am an acquaintance of his, but not a friend. 13. She thought them to be us. 14. He was a man whom I thought to be honest. 15. I like mine better than yours. 16. They considered her to be an artist. 17. This was the boy whom we believed to be the ringleader. 18. He was a friend of ours for many years. 19. John's is the best theme, but hers is more interesting. 20. I must be at the dentist's by four o'clock.

AGREEMENT OF THE PRONOUN AND ANTECEDENT

336. A pronoun must agree with its antecedent in person, number, and gender (see Sec. 45).

337. "Everybody," "Each." A singular pronoun is used with an antecedent consisting of the pronouns *everybody, each, anybody, somebody, neither, either,* or a word or series of words preceded by the adjective *every* or *each.*

> Everybody must do *his* duty (not *their* duty).
> Each of the parties will send *its* delegates.
> Somebody has lost *his* hat.
> Neither of the girls knew why *she* had failed.
> Every man and boy must do *his* part.
> Each pen, pencil, and eraser must be left where you found *it* (not *them*).

338. This rule offers no difficulties when the group indicated by the antecedent consists of males only or females only, for then the pronoun will be masculine or feminine, respectively.

> *Everybody* (at the Masonic lodge) took *his* seat.
> *Everybody* (at the sewing circle) took *her* seat.

339. When the antecedent refers to a mixed group, males and females, it is customary to use the masculine pronoun, singular number, *his* (*he, him*), since there is no singular, third person pronoun of common gender.

> *Everybody* in the church expressed *his* surprise (*everybody* includes both men and women).

This use of the masculine pronoun is, of course, entirely arbitrary, and involves an illogical gender relation between the pronoun and its antecedent.

Some writers, in an effort to avoid the ambiguous reference, use *his or her:* "Everybody expressed *his or her* surprise." This construction, however, is awkward and cumbersome, and should not be used unless the statement requires special exactness in the reference of the pronoun.
Sometimes it is better to reconstruct the sentence.

All the audience expressed *their* surprise.

Everybody expressed surprise.

340. "Either—Or." When the antecedent consists of two nouns connected by the conjunctions *either—or, neither—nor,* or *or,* a singular pronoun is used if the separate parts of the antecedent are singular, a plural pronoun if the parts are plural.

Either the *man* or the *boy* has deserted *his* post.

Neither the *men* nor the *boys* have deserted *their* posts.

I shall ask the *janitor* or the *doorman* for *his* key.

(a) When the parts are of different persons, numbers, or genders, the pronoun is made to agree with the nearer part, or the sentence should be reconstructed.

Neither the *mother* nor the *daughters* would admit *their* mistake.

341. Collective Nouns. A singular or a plural pronoun is used with a collective noun as antecedent, according to whether the group which it names is thought of as acting as a unit or as individual members.

The jury has agreed on *its* verdict.

The committee are too much occupied with *their* personal affairs.

342. "One." When the indefinite pronoun *one* (meaning *anyone, a person*) is used as an antecedent, some writers always refer to it later by *one* or *one's*. It is, however, also correct to use *his, he,* or *him*.

One soon discovers that *one's* income is insufficient for all that *one* wants.

One soon discovers that *his* income is insufficient for all that *he* wants.

Pronouns Without Definite Antecedents

343. Indefinite Plurals. The plurals of all three persons of the personal pronouns are used indefinitely in the sense of *one, a person, people in general*.

On closer examination, *we* find that the theory is unsound.

On entering the building, *you* will see a marble statue.

They say that the commander has resigned.

344. Indefinite "Your." The possessive case *your* is similarly used in a few expressions like:

Your truly brave man never falters.

Note. These indefinite constructions should not be used when there is any danger of ambiguity.

345. Indefinite "It." The pronoun *it* is used indefinitely and impersonally in a number of constructions.

(1) In certain statements about the weather, time, etc.

It is warm today.
It is snowing.
It feels like rain.
It is nearly midnight.
It is time to go to work.

(2) As an introductory word whose function it is to bring into a prominent place near the beginning of the sentence some word or words which are to be emphasized.

It is John that I want to see (emphasizes *John*).
It was here that we found him (emphasizes *here*).
It is a long journey to Rome.
It is five miles to the nearest town.
It seems only a short time since you were here.
It was twenty years before I saw him again.
It was in London that I met him.
It was for this reason that I objected.
It is what we do that counts.

The gain in emphasis is obvious in these sentences, when they are compared with the following forms.

I want to see *John*.
We found him *here*.

(3) As an expletive standing for an infinitive or a clause which follows the verb and is the real subject of the sentence (see Secs. 286–7).

It is reported that he was surprised at the result (*that he was surprised at the result* is reported).
It is hard to select the winner (*to select the winner* is hard).

(4) As an expletive standing for the direct object (see Sec. 362 (a)).

He found *it* difficult to escape (he found *it*, namely, *to escape* (*escaping*), difficult).

(5) As a sort of general impersonal object after certain verbs.

He lorded *it* over his neighbors.

They are roughing *it* this summer.

We will fight *it* out on this line if it takes all summer.

(6) In sentences like the following, *it* is used to refer to persons, contrary to the ordinary rules for the agreement of pronouns.

It is *I.*

It was my *brother.*

It is *they* who are responsible.

In the first sentence *I* is first person, whereas *it,* in the ordinary uses, is third person. In the second, *brother* is masculine, whereas *it* is supposedly neuter. In the third, *they* is plural, whereas *it* is singular. In other words, in these constructions *it* may refer indefinitely to words of any person, number, or gender.

Exercise 64

Supply the correct pronoun. The pronoun must agree with its antecedent in person, number, and gender.

1. The voters have already given _____ verdict.
2. Either Mary or Helen will drive _____ car.
3. If you see John or his brother, will you tell _____ what has happened?
4. Dr. Morton is studying the phenomena to determine _____ significance in the field of chemistry.
5. The company has prepared a prospectus to be sent to all _____ customers.
6. Everybody felt that the new rules were directed at _____ personally.
7. Neither the book nor the papers could be found when the students needed _____.
8. The committee cannot agree on how _____ should vote.
9. The committee is convinced that _____ report presents a true picture of _____ findings.
10. One or the other of the women will be prepared to tell about _____ personal experiences in Germany.
11. Neither of the countries would admit _____ guilt in beginning the war.
12. One cannot always tell how _____ will conduct _____ in an emergency.
13. Every senator and congressman will be asked to give _____ support to these bills.
14. Each of the candidates will be invited to present _____ views on the proposed law.

15. Somebody in authority should have told us what ———— wanted us to do.

16. The company was held responsible for the conduct of ———— employees.

Exercise 65

Explain the uses of *it* and of other pronouns without definite antecedents.

1. It was January, and the weather was beautiful. (Joseph Conrad.) 2. It is notorious that important elections are decided by votes bought with money. (J. R. Lowell.) 3. We considered it an honor to be invited. 4. They say that it takes two to make a quarrel. 5. You fight, sweat, nearly kill yourself, sometimes do kill yourself, trying to accomplish something—and you can't. (Joseph Conrad.) 6. It was twelve miles to the nearest post office. 7. I take it that he had little to fear on that score. (Arthur Machen.) 8. They had been roughing it for a month in the Canadian Rockies. 9. One would like to make up one's mind exactly what a short story is. (W. S. Maugham.) 10. It seemed possible to carry out the programme after all. (Thomas Hardy.)

11. It was I who made the discovery. 12. For if any man was happy, it was surely he. (Aldous Huxley.) 13. It was dark, but many stars shone now. (John Galsworthy.) 14. Your real golf enthusiast will be waiting to play at the crack of dawn. 15. Now it was distinctly a feat for me to stay in school. (Mary Antin.) 16. At four o'clock we called it a day and went home. 17. At times we are all too much concerned with material things. 18. It is strange the power that a mind of deep passion has over feeble natures. (Herman Melville.) 19. "Go it," I almost cried, "and go it stronger." (William James.) 20. It was in March that I first saw them.

Chapter XIV   ADJECTIVES

346. Any word or group of words that modifies a noun is an adjective. The following constructions are commonly thus used.

(1) Regular Adjectives: *brave* soldiers; *large* apples.

(2) Nouns or Pronouns: *Christmas* presents; *that* book.

(3) Nouns or Pronouns in the Possessive Case: *John's* hat; *my* coat.

(4) Participles or Participial Phrases: *running* water; a man *reading the paper;* a fish *caught in the net.*

(5) Infinitives or Infinitive Phrases: houses *to rent;* an attempt *to find a solution.*

(6) Prepositional Phrases: the house *on the alley.*

(7) Clauses: the man *who was hungry.*

(8) A Past Participle followed by an Adverb: a *broken-down* carriage; a *worn-out* overcoat; a *trumped-up* charge.

(9) A Noun, equivalent to a Prepositional Phrase, used as follows: a coat a *size* too small (*of a size*); ink the *color* of blood (see Sec. 315).

(10) A Preposition, without an Object expressed: "They live in the room *above*" (*above this one*) (see Sec. 533).

(11) Idiomatic Expressions like "a *ten-foot* pole" and "a *five-mile* walk," consisting of a plural numeral combined with a singular noun to form a single unit-adjective.

Note. The constructions in (11) are used only before a noun, and a hyphen should be placed between the two parts. When a corresponding expression is placed after the noun that it modifies, the plural form—*feet, miles,* etc.— is used, and the hyphen is omitted: "This pole is *ten feet* long."

NUMBER

347. The pronominal adjectives *this* and *that* (plural *these* and *those*) are the only adjectives in English which have different forms before singular and plural nouns.

this paper, *these* papers; *that* child, *those* children.

348. Before the nouns *kind* and *sort,* which are singular, the singular forms *this* and *that* must be used, not the plural forms *these* and *those.*

> *this* kind of people (not *these* kind).
> *that* sort of peaches (not *those* sort).

Before the plurals of these nouns, *these* and *those* are used: *those* kinds, *these* sorts.

349. Other adjectives have the same form for singular and plural: *good* boy, *good* boys.

POSITION OF ADJECTIVES

For the regular position of single adjectives, generally before nouns, see Sec. 91.

350. A pure adjective phrase or clause, or a pure adjective modified by a phrase or clause, regularly follows the noun.

> The name *of the man* is Harry Drake (phrase).
> He gave us instructions *to bring the papers.*
> The messenger *who brought the papers* has gone (clause).
> A plank *black with age* was lying near (adjective modified by a phrase).
> The men *working in the field* were notified.

Note. The expression "*pure* adjective" is used above to distinguish these constructions from those having a dual adjective and adverbial meaning (see Sec. 494). The latter type, when they refer to the subject of a sentence, may be placed before the subject or after it.

> *Fearing* trouble, the officer summoned the guard.
> The officer, *fearing* trouble, summoned the guard.
> *Weak* from his effort, John fell to the ground.
> John, *weak* from his effort, fell to the ground.

351. A few adjective phrases which have become closely united into permanent units may precede the noun.

> This is an *up-to-date* hotel.
> He is a *dyed-in-the-wool* Republican.

PREDICATE ADJECTIVE

For a previous discussion, see Sec. 92.

352. In addition to regular adjectives, the following constructions may be used as predicate adjectives.

(1) A Participle.

    The book is *interesting*.
    His address was *inspiring*.

A participle used as a predicate adjective should be carefully distinguished from one used as a part of a progressive verb-phrase.

    The book is *interesting* (predicate adjective).
    The man *is interesting* the farmers in tractors (part of a verb-phrase).

(2) An Infinitive.

    The third apartment is *to rent*.
    This bread is *to eat*.

(3) A Prepositional Phrase.

    His demand is *out of reason* (*unreasonable*).
    They were *in high spirits* (*happy*).
    The illustrations are *in colors* (*colored* illustrations).
    The man is *from the city* (a *city* man).
    The officer was *of gigantic size* (*large*).
    These books are *by an unknown writer* (*anonymous*).

(4) A Clause.

    That is *what I call cheap*.

Uses of Predicate Adjectives

353. A predicate adjective may follow a verb in the passive voice, as well as one in the active voice.

    The guide is considered *trustworthy* (passive voice).
    The body was found *frozen*.
    The house was painted *green*.
    His father became very *wealthy* (active voice).
    The prisoner turned *pale*.

354. A predicate adjective may describe the subject in a simple adjective relation.

    The Jonathan apples are *ripe*.
    This book on earthquakes is *reliable*.
    The report has been found *true*.
    The man was declared *guilty*.

355. After certain verbs denoting *making*, *doing*, or *turning*, the predicate adjective describes the subject as it is after the action indicated by the verb has taken place.

    The iron is hammered *square*.

The ore is heated *red hot.*
The line was made *straight.*
The milk turned *sour.*

These adjectives are similar in meaning to clauses introduced by *until* or *so that:* "The iron is hammered *until* (or *so that*) it is square."

356. A predicate adjective after a passive verb sometimes has much the same meaning as an adverbial clause of time.

The mortar is applied *wet* (while it is wet).

Note 1. The predicate adjectives in Secs. 355–6 show the dual relation of adjective and adverb. Thus, in "The ore is heated *red hot,*" the adjective *red hot* both describes the noun *ore* and tells the result produced by the action indicated by the verb.

Note 2. If the passive verb is changed into the active voice, the predicate adjective which follows it becomes an objective complement (see Secs. 363 ff.): thus, "The ore is heated *red hot*" becomes "They heated the ore *red hot.*"

DISTINCTION BETWEEN PREDICATE ADJECTIVE AND ADVERB

357. After certain verbs care should be taken not to use an adverb when a predicate adjective is required to convey the intended meaning.

The flower smells *sweet* (not *sweetly*).
The medicine tastes *bitter* (not *bitterly*).
The boy looked *stupid* (not *stupidly*).
The tone sounds *flat* (not *flatly*).
The note rang *true* (not *truly*).

In the first sentence, for example, *sweet* describes the flower—it is a *sweet flower;* the second makes a statement about a *bitter medicine;* the third, about a *stupid boy.* Yet in all the sentences given above the qualifying words do, in some degree, modify the verbs as well: they are adjectives which also have an adverbial meaning (see Sec. 494).

A test that may be used in determining whether an adjective or an adverb is to be employed is this: Does the modifier belong to the subject more particularly than to the verb? If it does, use the adjective. For instance, compare the two sentences:

The boy looked *stupid.*
The boy looked *stupidly* at the floor.

In the first, the adjective *stupid* describes the *boy;* in the second, the adverb *stupidly* shows his manner of looking at the floor.

Another test for determining whether an adjective or an adverb is correct may be made by substituting *is* or *was* (*are* or *were*) for the verb in the sentence, and placing the adjective form after it. If this can be done without materially changing the thought of the sentence, a predicate adjective is almost always the proper construction; if it cannot be done, the adverb should be used. Thus, for "The boy *looked* stupid," we can substitute "The boy *was* stupid" (in appearance); hence the adjective form is correct. In the sentence, "The boy *looked* stupidly at the floor," the change gives no meaning at all: "The boy *was* stupid at the floor"; hence the adverb must be used.

ADJECTIVES AS OBJECTIVE COMPLEMENTS

For a preliminary discussion, see Sec. 93.

358. A participle (present or past) may be used as an objective complement.

> They found the prisoner *missing.*
> They kept us *working* all day.
> We heard the man *coming.*
> We discovered him *mowing* the lawn.
> He found the house *locked* and his mother *gone.*

359. A phrase may be used as an objective complement.

> We considered him *of value* to the town (*valuable*).
> We found the family *in high spirits* (*high spirited* or *happy*).
> The report made him *out of humor* (*ill humored*).

360. The infinitive phrase in sentences like the following is sometimes called an objective complement.

> They knew him *to be honest.*
> The investigation proved the prisoner to be *insane.*

This classification may be followed or the expression *him to be honest* or *the prisoner to be insane* may be regarded as an infinitive phrase with a subject, used as the object of the verb (see Secs. 205; 313, *note*).

361. An adjective used as an objective complement may be introduced by *as*.

> We regarded him *as* entirely *trustworthy*. (Cf. "We considered him *trustworthy.*")

362. The adjective used as the objective complement precedes the direct object (the infinitive) in sentences like:

> We thought *best* to go. (We thought to go *best*.)

(a) Sometimes an impersonal *it,* anticipating the direct object (see Sec. 345 (4)), precedes this construction.

We thought *it* best to go. (We thought *it*—namely, *to go*—best.)

363. When used after verbs denoting *making* or *causing,* the objective complement describes the object as it is after its nature or appearance has been changed by the action indicated by the verb; it therefore shows the result of that action on the object.

The gift made her *happy.*
They made the ball *round.*
She wrung the clothes *dry.*
We stained the chair *brown.*

364. When used after some verbs it modifies or describes the object without indicating any change in its nature or appearance.

We consider the man *honest.*
They thought the story *absurd.*
The physician found the patient *sick* in bed.

THE ARTICLES

ARTICLES WITH NAMES OF MEMBERS OF A CLASS

365. An article is regularly used with a noun designating a member of a class of objects. The indefinite articles *a* and *an* indicate any member; the definite article *the* indicates a particular member (see Secs. 89 ff.).

I want *an* apple.
I want *the* apple on the table.

ARTICLES WITH PROPER NAMES

366. With proper names, we should expect that the article would be omitted, since the proper name itself regularly indicates a particular member of a class. In many cases it is omitted, but there are numerous exceptions. An idea of the diversity of usage may be gained from the following examples (the list is, of course, not complete).

367. Names Requiring an Article. The article *the* is regularly used when the name consists of a *class name preceded by an adjective,* in certain groups, such as:

(1) *Nations:* The United States, the French Republic, the British Empire.

(2) *Oceans, Seas, Rivers, and Channels:* The Atlantic Ocean, the Yellow Sea, the Mississippi River, the English Channel.

(3) *Mountains (when plural) and Valleys:* The Rocky Mountains, the Andes Mountains, the Berkshire Hills (also elliptical expressions: the Rockies, the Alps, the Andes, the Berkshires), the Yosemite Valley, the Mississippi Valley. Single mountains usually omit the article, with the class name standing either first or last: Lookout Mountain, Bald Mountain, Bunker Hill, Mt. Washington, Mt. White.

(4) *Corporations, Companies, Magazines, Buildings, etc.:* The Boston Store, the Auditorium Hotel (also the Auditorium), the Smith Dry Goods Company, the Economy Market, the State Street Bank, the Atlantic Monthly, the Colonial Theater, the Woolworth Building.

(5) *Any Name containing an "of" Phrase:* The City of Columbus, the Province of Quebec, the Republic of France, the Gulf of Mexico, the Bay of Naples, the Strait of Dover.

368. Names Omitting the Article. The article is regularly omitted in the following names, although they contain class names like those in Section 367.

(1) *Counties and Cities:* Hennepin County, Adams County, Atlantic City.

(2) *Single Islands:* Long Island, Roanoke Island (but *the* Shetland Islands, *the* Bahama Islands—plural (also *the* Bahamas)).

(3) *Lakes, Creeks, Bays, Sounds:* White Lake (cf. *the* White Sea), Moose Lake (also when the class name precedes: Lake Michigan, Lake George), Simpson Creek, Pigeon Creek, Hudson Bay, Puget Sound.

(4) *Streets, Avenues, etc.:* Market Street, Forty-second Street, Commonwealth Avenue, Drexel Boulevard, Roosevelt Road, Clinton Place.

(5) *Any Name having the Qualifying Word in the Possessive Case:* St. George's Channel, Sullivan's Theater, Tom's Café.

369. The article is regularly omitted with the names of persons, and with geographical names which do not contain a class name.

John Smith, General Grant, King George II; Europe, England, Siam, Germany, Indiana, Philadelphia.

Note. The is used to distinguish a particular person having a certain name from other persons of the same name.

The John Smith that I know is not *the* John Smith who signed the letter.

370. Abstract Nouns and Names of Classes without Units. With an abstract noun or a noun indicating a class which is thought of as bulk or material, not as being made up of individual units or members, the article is regularly omitted.

> *Loyalty* is always commendable.
> They fought for *freedom* from *oppression*.
> *Steel* is strong and hard.
> *Water* becomes *steam* under certain conditions.
> *Science* is classified knowledge.

Note. With some words the usage may vary with the context.

> *Night* is the time for sleep.
> At *night*, noises are intensified.
> In *the night*, noises are intensified.

371. Classes Composed of Individual Units. With a name indicating a class which is made up of individual units or members, the following forms occur.

(1) With plural class names, the article is regularly omitted.

> *Cats* are domestic pets.
> *Rubies* are precious stones.

(2) With the more general class names in the singular number, an indefinite, not a definite, article is used.

> *An animal* is a living creature (not *the* animal).
> *A jewel* is a precious stone (not *the* jewel).

(3) With the more specific class names in the singular number, either a definite or an indefinite article may be employed.

> *The cat* (*a cat*) is a domestic pet.
> *The ruby* (*a ruby*) is a precious stone.

372. It will be noted that in the case of singular class names the article regularly becomes more definite as the class becomes more definite and specific in its individual units. Thus, the article is omitted in the class names in Sec. 370—these classes have no individual units; an indefinite article is used with the names in Sec. 371 (2)—the individual units are comparatively general; the definite article is used with the names in Sec. 371 (3)—here the units are specific. The words *poetry*, *poem*, and *epic* may be taken to illustrate these three classes.

Poetry is a form of verse.
A poem (not *the poem*) is a form of verse.
The epic (*an epic*) is a form of verse.

373. This principle, however, is only a general one. In actual practice there are many subtle distinctions in the use of the article, which must be learned by observation and experience.

SPECIAL USES OF THE ARTICLES

374. "A" for "Each." *A* or *an* is used in the sense of *each* in expressions like:

two dollars *a* pound; fifty miles *a* day; ten cents *an* ounce.

A or *an* is preferable to *per* except in Latin phrases like *per diem, per annum,* etc.

The is also sometimes used in these expressions: as, "one dollar *the* copy."

375. "Such a." In expressions like *such a, many a,* and *what a,* the article follows the principal adjective instead of preceding it.

such a manner; *many a* boy; *what a* book.

The regular position of the article is before the principal adjective or adjectives: as, "*a* large boy"; "*a* fine, healthy baby."

376. "A Dozen." In idiomatic expressions like *a dozen eggs, a few boys,* etc., the article *a* seemingly modifies a plural noun.

This construction may be explained as having originated from the dropping of the preposition *of* from expressions like *a dozen* (*of*) *eggs,* in which *a* modified the singular noun *dozen,* which in turn was modified by the phrase *of eggs.* In parsing, however, the *of* is not to be supplied: the construction is a recognized idiom.

Note. Compare the expressions *a dozen of each kind,* and *a few of every class,* in which the *of* is retained.

377. "A-fishing." The *a* in *a-fishing, asleep, aboard,* etc., is not the article but a weakened form of *on.*

These expressions are derived from *on-fishing, on sleep, on board,* etc.: that is, they were originally prepositional phrases. Compare "*aboard* the ship" and "*on board* the ship," in which we have a weakened and a full form of the same construction, both in present-day use.

378. Emphatic "The." *The* is used to point out an object with special emphasis.

This is *the* book of the year.
He is *the* man of the hour.

379. "The" as an Adverb. In the following expressions *the* is used, not as an article, but as an adverb of degree.

The more you eat, *the* more you want.
The more, *the* merrier.
He writes *the* most effectively when he has a congenial subject.

380. Archaic "Ye." The form *ye,* used in such expressions as *Ye Olde Inne* to give them an archaic turn, is not the pronoun *ye* but the article *the*. Formerly, the combination *th* was represented by a character called "thorn," which was similar in appearance to a *y* with a closed top. In early printing the *y* was substituted for the "thorn," and the word appeared as *ye*. It is pronounced like *the*.

Exercise 66

Point out the adjective constructions—words, phrases, and clauses—used as predicate adjectives and objective complements (see Secs. 352–364). For each phrase and clause thus used, try to substitute a single word which expresses about the same meaning.

1. He was one of those actors who are always in luck. (Hamlin Garland). 2. I found the meadow and the other fields too dry for cultivation. 3. The houses were all in darkness, because evening meals were laid in the kitchens. (Frank Swinnerton.) 4. In the early years the colonists regarded the natives as unfriendly and treacherous. 5. Our growth in wealth and power was without precedent. (J. R. Lowell.) 6. He saw himself saving people from sinking ships. (Joseph Conrad.) 7. That silence and brooding obscurity would make a man contrite and willing to learn. (H. M. Tomlinson.) 8. He was a man of passionate temper who had always kept himself suppressed. (D. H. Lawrence.) 9. His eyes were on fire. (Hugh Walpole.) 10. Rip now felt a vague apprehension stealing over him. (Washington Irving.)

11. Dick had just waked to another morning of blank despair, and his temper was of the shortest. (Rudyard Kipling.) 12. Everything was as we had left it—not a book, not a paper had been disturbed. 13. This development made all our previous arrangements of no avail. 14. These efforts have kept my mind distracted and ill at ease, and made my narrative broken and disjointed in places. (Mark Twain.) 15. They left the village in ruins and the inhabitants desperately in need of food. 16. I found myself shy and a little dumb in the presence of bright and brilliant spirits. (Edgar Lee Mas-

ters.) 17. This young man was of a ruddy complexion, with a compressed, red mouth. (Willa Cather.) 18. Indeed, that was as it should be. (R. L. Stevenson.) 19. He found the house gone to decay—the roof fallen in, the windows shattered, and the doors off the hinges. (Washington Irving.)

Chapter XV   VERBS

For a preliminary discussion of verbs, their classification, properties, and use, see Chapter IV.

TRANSITIVE VERBS WITH IMPLIED OBJECTS

381. A verb which is transitive by nature is sometimes used without an expressed object.

> The men *ate* in silence.
>
> I *can hear* perfectly well.

These verbs have the appearance of intransitive verbs, but there is an implied object: thus, one doesn't eat without eating *something*. They are sometimes called *Transitive Verbs used Absolutely*. The difference between them and the real intransitive verbs may be seen by comparing the following sentences with the examples given above:

> Water *freezes* in winter (intransitive).
>
> The answer *came* quickly (intransitive).

(In Part I (see Sec. 99) no distinction was made between the two groups, but in a complete analysis they are to be classified separately.)

VERB-GROUPS

VERB PLUS PREPOSITION OR ADVERB

382. Sometimes a preposition or an adverb is so closely related to a preceding verb that it seems to help in expressing the verbal idea. The two may be regarded as forming a Verb-group.

> They *looked up* his address (cf. "They *found* his address").
>
> We *ate up* the food (*consumed*).
>
> The workmen *tore down* the building (*demolished*).
>
> He *has built up* a prosperous business (*established*).
>
> The guide *pointed out* the trail (*indicated*).

In these sentences, *up, down,* and *out* are not prepositions introducing phrases, as may be seen by comparing "looked up *his address*" with "looked *up the stairway*," in which the prepositional relation is obvious.

Words like *up, down*, etc., in these constructions are sometimes called adverbs modifying the verbs. This is a legitimate classification; yet the relation between these words and the verbs is so close that the combinations may also be considered as verb-groups. Either classification may be used.

Note. In the first sentence above, the verb-group *looked up* is, in effect, a transitive verb—having *address* as its object—although *looked* alone is intransitive.

383. The constructions in the following sentences are somewhat different in nature.

> He *came up* the hill (*ascended*).
>
> They *ran after* the fugitive (*pursued*).

In these sentences, *up the hill* and *after the fugitive* would usually be parsed as prepositional phrases modifying the verbs. This classification may be used, or *came up* and *ran after* may be regarded as verb-groups.

Verb Plus Infinitive

384. A form of *be, have*, or *ought* combined with an infinitive (*is to go, have to study, ought to come*), or a form of *be* combined with *going* or *about* and an infinitive (*is going to fail, is about to shoot*), makes a verb-group which is closely equivalent to a verb-phrase having *will, must, should*, etc., as an auxiliary.

> He *is to pay* the freight (*will pay*).
>
> They *have to be* at home tomorrow (*must be*).
>
> We *ought to try* harder (*should try*).
>
> I *am going to read* this book (*will read*).
>
> They *are about to sail* for Europe (*will soon sail*).
>
> His statements *are to be trusted* (*can be trusted*).

Similarly, *used* combined with an infinitive makes a verb-phrase about equivalent to a past tense of a verb, modified by the adverb *formerly*.

> He *used to play* golf (*formerly played*).

Exercise 67

Point out the verb-groups in the following sentences, and give their equivalents in other verb forms.

1. The savages had to be fought; the land had to be cleared. (J. T. Adams.)
2. But the most terrible ordeal was to come. (Thomas Hardy.) 3. Mrs. Norris is going to have a fine crop of apples this fall. (Edgar Lee Masters.) 4. The ship was about to start on its annual cruise to the South Seas. 5. They very soon found out in the steamer that the rope was gone. (Joseph Conrad.) 6. Innumerable writers are showing up the bestial side of military service. (William James.) 7. (He) went to bed, feeling assured that sooner or later he would hit upon the right track. (Arthur Machen.) 8. Labor had to choose other means for raising its standards of living. (Charles A. Beard.) 9. They had kept up a desultory correspondence after graduating from college. 10. Here they used to sit in the shade through a long, lazy summer's day. (Washington Irving.)

11. Did you think you were going to escape like this? (H. M. Tomlinson.) 12. They will have to raise the money by private subscription. 13. And now in a few thousand words I am to try to reproduce some of the beauty and interest of these islands. (William Beebe.) 14. We had made out the red light in that bay and steered for it. (Joseph Conrad.) 15. The war against war is going to be no holiday excursion or camping party. (William James.) 16. They ought to go to the meeting.

TENSE

385. The uses of the six tenses in English were stated in general terms in Sections 114, 115. This explanation, however, presented only part of the truth: it outlined the fundamental principles in the distinction of tenses, but did not take into account a number of exceptions.

The first step in a more thorough study of this subject is to distinguish clearly between *grammatical tenses* and the *actual time* represented by them. When we speak of *grammatical tenses* we have reference to the forms of the verbs. These forms follow definite rules of construction (see Sec. 116): the future tense is formed by means of the auxiliary verbs *shall* or *will;* the present perfect tense by *have* or *has;* the past perfect by *had,* etc. The distinguishing of the grammatical tenses, then, is largely a matter of the mechanical recognition of form.

The *grammatical tenses,* however, do not always represent the *actual time* which their names would lead us to expect. For example, the present tense does not always show that the action is taking place in present time, and the future tense is not the only one that may indicate future time. The following list covers the principal uses of the different tenses.

TENSES IN THE INDICATIVE MOOD

Uses of the Present Tense

386. The principal uses of the Present Tense are:

(1) To indicate an action that is taking place in actual present time.

>He *is* at the office.
>
>His hands *feel* warm.
>
>I *am writing* a letter to my sister.

(2) To express a fact that is always and universally true.

>God *is* just.
>
>Water *flows* downhill.

In this use, the present tense covers past, present, and future time.

(3) To indicate habitual or customary action.

>I *walk* to the office every morning.
>
>John *writes* to his mother daily.
>
>He *is selling* stocks and bonds for a New York firm (meaning that this is his business).

In this use, the present tense includes past and present time, and implies continued action in the future.

(4) To indicate an intended action in future time (the context shows the future meaning).

>I *leave* next Monday for New York.
>
>He *is coming* tomorrow.

387. **Combined with an Infinitive.** The present tense forms of *be* and *be going,* combined with an infinitive, frequently indicate future time (*about* is sometimes used with *be* in this construction).

>He *is to be* here next week.
>
>I *am going to do* the work tomorrow.
>
>He *is about to begin* his speech (cf. "will soon begin").

388. **The Historical Present.** The present tense may be used to give vividness to an account of a past event.

>Imagine, for a moment, the scene which greeted the travelers in this Italian village. It *is* Christmas morning, and the bell of the little church *is ringing* cheerily to summon the villagers to the morning service, etc. (Notice the change from the past tense to the present tense when the description of the actual scene begins.)

By this use of the **Historical Present,** as it is commonly called, the narrator makes a past scene or action more vivid by describing it as if it were actually present before him.

(a) In the following sentences, also, the present tense gives a past action a definite connection with present time.

I *hear* that the State Street Bank has failed.

I *see* that Williams has been made vice-president.

The first sentence, for instance, does not necessarily mean that I am hearing the news *now* for the first time; it indicates rather that I *have heard* the report, and am recalling it *now*.

Uses of the Past Tense

389. The Past Tense in its ordinary uses places an action unreservedly in past time, and cuts it off completely from any connection with present time. Its two principal functions are:

(1) To indicate an action that occurred at a specific time in the past (the specific time may be expressed, or understood from the context).

He *arrived* on Saturday.

They *entered* the room noiselessly.

She *was waiting* at the door.

(2) To indicate habitual or customary action in past time.

The Indians *lived* in wigwams.

The Romans *were* valiant fighters.

All the poor *brought* their troubles to him.

390. Idiomatic Uses. Besides these, the past tense has two idiomatic uses, as illustrated below.

(a) I *was going* tomorrow (meaning that I did intend to go tomorrow, but I have changed my mind).

Here the past tense indicates that some future action was contemplated in the past, but is no longer probable.

(b) I *knew* that it *was* late (in reply to some remark, such as "It is past midnight").

I *thought* you *seemed* tired (in reply to some remark, such as "I am tired").

In each of these sentences the verb in both the main and the subordinate clause is in the past tense, although the sentence distinctly implies that the condition which it describes is still continuing. Thus the first example means primarily "I knew (before you said so) that it was late," but it also implies that I still *know* that it *is* late. The past tense in the subordinate clause is due to attracted sequence of tenses (see Secs. 406 ff.).

USES OF THE FUTURE TENSE

391. The Future Tense is used:

(1) To indicate an expected future action.

> We *shall arrive* next Monday morning.
>
> The work *will be finished* within a month.

(2) To indicate customary action—present, past, and presumably future.

> Often she *will eat* a box of candy in an evening.

(3) To indicate—under certain conditions—a fact true at the present time.

> He *will be* at home now.
>
> You *will find* him in his office now.
>
> He *will* not *be* there so early as this.

The future tense is used in these sentences because they imply some possible future action. Thus the first sentence, in addition to stating that the man is at home now, suggests that if you will go there you will find him. The present meaning is shown by the context: for example, the adverb *now*.

Sometimes this construction expresses a hope or desire that something may be true at the present time.

> They *will* surely *be* ready by this time.

392. A verb having *will* as an auxiliary may indicate determination or persistence.

> He *will eat* mince pie, though it makes him ill.

Here the implication is that he has eaten mince pie in the past, eats it at present, and will continue to eat it.

For uses of the future perfect tense, see Sec. 115 (3).

USES OF THE PRESENT PERFECT TENSE

393. The Present Perfect Tense is regularly used to indicate an action completed at some time before the present.

> I *have solved* the problem.
>
> He *has filed* his income tax schedule.
>
> I *have seen* that picture somewhere.

394. The two principal characteristics of the present perfect tense, as regularly used, are: (a) it sets up the present as the limit of the period in which the action occurred; (b) it places the action *indefinitely* in that period.

395. The important point to remember about this tense is that it is not used when an action is to be placed at a definite point in past time.

I *have seen* him *yesterday* (incorrect).

He *has worked* on a farm *last summer* (incorrect).

In 1492 Columbus *has discovered* America (incorrect).

For these definite references, the past tense is used.

I *saw* him *yesterday* (correct).

He *worked* on a farm *last summer* (correct).

In 1492 Columbus *discovered* America (correct).

396. If any definite indication of time is used with the present perfect tense, it must be closely connected with the present.

I *have spoken* to him *this afternoon.*

He *has sold* some books this summer.

Compare also the use of this tense in connection with *since:*

Since 1916, prices *have risen* rapidly (correct).

Here the statement is made, not about a definite point of time in the past, but about a period extending from 1916 to the *present.*

Notice that it would be incorrect to say, "*After 1916,* prices *have risen* rapidly," for *after* does not connect the statement with the present. The past tense *rose* would be used here.

397. Action Continuing into the Present. The present perfect tense sometimes indicates an action which was begun in the past and continues into the present.

He *has worked* for five hours on this problem (he is still working on it).

They *have lived* in the country ten years (they still live there).

In statements of this sort the progressive forms, *has been working* and *have been living,* are often used.

Use of the Past Perfect Tense

398. The regular function of the Past Perfect Tense is to indicate that an action occurred before some other past action, or before some certain time in the past.

I *had written* to you before your letter came.

When the clock struck six, he *had copied* twenty pages.

He succeeded because he *had studied* the problem thoroughly.
They went to his assistance after he *had called* twice.

Note 1. The previous action represented by the past perfect tense may be placed in a main clause (as in the first two examples above), or in a subordinate clause (last two examples).

Note 2. The subsequent action is usually expressed by the past tense.

399. In narrative writing the past perfect tense is used to indicate any action that preceded the time of the main story, when the latter time is expressed by the past tense.

We found a stranger there, looking at a notice tacked on the front of the building. It *had been put* up months before, and was stained and torn by the weather. This paper *had been sent* out by the sheriff from the county seat, and gave a picture and a description of an outlaw who *had escaped* from prison.

400. Sometimes the past perfect tense is used in a subordinate clause beginning with *before* or an equivalent word, to indicate an action which *should have preceded* the action expressed in the main clause, but did not actually do so.

He gave his decision before he *had studied* all the data.
The manager came before I *had read* the report.

Thus the past perfect tense in the first example emphasizes the fact that all the data should have been studied before the decision was given.

401. In modern English, the past tense is frequently used instead of the past perfect tense when the time of the previous action is clearly shown by the context, and does not need to be emphasized.

He won because he *studied* the problem thoroughly (*had studied*).

The past perfect form, however, should always be employed when it is needed for clearness.

Exercise 68

Name the grammatical tenses of the verbs, and explain the actual time relations that they represent.

1. He has been the Washington correspondent for the *Times* since 1922. 2. Misers get up early in the morning; and burglars, I am informed, get up the night before. (G. K. Chesterton.) 3. The sun is setting and I see the shadows stealing across the lake. 4. My father liked my class poem when he

heard me read it at commencement. (Carl Van Doren.) 5. "I'm going down to the office immediately after breakfast," he said. "What are you going to do with yourself?" (W. S. Maugham.) 6. The books of an older generation will not fit this. (Nathaniel Hawthorne.) 7. Character is higher than intellect. (R. W. Emerson.) 8. You must hurry, for the play is about to begin. 9. These lagoons have long since disappeared, but they were beautiful things in their time. (Willa Cather.) 10. Don't be afraid that I am going to talk of the "romance" of the inn. (Thomas Burke.)

11. The door was swung open for him by a page. (J. B. Priestley.) 12. When the men of other days put out to sea they trusted their lives to small wooden vessels propelled by oars. (Joseph Husband.) 13. He had not risen, but he accompanied his words with a smile. (R. L. Stevenson.) 14. Some nights they (thrushes) will sing in universal chorus. (L. B. Gillet.) 15. Into the street rode a tall figure seated upon a white horse. (Sherwood Anderson.) 16. We were going to town tomorrow, but the roads are almost impassable. 17. He had placed in prominent positions the books that he had inherited from his father, who had been a schoolmaster. (May Sinclair.) 18. Sometimes he will sit for an hour looking at a book but seeing nothing. 19. The *Queen Mary* sails on May 25 from New York. (Express the same time relation in three other ways.) 20. Jane *will* dress in red, although that color is unbecoming to her.

21. He lived in Paris after the close of the war. 22. He has lived in Paris since the close of the war. 23. He has lived in Paris, and during his visit this summer he will meet many old friends. 24. He has been living in Paris for twenty years. 25. I hear that you were in New York recently. 26. They were coming next week, but Mr. Adams is ill.

Exercise 69

Supply the tense form (present, past perfect, etc.) that expresses the time indicated in the sentence. If more than one tense form can be used, explain the difference in meaning.

1. They _____ in the city yesterday (visit).
2. The boys _____ every day since New Year's (work).
3. I _____ in Chicago now (live).
4. For the meeting this evening, the committee _____ a long, detailed report (prepare).
5. Yesterday we _____ an order from a firm in Brazil (receive).
6. I _____ to the theater every night this week (go).
7. I _____ to the theater every night so far this week (go).
8. I _____ to the theater every night last week (go).

9. I _____ to the theater every night since last Sunday (go).
10. They _____ before we came (leave).
11. By the time we were ready, the legislature _____ in session for over a week (be).
12. When I met him he said that he _____ in the city for the past month (be).
13. We _____ to him on Tuesday about this report (speak).
14. We _____ to him already about this report (speak).
15. When we finally heard from him, he _____ away from home two months (be).
16. At noon yesterday he received the telegram that he _____ to get last week (expect).
17. They _____ if you ask them (come).
18. We _____ this play when we were in Boston (see).
19. We _____ this play twice since it came to Chicago (see).
20. We _____ this play twice after it came to Chicago (see).
21. They _____ on us twice yesterday (call).
22. They _____ on us twice today (call).

TENSES OF THE SUBJUNCTIVE MOOD

For the forms and uses of the subjunctive mood, see Secs. 131 ff.

402. Time Indicated by the Present Tense. The present tense of the subjunctive mood indicates present time (or future time when the context shows the future meaning).

If that *be* the case, our cause is lost.
If it *be* raining tomorrow, they will not go.

403. Time Indicated by the Past Tense. The past tense of the subjunctive mood has no definite connection with actual past time. Like the present tense, it regularly refers to present time.

If I *were* wealthy, I would give you the money (now).
I wish that he *were* here (now).
He acts as if he *were* ill (now).

The difference between the two tenses in conditional statements is that the present subjunctive indicates a condition which *may or may not be true to fact,* whereas the past subjunctive indicates a condition which is *contrary to fact* (see Secs. 136, 137). Thus in this kind of statement the past tense has lost practically all its force as an indicator of time, and has become a means of showing the kind of condition that is being expressed.

Note. When the verb of the main clause is in the past tense, the past sub-junctive in wishes and after *as if* and *as though* indicates the same time as the main verb—that is, it represents what was present time when the action of the main verb occurred.

I wished that he *were* there (at the time of the wishing).

She walked as if she *were* tired.

404. The past subjunctive may refer to actual future time, or to time subsequent to that of the main verb, when the context shows this kind of relation.

If he *were to ask* me tomorrow, I might consent.

I wish that she *were going* next week.

He talked as though he *were going* to be a millionaire.

405. **Time Indicated by the Past Perfect Tense.** For indicating actual past time in the subjunctive mood, a past perfect form is used.

If she *had been* there, the accident would not have occurred.

If he *had come,* the officers would have seen him.

I wish that I *had seen* you.

He looks as if he *had been injured.*

Exercise 70

(A) Name the grammatical tenses of the verbs in the subjunctive mood, and tell what actual time they represent.

1. If that were true, he would be a hero. 2. If that be true, he should be rewarded. 3. I wish that he were here so that you could talk with him. 4. I wish that he had been here so that you could have seen him. 5. I wish that he were going with us to the next convention. 6. If everyone were as kind as Uncle John, how nice the world would be. (Hugh Walpole.) 7. It makes no difference whether the actors be many or one, a tyrant or a mob. (R. W. Emerson.) 8. If I knew his name, I would introduce him. 9. I wish that she had been less generous with her praise. 10. Then it [the sheep] began to pant heavily and to shake as if a spasm were upon it. (Elizabeth M. Roberts.)

11. Had they been regular troops, the results would have been most fatal. (Francis Parkman.) 12. I wish that I had time to read the book. 13. She felt as if she were living in a world of dreams. 14. He acted as if he had heard the story before. 15. Even if they traveled all next week, they could not get here in time.

(B) Which verbs in the conditional clauses are in the indicative mood and which are in the subjunctive mood? What actual time does each represent?

1. If they work all night they may finish the investigation. 2. If they worked all night they might finish the investigation. 3. If they had worked all night they might have finished the investigation. 4. If he speaks slowly, we can understand him. 5. If he spoke more slowly, we could understand him. 6. If he was tired, he stopped working. 7. If he were tired, he would stop working.

SEQUENCE OF TENSES

406. Sequence of Tenses is the principle which governs the tense relations between the verb in a main clause and one in an accompanying subordinate clause.

The verbs may be in Natural or Attracted Sequence.

Verbs are in **Natural Sequence** when they indicate the natural or logical time relation existing between the actions which they represent.

For instance, when the actions in the main clause and in the subordinate clause take place in present time and in future time respectively, natural sequence requires that the verbs shall be in the present tense and the future tense: "He *knows* that you *will come.*"

In cases of **Attracted Sequence,** the verb in the subordinate clause is "attracted" from its natural tense form into one which harmonizes with the tense of the verb in the main clause, without regard to the actual time represented.

For example, if a person says, "I *am* ill," that remark may be immediately repeated by someone in the form, "He *said* that he *was* ill." Here the verb *am* is attracted into the past tense *was* to make it conform with the past tense *said,* in spite of the fact that the original speaker may still be ill.

ATTRACTED SEQUENCE

407. Attracted sequence is the only one of the two types that involves possible complications, and it is largely restricted to *indirect discourse and to clauses of purpose when these constructions follow main verbs in the past and past perfect tenses.*

408. In Indirect Discourse. Indirect Discourse is a form of statement in which the thought of a speaker is repeated in substance but in a different form from that originally used.

He said, *"I will go"* (direct discourse).
He said *that he would go* (indirect discourse).

409. When the verb of the main clause is in the past or past perfect tense, attracted sequence occurs.

(1) A present tense in the original direct statement becomes a past tense in indirect discourse.

She *said* that you *were* wrong. (Direct—"you *are* wrong.")
I *told* you that he *was* at home. (He *is* at home.)
They *asked* whether we *were* ready. (*Are* you ready?)
I *remarked* that I *might be* there. (I *may be* there.)

Exception. The present tense is regularly used in the subordinate clause, with a past tense in the main clause, to express a universal or general truth.

He *declared* that the earth *is* round.
They *said* that virtue *is* its own reward.

(2) A present perfect tense becomes a past perfect tense.

They *said* that he *had gone*. (Direct—"He *has gone*.")

(3) A future or a future perfect tense assumes a form having as an auxiliary *would* (*should*) or *would have* (*should have*), respectively.

She *said* that she *would go*. (Direct—"I *will go*.")
I said that you *would have finished* the work by that time. (You *will have finished* the work by that time.)

(4) A past or a past perfect tense, since it is already in harmony with the tense of the main verb, regularly remains a past or a past perfect tense, respectively.

I *said* that you *were* at home yesterday. (Direct—"You *were* at home yesterday.")
They *knew* that he *had been* there before the war. (He *had been* there before the war.)

410. The same kind of attracted sequence occurs after such verbs as *expect, suppose, think,* and *know,* and after predicate adjectives like *evident, certain,* and *sure.* These constructions are similar to indirect discourse, although they do not actually state that someone said something.

Thus, on going to a place and finding a person there, one may say, "I was sure that you *were* here." The verb in the subordinate clause is attracted into the past tense by the past tense in the main clause, in spite of the fact that you are still here. Compare also "I thought that you *would go*," made in response to a statement, "I *will go*."

Note. When the verb of the main clause in indirect discourse is in any other tense than the past and past perfect, the verb of the subordinate clause regularly has natural sequence (see Sec. 412).

> He *says* that he *is* a soldier.
> He *says* that he *was* formerly a soldier.
> He *says* that he *will be* a soldier.
> He *says* that he *had been* a soldier before he became a painter.
> She *has said* that you *will receive* the money.
> She *has said* that you *received* the money.
> He *will think* that you *were* guilty.

411. In Clauses of Purpose. When the verb of the main clause is in the past or past perfect tense, the past tense of a verb, usually a modal auxiliary like *might, could, would,* or *should,* is used in a subordinate clause of purpose (attracted sequence).

> He *bought* the house in order that he *might live* in comfort.
> He *had bought* the house in order that he *might live* in comfort.
> He *bought* a house so that he *could have* a home of his own.
> We *took* care that we *should* not *be seen.*

Note. When the verb of the main clause is in any other tense, the present tense is used in the subordinate clause.

> He *is buying* the house in order that he *may live* in comfort.
> He *will buy* (*has bought*) a house in order that he *may live* in comfort.
> He *is buying* a house so that he *can have* a home of his own.

NATURAL SEQUENCE

412. Natural Sequence occurs regularly in clauses other than those covered in Secs. 407 ff. The principle governing the sequence of tenses in these constructions is simple.

No matter what the tense of the verb in the main clause is, the verb of the subordinate clause may be in any tense whatsoever that is required by the meaning of the sentence.

> He *was* once stronger than he *is* now.
> The general once *lived* where the new depot *will be built.*
> He *was* once a tramp, although he *is* now wealthy.
> The Romans *did* not *dress* as we *do* now.

He *worked* harder than you ever *will* (work).
She *is* unhappy because she *is* poor.
She *is* unhappy because she *lost* her money.
He *will* take what I *brought.*
He *will read* the book when I *have finished* it.
They *have* always *lived* where the winters *are* warm.

For combinations of tenses in conditional sentences, see Sec. 442.

Exercise 71

Change the following sentences from direct to indirect discourse, or
from indirect to direct discourse—with especial attention to the shift
in the grammatical tenses of the verbs.

1. He replied, "I live in New York."
2. I said, "We are going to the theater tonight."
3. "Will you come tomorrow?" he asked.
4. "I have found the lost papers," I announced.
5. "Honesty is always the best policy," she declared.
6. "I know that I feel better," he said.
7. "May I see the president?" he inquired.
8. "I have worked since sunrise," I replied, "and I am tired."
9. They promised that they would send the money tomorrow.
10. I said that I was willing to sell the house.
11. I argued that I had a right to present my side of the case.
12. He says that good tickets are still available.
13. He said that good tickets were still available.

SIMPLE AND PROGRESSIVE VERB FORMS

For the Simple and the Progressive Forms of the tenses, see Secs. 120,
121.

GENERAL DISTINCTION

413. In general, the progressive form of the verb, as distinguished from
the simple form, makes the action seem more vivid and emphasizes
the fact that the action is *in progress* at a certain time.

In the following sentences this is practically the only consideration
which governs the choice of one form or the other.

He *feels* tired.
He *is feeling* tired.

An hour later the sun *shone* brightly.
An hour later the sun *was shining* brightly.
He *will talk* for an hour at least.
He *will be talking* for an hour at least.
He *has fished* in this lake for five summers.
He *has been fishing* in this lake for five summers.

In other instances, however, there are more specific differences in use.

SPECIFIC DISTINCTIONS

414. Present Tense. In the Present Tense the two forms sometimes have radically different functions.

(1) With many verbs the simple present indicates only habitual action, the progressive form being used when an action is placed in actual present time.

John *talks* very rapidly (habitual action).
The soldiers *drill* on the parade ground.
John *is talking* to a friend (actual present).
The soldiers *are drilling* on the parade ground.

(2) With some verbs, however, the simple present may indicate actual present time.

I *think* that he is right.
That medicine *seems* harmless.
This rose *smells* sweet.
He *hears* a noise in the house.
I *see* the house now.
I *respect* your motives.

The distinction between groups (1) and (2) seems to be that the verbs in the first one are concerned with *action or activity,* as *walk, run, talk,* etc. (sometimes cessation of activity—as *stand, sit,* etc.); whereas those in the second group generally represent a *state or condition,* as *seem, feel, know, think,* etc. This is only a rough statement of the difference, and certain exceptions will be found; but it shows the general tendency in the two groups.

The basis for the distinction seemingly is that the progressive form expresses an idea more vividly than a simple form and is therefore better suited to indicate action, which, by nature, is more vivid than a condition or a state.

415. It will be noted that, in harmony with the principle just given, some of the verbs in group (2) take the progressive form to indicate actual present time when they are used in a sense that brings them into connection with a definite action.

I *am thinking* of going to Los Angeles (cf. "I *think* you are right").

He *is saying* his prayers (cf. "He *says* that he is ready").

416. Tenses Indicating Past Time. In the tenses representing past time (past, present perfect, and past perfect), the progressive form is used to give the impression that the action was not completed. Compare:

He *was writing* the letter yesterday (progressive form—the letter may not have been completed).

He *wrote* the letter yesterday (simple form—the letter was completed).

She *has been reading* the book.

She *has read* the book.

Before I came they *had been framing* a new constitution.

Before I came they *had framed* a new constitution.

417. In the past tense, when one action of comparatively brief duration occurred while another action of longer duration was in progress, the briefer action is generally represented by the simple past, the longer one by the progressive past.

He *was waiting* for the train when I *saw* him.

The man *was carrying* a revolver when he *was arrested*.

John *was standing* on the corner as the car *passed* by.

418. When the two actions are of about the same duration, either the simple past or the progressive past may be used to represent both actions, the latter being chosen when especial emphasis or vividness is desired.

He *spoke* as I *entered* the room.

He *was laughing* all the time that the officers *were searching* him.

Notice the difference in meaning in the following sentences.

He *spoke* as I *entered*.

He *was speaking* as I *entered*.

In the first, he made some brief remark, perhaps gave a word of greeting, when I entered. In the second, he was in the midst of a statement which he had begun before my entrance.

Exercise 72

Explain the difference in meaning and time relation expressed by the simple and the progressive verb forms.

1. In the evening we go to the theater or play bridge. 2. We are going over sixty miles an hour. 3. Everyone looks sleepy. 4. Everyone is looking at the clock. 5. Night came, and the wolves began to howl. (Francis Parkman.) 6. Night was coming, and the wolves were beginning to howl. 7. He reads French easily. 8. He is reading one of Hardy's novels. 9. I have read the latest report of the committee. 10. I have been reading the latest report.

11. They had left the square and were passing up Harley Street. (Hugh Walpole.) 12. They passed the police station on their way home. 13. All this time the third stranger had stood in the doorway. 14. All this time the third stranger had been standing in the doorway. (Joseph Conrad.) 15. She smiled when he looked at her. 16. She was smiling when he looked at her. 17. I make it my business, when I am in France, to preach political good-will and moderation. (R. L. Stevenson.) 18. I am making it my business, while I am in France, to become familiar with colloquial French. 19. He climbed to the top of the mountain. 20. He was climbing to the top of the mountain. 21. They have been making money on the stock exchange. 22. They have made money on the stock exchange.

PARTICIPLES

For a previous discussion of participles, see Secs. 159 ff.

Uses of the Participle

419. A participle or a participial phrase may be used:
(1) As an Adjective.
> The *running* water is pure.
> The man *reading the paper* is the auditor.
> His *rejected* manuscript was returned.

(2) As a Predicate Adjective.
> That condition was *exasperating*.
> The arm is *swollen*.
> The man was found *dying*.

(3) As an Adverb in a Dual Relation (see Secs. 200, 494).
> *Fearing more trouble*, the sheriff sent for help.
> The boy came *jumping up the steps*.
> They ran down the street, *shouting and waving their hats* (see Sec. 527).

(4) As an Objective Complement (see Sec. 358).
> We found the family *starving*.

(5) In the Nominative Absolute Construction (see Secs. 25 and 204).
   That *being* the case, he will not come.
   It was very cold, the thermometer *registering* zero.
   He faced the audience, his hand *raised* for silence.
(6) Parenthetically.
   Generally *speaking,* there are three kinds of cats.
   This result, *assuming* that it is correct, is startling.

A participle used parenthetically does not need to refer to a definite noun.

(7) As Part of a Verb Phrase (see Sec. 203).
   He *is writing* a novel.
   The artist *has finished* the picture.

TENSE

See Sec. 160 for the tense forms of participles.

420. Present and Past Participles do not represent the actual present or past time which their names suggest, but regularly indicate time relative to the time of the verb in the sentence.

421. The Present Participle regularly indicates an action which is occurring at the time represented by the verb.
   Every man *carrying* a rifle *was arrested.*
   Every man *carrying* a rifle *is being arrested.*
   Every man *carrying* a rifle *will be arrested.*
In these sentences the men are carrying the rifles at the time of their arrest, and the arrests are placed in past, present, and future time, respectively.
Sometimes the Present Participle represents an action as taking place at the time the sentence was written or spoken, instead of at the time indicated by the verb.
   That man *sitting* at the desk *was promoted* last week.
   That man *sitting* at the desk *will be discharged* next week.

422. The Past Participle regularly indicates an action which occurred before the time represented by the verb in the sentence.
   The house *destroyed* by fire *is being* rebuilt.
   The house *destroyed* by fire *was* rebuilt.
   A letter *mailed* tomorrow *will be* delivered the following day.
The Past Participle may indicate an action which was begun before

the time represented by the verb, and the results of which are still in effect at the time of the verb.

She saw a child *clothed* in rags.

The factory *located* in Boston is closed for repairs.

423. The **Perfect Participle** indicates that the action which it represents occurred definitely before the time of the verb, and emphasizes the fact that the action was completed before that time.

The student, *having solved* the problem, asked for more work.

The man, *having found* the watch, is going home.

The watch *having been found*, the man is going home.

Voice

424. The **Present Participle** shows that the person or thing named by the noun which the participle modifies is performing the action indicated by the participle.

The boy *writing* the letter is the president's son.

425. The **Past Participle** regularly shows that the person or thing which the noun represents is receiving the action indicated by the participle.

The tree *struck* by lightning was destroyed.

In the first sentence the present participle *writing* modifies *boy*—and the boy is doing the writing. In the second sentence the past participle *struck* modifies *tree*—and the tree received the action.

Some past participles are used as simple adjectives with little, if any, passive meaning: a *retired* farmer, a *returned* missionary.

Exercise 73

(A) Explain the uses of the participles and participial phrases. Point out those that have a dual function as adjective and as adverb.

1. The stone steps leading down to it from the level of earth were quite unlighted. (Arnold Bennett.) 2. These two reports by the Bureau of Fisheries are interesting and well written. 3. I had seen them coming back that night. (R. L. Stevenson.) 4. Living at home, I was never absorbed in the life of the university. (Carl Van Doren.) 5. A few years ago they had bought this farm, paying part, mortgaging the remainder in the usual way. (Hamlin Garland.) 6. The rural population, impoverished and often enslaved, frequently revolted. (R. G. Tugwell.) 7. The next morning they heard the Squire moving about in his room. (W. D. Howells.) 8. A few scattering clouds were drifting on the west wind, their shadows sliding down the

green and purple slopes. (Hamlin Garland.) 9. About an hour before sundown, having stowed our water-casks, we commenced getting under way. (R. H. Dana.) 10. The door, being bolted on the inside, could not be opened.

11. Toiling and resting and toiling again, we wore away the morning. (H. M. Tomlinson.) 12. Their identity having been established, they were released by the customs officials. 13. Colet watched the papers sprawling and scattering. (H. M. Tomlinson.) 14. I had followed him, thinking of answers to each point as he made it. (Edgar Lee Masters.) 15. The people seemed a little tired, maybe from that long drive. (Ruth Suckow.) 16. When we came on deck at four o'clock, we found things much changed for the better. (R. H. Dana.) 17. Strictly speaking, he was not eligible for the prize. 18. Before the ticket wagon a straggling, excited crowd wrestled, suspicious, determined, hurried. (Hamlin Garland.) 19. He began to pace the room, his head bowed in thought. (H. M. Tomlinson.)

(B) Name the voice, and the time indicated by each participle in the preceding sentences.

Exercise 74

Supply the proper tense form of the participles—present, past, or perfect; active or passive—of the verbs indicated in parentheses. Explain the relation in time between the participle and the main verb in each sentence.

1. _____ the play before, I knew what the ending would be (see).
2. _____ the book aside, he began to write his impressions of it (lay).
3. Two attacks _____, the garrison waited anxiously for the next attempt (repulse).
4. The weather _____ cold, we wore our heaviest clothing (be).
5. The weather _____ cold, we are wearing our heaviest clothing (be).
6. The weather _____ much colder during the night, we wore our heaviest clothing the next day (turn).
7. She will be at the door, _____ for him (wait).
8. _____ the telegram the night before, we were naturally concerned because we had not received a reply (send).
9. A letter _____ by Franklin is in the collection (write).

INFINITIVES

For previous discussions of infinitives and infinitive phrases, see Secs. 152 ff., 193 ff.

Uses

426. As a Noun. An infinitive or infinitive phrase may be used as a noun.

(1) Subject of a Verb.

To falter would be fatal.
To send the message was unnecessary.
It is hard *to select a subject* (see Sec. 345 (3)).

(2) Predicate Noun.

His ambition is *to study law.*

(3) Object of a Verb.

He promised *to come.*
They wanted *to see the parade.*
We found it easy *to cross the river* (see Sec. 345 (4)).

(4) Retained Object of a Verb (see Secs. 301 ff.).

He was forced *to sign a contract.*

(5) Object of a Preposition.

She has no choice but *to obey* (see Sec. 539 (1)).

(6) In Apposition with a Noun.

His first proposal, *to borrow the money,* was rejected.

427. As an Adjective. An infinitive or infinitive phrase may be used as an adjective.

A desire *to travel* is his reason for resigning.
He has an opportunity *to prove his ability.*
This house is *to rent* (predicate adjective).

428. As an Adverb. An infinitive, or infinitive phrase, may be used as an adverb—to modify, or complete the meaning of, a verb, adjective, or adverb.

He went *to get a book* (modifies a verb).
The man stooped *to pick up the paper.*
He came *to believe that the story was true.*
They are sure *to fail* (modifies an adjective).
This problem is easy *to understand.*
She was careful *to lock the door.*
He was too weary *to talk* (modifies the adverb *too*).
They were angry enough *to fight* (modifies the adverb *enough*).

Some of these infinitives have so general a relation with the words which they modify that it is useless to attempt to classify them according to their meanings. In such cases they may be called "Complementary Infinitives used as Adverbs." In other instances they clearly fall into one of the regular adverbial groups. For example:

He is too small *to do this work* (degree).
They came *to get their wraps* (purpose).

429. In a Verb-phrase. An infinitive used with a form of *be* or *have* makes a verb-phrase.

He *is to go* next week (see Sec. 384).
She *has to write* a letter.

Sometimes the infinitive is combined with *going, about, ought,* or *used*.

I *am going to tell* your father.
The firm *is about to fail*.
He *used to sleep* all day.

430. Used Parenthetically. An infinitive may be used parenthetically.

This statement, *to speak frankly,* is untrue.
To be sure, he is not entirely at fault.

431. Used Absolutely with a Noun. An infinitive with a noun may form a construction similar to a nominative absolute with a participle.

A purse of $5,000 has been offered, *the winner to take two-thirds*.

432. Combined with "How," etc. An infinitive combined with *how, when, where, which, whether,* and similar words forms an equivalent of a noun clause (see Sec. 322).

I don't know *how to write the letter* (object of a verb).
She will tell you *where to find it*.
The question is *which to select* (predicate noun).
What to do is our next problem (subject).

433. Infinitive with a Subject. For infinitives with subjects and *for* plus an infinitive with a subject, see Secs. 205-207. Examples are:

We expected *them to come on Sunday*.
For them to do that was inexcusable.

434. Infinitive without "to." An infinitive with the sign *to* omitted (see Sec. 158) may be used:

(1) After certain verbs like *dare,* etc.

I dare not *try* it (to try).
I saw them *fall* (to fall).
We made him *laugh* (to laugh).

(2) After auxiliaries to form verb-phrases (see Sec. 154, *note* 1).
    She will *come.*
    He can *sing.*
    They should *write.*
(3) As the object of the preposition *except* or *but.*
    This dog can do everything except *talk* (to talk).
    He does nothing but *complain.*

Note. For the idiom *cannot but* in sentences like "He *cannot but* agree," see Sec. 539 (2).

TENSES OF THE INFINITIVE

435. The infinitive has two tenses—the Present and the Perfect: for example, *to see* (present), *to have seen* (perfect). Both tenses have progressive and passive forms: *to be seeing, to be seen; to have been seeing, to have been seen* (see Sec. 156).
The tenses of the infinitive do not represent the actual present or past time which their names suggest; they indicate time relative to that of the verb with which they are used.

PRESENT INFINITIVE

436. The Present Infinitive may be used with any tense of a verb. It may represent:
(1) An action occurring at the same time as that of the verb which it accompanies.
    I *like to study.*
    He *seemed to lift* the weight easily.
    They *will help* you *to find* a position.
    I *had refused to accept* money for these services.
    He appears *to be working* hard.
    She likes *to be seen.*
(2) An action occurring after the time of the verb which it accompanies.
    I *expect to go* home tomorrow.
    Yesterday he *promised to see* me again next week.
    He *will leave* tomorrow *to attend* the meeting of the directors on Thursday.
    They *have invited* us *to attend* the opening performance.

Perfect Infinitive

437. The Perfect Infinitive regularly represents an action which occurred before the time of the verb which it accompanies.

It is generally used with a verb in the present tense; sometimes with one in the future tense; less frequently with one in the past tense.

(1) With a verb in the present tense.

I *am* sorry *to have troubled* you.
I *am* glad *to have had* this opportunity to speak to you.
He *is supposed to have been wounded* in the battle.

(2) With a verb in the future tense.

They *will find* him *to have been* a traitor.
As the years pass, he *will seem* more and more *to have represented* the highest ideals of his time.

(3) With a verb in the past tense.

When he left, he *appeared to have enjoyed* the program.
He *was reported to have been captured* by the Indians.

Before using this combination of a perfect infinitive with a verb in the past tense, the writer should be sure that the action which is expressed by the infinitive really belongs to a time previous to that of the verb. Usually he will find that such is not the case, and that the present infinitive is the proper form to use.

I hoped *to have seen* you (incorrect).
I hoped *to see* you (correct).
He would have liked *to see* you (correct).

Exercise 75

Explain the uses of the infinitives and infinitive phrases.

1. To do the work properly would require at least a month. 2. Still the young man would have to be disciplined, to get him back in his place. (H. M. Tomlinson.) 3. A house supposed to have been built by Lincoln, has been preserved. 4. I did not know whether to laugh or cry. (R. L. Stevenson.) 5. He is planning for you to meet him in Boston. 6. At first the plan seemed feasible, but later they found it to be impractical. 7. Nobody likes to be asked favours. (Oscar Wilde.) 8. We have the power, but we have still to learn how to use our power. (H. G. Wells.) 9. For a hundred years America had been in a position to supply land to all immigrants who cared

to till the soil. (Charles A. Beard.) 10. We intimated that the prairie was hardly the place to enjoy a quiet life. (Francis Parkman).

11. The exiles were forbidden to return at the peril of their lives. (Bret Harte.) 12. She lets her clever tongue run away with her sometimes. (Oscar Wilde.) 13. There was no alternative except to take the case to a higher court. 14. The weight, to be exact, was ten pounds and six ounces. 15. Where to get the money was the next question. 16. Under these conditions, for him to go was impossible. 17. It is better to have loved, and lost. 18. In that case, he urged the states to build better highways. (Charles A. Beard.) 19. He found it hard to believe that. (H. M. Tomlinson.) 20. But at that depth my feet began to leave me, and I durst venture no further. (R. L. Stevenson.)

21. Beyond the captain Colet saw a dire spectre loom and bear down on them. (H. M. Tomlinson.) 22. The difficulty of literature is not to write, but to write what you mean. (R. W. Emerson.) 23. There is still one possibility —namely, to rent the house and live in a hotel. 24. This was not due to any deliberate avoidance, or any attempt to be singular. (Alfred Noyes.) 25. The bad side was the difficulty in getting them to obey orders. (William McFee.) 26. For years he has done nothing but write for the pulp magazines.

(A) Name the tense and voice of each infinitive in the preceding sentences.

Exercise 76

Supply the proper tense form of the infinitives—present or perfect, active or passive. Explain the relation in time between the infinitives and the main verb in each sentence. If two tense forms are possible, explain the difference in meaning. (Use the infinitive of the verb given in parentheses.)

1. In January the company was said to ———— near bankruptcy (be).
2. The fugitive was reported yesterday to ———— in New York on various occasions (see).
3. They want to ———— next week (go).
4. He was believed to ———— a cousin of the prisoner (be).
5. I am glad to ———— you so cheerful today (find).
6. I am glad to ———— him speak at the last convention (hear).
7. I was glad to ———— so good an opportunity to see the House of Commons in session (have).

8. He would have been glad to —————— you when he was here (meet).
9. She ought to ————— early enough to be here by this time (start).
10. She ought to ————— early enough to be here early tomorrow (start).
11. He is said to ————— engaged to the actress, Marie Culoa (be).
12. They believe him to ————— the master mind of the gang (be).
13. This play was once thought to ————— by Shakespeare (write).
14. When the directors meet next Tuesday, they will expect us to —————
   the report before the session begins (finish).

THE MODAL AUXILIARIES

438. Verb-phrases indicating permission, possibility, probability, ability, obligation, and kindred ideas are often made with the aid of the Modal Auxiliaries: namely, *may, can, must, might, could, would,* and *should.* In many instances these serve as substitutes for older verbs in the subjunctive mood.

For the various tense forms of the modal auxiliaries, see Sec. 145.

439. Time Indicated by the Modal Auxiliaries. *Might, could, would,* and *should,* although they are classified as past tenses of *may, can, will,* and *shall,* do not ordinarily indicate actual past time. They may indicate either present or future time, just as the present forms do.

The distinction in the use of the present and past tenses is sometimes a matter of different shades of meaning, the past tense forms expressing an idea less definitely—with a greater degree of doubt.

> I *can* go today.
> I *could* go today (more doubtful).
> You *may* find it.
> You *might* find it (more doubtful).

Frequently the past tense form is due to sequence of tenses (see Secs. 407 ff.).

> I thought that he *might* come. (He *may* come.)
> He said that John *would* refuse. (John *will* refuse.)

440. In order to place an action definitely in past time, the present perfect or the past perfect form is regularly used. The latter generally expresses greater doubt.

> He *may have* gone yesterday.
> He *might have* gone yesterday (more doubtful).
> We *could have* seen them.

Note. In some uses, *could* and *would* without *have* may indicate past time: "He *would* eat the entire apple" (was determined to eat it). "He *could* read when he was four years old."

GENERAL USES

441. In sentences expressing condition, necessity, concession, and purpose the modal auxiliaries have the following uses.

442. In Main Clauses. (1) When there is a past tense of the subjunctive mood in a conditional clause contrary to fact, the verb of the main clause regularly has *might, could, would,* or *should* as its auxiliary.

If he *were* younger, he *would* work harder.
If they *knew* the way, they *could* come alone.
If he *had* more money, he *might* be happier.

(2) When there is a past perfect tense of the subjunctive mood in a conditional clause contrary to fact, the verb of the main clause regularly has *might have, could have, would have,* or *should have* as its auxiliary; occasionally it has *might, could, would,* or *should.*

If he *had been* younger, he *would have* worked harder.
If they *had known* the way, they *could have* come alone.
If I *had done* that, I *would* tell you.

Note. In sentences expressing a condition which may or may not be true to fact, the verbs in both the main and the subordinate clause may have any form or be in any tense required by the thought, and a modal auxiliary is not necessarily present.

If you *come, bring* me the paper.
If he *is* sick, he *brought* the trouble on himself.
If that *be* (*is*) true, I *was* mistaken.
If she *goes,* she *will be* sorry.
If he *was* there, I *am* sure that he *regrets* it.
If he *went,* he *will tell* you.
If she *knew* it, she *said* nothing to us.
If they *were* there, they *should have telephoned.*
If he *has seen* her, he *will come.*

443. In Subordinate Clauses. Verb-phrases formed with modal auxiliaries are used as subjunctive equivalents in a number of constructions where the subjunctive was formerly the rule. The subjunctive mood is still occasionally found in these constructions, but the forms with the auxiliaries are more common.

(1) *Should* is used in conditional clauses which may or may not be true to fact to indicate doubt that the condition will be fulfilled.

> If they *should* fail, please write to me at once.
> If he *should* forget to come, you can take his place.

Compare "If he *forgets* to come" and "If he *forget* to come" (see Sec. 136 (1)). *Forgets* (indicative), *forget* (subjunctive), and *should forget* (with the modal auxiliary) indicate increasing degrees of doubt.

(2) *Should* (or *shall*) is sometimes used instead of the present subjunctive in certain clauses depending upon a verb, noun, or adjective which expresses some form of wish, command, or urgency (see Sec. 136 (4), *note*).

> He insisted that the order *should* be obeyed at once.
> It was necessary that the messenger *should* leave immediately.
> His command was that we *should* be released.
> The instructor requires that all papers *shall* be typewritten.

(3) *May, might,* or *should* is used in concessive clauses which admit something as doubtful or possible, not as accomplished.

> Although that *may* be true, I refuse to go.
> Even though the house *should* burn, the contents are insured.
> Even though I *might* be late, I will finish the work.

"Although it *is* true," "Although it *be* true," "Although it *may be* true," and "Although it *might be* true" indicate increasing degrees of doubt.

(4) *May* or *might* (sometimes *should* or *would*) is used in purpose clauses (see Sec. 515).

> She studies hard in order that she *may* get a passing mark.
> He talked rapidly so that he *might* finish his speech.
> He started early so that he *would* be on time.

SPECIFIC MEANINGS OF THE MODAL AUXILIARIES

444. "May" (past tense, *might*) denotes:
(1) Permission.

> You *may* go home (you have my permission).
> *May* I suggest a change in the plan?
> He says that you *may* buy the hat.
> He said that you *might* buy the hat.

(2) Possibility.

> They *may* find the book.
> They *might* find the book (more doubtful).
> I think that I *may* see him.

I thought that I *might* see him.

(3) A wish (*may* only).

May the flag wave forever!

May that time never come!

(4) For the use of *may* or *might* as subjunctive equivalents, see Sec. 443.

Note. For the distinction between *may* and *might,* see Sec. 439.

445. "Can" (past tense, *could*) denotes:

(1) Ability.

He *can* easily carry the bundle.

He *could* easily carry the bundle (if he tried).

He says that he *can* speak French.

He said that he *could* speak French.

(2) Refusal of permission—in negative statements.

You *cannot* go now (I forbid you to go).

446. "Must" denotes:

(1) Necessity or obligation.

She *must* write the letter at once.

The officer *must* do his duty.

Note. To indicate necessity or obligation in past time, the verb *had* with an infinitive is used.

He *had to see* a client in the city yesterday.

Must, however, may refer to past time when used in sequence with a verb in a past tense.

He *told* them that they *must* stop quarreling.

(2) Emphasis in the statement of some inference.

It *must* be after midnight (judging from the way I feel, I infer that it is after midnight).

He *must* think that you are foolish (from what he says to you I infer that he considers you to be foolish).

For past time, *must have* is used.

It *must have* been late when he came.

447. "Would" denotes:

(1) Habitual action in the past.

Every evening I *would* walk five miles.

People *would* come many miles to see him

(2) Determination.

> I simply *would* not listen to him any longer.
>
> He *would* come in spite of our objections.

(3) Willingness to do something.

> He *would* help you if he could.
>
> I *would* come if I were able.

(4) Simple futurity (in the second and third persons—see Sec. 456).

> They *would* be arrested if they came.
>
> You *would* find him congenial if you knew him better.

(5) A wish.

> *Would* that I were there!
>
> *Would* that tomorrow were here!

This use is largely oratorical or poetical. The ordinary form is, "I *wish* that I were there."

Note 1. In sequence with a verb in the past or past perfect tense *would* may represent a *will* used in direct discourse: "He said that he *would* call" (direct discourse, "I *will* call").

Note 2. Would may be used with a subject in the first, second, or third person in all the instances cited above, except (4).

448. "Should" denotes:

(1) Duty or obligation—equivalent to *ought to; should* indicates a weaker degree of obligation than that expressed by *must.*

> I *should* be there at this minute.
>
> You *should* give him the money.
>
> He *should* not work so hard.

(2) Inference.

> He *should* be at home by this time (from the time that has elapsed, I infer that he is probably there).
>
> We *should* arrive before dark, if everything goes well.

(Compare the use of *must* to emphasize an inference of this sort—see Sec. 446 (2)).

(3) Simple futurity—in the first person (see Sec. 456).

> I am sure that I *should* have a good time if I went.
>
> I *should* be glad to talk with him.

(4) For the use of *should* as a subjunctive equivalent in clauses expressing condition, necessity, concession, and purpose, see Sec. 443.

(5) In expressions like "I *should say,*" "I *should think,*" etc., *should*

makes the statement less abrupt, more deferential, than *I say* and *I think*.

    I *should say* that he is lucky. (Compare, "I *say* that he is lucky.")
    I *should think* that she would be angry.

Note 1. In sequence with a verb in the past or past perfect tense *should* may represent a *shall* used in direct discourse: "I said that I *should* be glad to see him" (direct discourse, "I *shall* be glad to see him").

Note 2. Should may be used with a subject in the first, second, or third person in all the cases cited above, except (3) and (5).

DISTINCTION BETWEEN "SHALL" AND "WILL"

449. The distinctions between *shall* and *will* are not so rigidly observed now as they once were, the modern tendency being to use *will* in a number of cases where *shall* was formerly required. Certain differences, however, are still recognized by careful speakers and writers.

450. "Shall." In the **First Person** *shall* denotes simple futurity—the fact that something is going to occur.

    I *shall go* to town on Saturday.

451. In the **Second and Third Persons** *shall* denotes determination or a command on the part of the *speaker*.

    You (he) *shall go* to school (I am determined that you (he) shall go).

Note. In "polite" commands *will* is frequently used.

    You *will* report for duty tomorrow.

452. "Will." In the **First Person** *will* always denotes willingness, determination, or a promise.

    I *will come* when you call.
    We *will go* in spite of this fact.

453. In the **Second and Third Persons** *will* denotes:

(1) Simple futurity.

    You *will find* him at home.
    She *will be* here tomorrow.

(2) Willingness or determination on the part of the *doer* of the action.

    Of course, you (he) *will help* in this work.
    You (he) *will eat* pie for breakfast (that is, persist in eating pie).

Notice the difference between the *doer* here and the *speaker* in Sec. 451.

454. Mistakes most frequently occur in expressing simple futurity. Note the distinction: Simple futurity is expressed by *shall* in the first person, by *will* in the second and third persons.

I *shall* come.
You *will* come.
He *will* come.

455. "Shall" and "Will" in Questions. In questions the form that is anticipated in the answer is used in all persons.

Shall I pay this bill? (You *shall*—command)
Will I have some candy? (I *will*—willingness)
Shall you be there? (I *shall*—futurity)
Will you accept the gift? (I *will*—willingness)
Shall he bring the book? (He *shall*—command)
Will he go with me? (He *will*—willingness)

456. "Should" and "Would." In expressing simple futurity, *should* and *would* are subject to the same rule as that given for *shall* and *will* (see Sec. 454).

I *should* be glad to meet him.
We *should* be surprised to find them there.
You *would* receive a hearty welcome.
He *would* find the book interesting.

For other uses of *should* and *would,* see Secs. 447–8.

Exercise 77

Point out the modal auxiliaries, and explain their meaning.

1. At such times his thoughts would be full of valorous deeds. (Joseph Conrad.) 2. Indeed, as a class, I should say that men of science were happier than other men. (Aldous Huxley.) 3. Of course, I should go tomorrow, but I cannot leave my work. 4. The long-boat would have taken the lot of us; but the skipper said we must save as much property as possible. (Joseph Conrad.) 5. He would often spend the day in the mountains, collecting ferns and mosses. 6. And I would that my tongue could utter the thoughts that arise in me. (Alfred Tennyson.) 7. He would buy the car, in spite of all we could do to dissuade him. 8. There may be a reduction in price later in the month. 9. About his internal life we can only speculate. (H. G. Wells.) 10. But I knew that my visit must be measured by days, almost by hours. (William Beebe.)

11. It seemed to him he cared nothing for the gale. He could affront greater perils. He would do so. (Joseph Conrad.) 12. "You must not—you shall not

behold this," I said shudderingly to Usher. (E. A. Poe.) 13. He might find the book if he would look more carefully. 14. You may go at four o'clock if your work is finished. 15. At the foot of these fairy mountains, the voyager may have descried the light smoke curling up from a village. (Washington Irving.) 16. May your shadow never grow less. 17. This report should be filed with the Department of Labor. 18. There must have been at least forty people at that table. (Arnold Bennett.) 19. Here I would stay for the night, at all events; if the weather cleared, I might be glad to remain for two or three days. (George Gissing.) 20. We should like to read the sequel of this story. 21. He would like to read the sequel of this story.

Exercise 78

Explain the use of *shall* and *will, should* and *would*.

1. He will not make that sacrifice for us. 2. He shall not make that sacrifice for us. 3. I shall try to focus that feeling and make inexpert efforts to find where it leads. (A. S. Eddington.) 4. The French army had said, "They shall not pass." 5. I shall presently find means to smuggle you out of here. (Joseph Conrad.) 6. I will find some kind of work for you tomorrow, without fail. 7. I shall drown; no one will help me. 8. I will drown; no one shall help me. 9. Will he take the proofs to the printer? 10. Shall he take the proofs to the printer?

11. Will they walk, or shall I go for them in the car? 12. Shall I tell them the whole story, or will you do it? 13. Shall we send the package by mail or by express? 14. Will we be held responsible for the accident? 15. Shall I refuse the invitation? 16. If we got rid of the others we should want you to help work the vessel home. (R. L. Stevenson.) 17. Under any other circumstances I would not have held on a moment longer. (Joseph Conrad.) 18. I dare not say what I should like to say about painting. (John Galsworthy.) 19. But I should be untrue to science if I did not insist that its study is an end in itself. (A. S. Eddington.) 20. I should think that you would be too tired to go.

21. My father was always saying the inn would be ruined. (R. L. Stevenson.) 22. I shouldn't think that this result would be possible. 23. He wouldn't believe that it was possible.

Exercise 79

Use the proper form of *shall* and *will, should* and *would*, and give your reason.

1. We _____ be too late for the first act of the play.

2. The guide _____ be at the station to meet you.
3. All right, then, I _____ go, since you insist.
4. We _____ be surprised if the plan is successful.
5. I _____ expect a reply by noon tomorrow.
6. He _____ be glad to mail the letter for you.
7. I _____ be glad to help you.
8. We _____ have to hurry, or we _____ be late.
9. I _____ find the answer to this problem if I have to work all night.
10. I hope that I _____ find them at home.
11. He _____ be on duty at the main entrance, and I _____ be at the side door.
12. I _____ probably hear from him some time today.
13. _____ I call for you this evening?
14. _____ I be too early if I come at 8 o'clock?
15. _____ she bring the flowers, or _____ I send for them?
16. _____ I go now, or _____ I wait?
17. _____ they give their consent freely?
18. _____ I lock the door, or _____ he do it?
19. _____ I have time to send a telegram?
20. I want to know whether I _____ include my traveling expenses.
21. I _____ say that his estimate of the cost is too high.
22. I _____ go if I had the time and money to spend.
23. You _____ be foolish to do that.
24. We _____ be disloyal to the school if we refused.
25. They _____ be disloyal if they refused.
26. I _____ like to believe that he is honest.
27. She _____ like to make the trip by plane.
28. We _____ be glad to get your approval of the plan.
29. Of course, I _____ enjoy seeing all my good friends again.

WEAK AND STRONG VERBS

Irregular Forms of Weak Verbs

457. For a preliminary discussion of strong verbs and weak verbs, see Secs. 169 ff. In that discussion it was stated that weak verbs regularly form their past tense and past participle by adding *-ed, -d,* or *-t* to the present tense.

458. Many weak verbs have irregular forms.

(1) In addition to adding *-ed, -d,* or *-t,* some weak verbs also change the vowel, and in some cases other letters as well.

PRESENT	PAST	PAST PARTICIPLE
tell	told	told
teach	taught	taught
seek	sought	sought

Note. In some instances the change in vowel is merely a shift from a long to a short vowel: as, *creep, crept; leave, left.*

(2) Some weak verbs which end in *-d* or *-t* in the present tense do not add another *-d* or *-t* in the past tense and past participle.

PRESENT	PAST	PAST PARTICIPLE
shed	shed	shed
rid	rid	rid
set	set	set

(a) One group of verbs changes the *d* of the present tense to *t* in the other two forms.

PRESENT	PAST	PAST PARTICIPLE
bend	bent	bent
build	built	built

(b) A second group shows a shift from a long to a short vowel: for example, from a long *e* (it may be spelled *ee* or *ea*) to a short *e*.

PRESENT	PAST	PAST PARTICIPLE
bleed	bled	bled
lead	led	led
meet	met	met

(3) The weak verbs *have* and *make* change the *v* and *k* to *d:* as, *have, had, had; make, made, made.*

MIXED STRONG AND WEAK VERBS

459. Some verbs have both strong and weak forms for either the past tense or the past participle, or for both. In some instances the two forms have different meanings.

PRESENT	PAST	PAST PARTICIPLE
wake	woke, waked	waked
thrive	thrived, throve	thrived, thriven
swell	swelled	swelled, swollen
show	showed	showed, shown
hang	hung, hanged *	hung, hanged *

* The form *hanged* is used only for execution by hanging.

460. Thus the line of demarcation between strong and weak verbs is not always clearly drawn. In fact, there is constantly at work a tendency to bring weak forms into originally strong verbs, and vice versa. This tendency is illustrated by the habit among illiterate speakers of substituting the weak forms *growed* and *throwed* for the correct strong forms *grew* and *threw*. These extreme substitutions probably will never be regarded as correct, but the process is similar to that by which the mixture of forms described above has been produced. Some of the substitutions gradually force themselves into good use and are finally accepted by everyone.

SOME TROUBLESOME VERBS

461. Mistakes in the use of the past tense and past participle are common. Some are so crude that only the illiterate, or grossly careless, speaker would be guilty of making them; others are found in the speech of fairly well educated people. The mistakes are of various sorts, but the majority of them may be traced to one of two causes.

(1) **Confusion of One Tense Form with Another.** This mistake is illustrated in expressions like "I *seen* it" and "I *done* it," in which the past participles *seen* and *done* are misused for the past tenses *saw* and *did*.

(2) **False Analogy.** This means that a form of one verb is made to correspond with that of another verb which is similar in appearance. Thus the incorrect past tense forms *growed* and *throwed* are the result of false analogy with words like *flowed* and *glowed*, which are the correct past tenses for *flow* and *glow*. Likewise, the use of *dove* for *dived*, as in "I *dove* into the water," is due to the influence of verbs like *drive, drove; strive, strove*.

462. List of Verbs. A list of troublesome verbs is given below. It includes not only some of those in which the mistakes discussed above are frequently made, but also others which for various reasons cause difficulty.

PRESENT	PAST	PAST PARTICIPLE
abide	abode	abode
arise	arose	arisen
awake	awoke, awaked	awaked, awoke
bear	bore	borne, born

PRESENT	PAST	PAST PARTICIPLE
beat	beat	beaten
begin	began	begun
beseech	besought, beseeched	besought, beseeched
bid	bade	bidden (to order)
bid	bid	bid (to offer)
bite	bit	bitten
blow	blew	blown
burst	burst	burst (not *bursted*)
cast	cast	cast
creep	crept	crept
deal	dealt	dealt
dive	dived	dived
do	did	done
draw	drew	drawn
drink	drank	drunk
drive	drove	driven
dwell	dwelt, dwelled	dwelt, dwelled
eat	ate	eaten
fall	fell	fallen
fly	flew	flown
forget	forgot	forgot, forgotten
go	went	gone (not *had went*)
grow	grew	grown
hang	hung, hanged	hung, hanged
hide	hid	hidden, hid
know	knew	known
lay	laid	laid
lead	led	led
lie	lay	lain
light	lighted, lit	lighted, lit
loose	loosed	loosed
lose	lost	lost
pay	paid	paid
prove	proved	proved
rend	rent	rent
rid	rid	rid
ride	rode	ridden
ring	rang	rung
run	ran	run
see	saw	seen

PRESENT	PAST	PAST PARTICIPLE
shine	shone	shone
shoe	shod	shod
shrink	shrank	shrunk
sing	sang	sung
sink	sank	sunk
sit	sat	sat
slide	slid	slid, slidden
slink	slunk	slunk
sow	sowed	sowed, sown
speak	spoke	spoken
spin	spun	spun
spit	spit	spit
swell	swelled	swelled, swollen
swim	swam	swum
swing	swung	swung
take	took	taken
tear	tore	torn
throw	threw	thrown
wake	woke, waked	waked
write	wrote	written

Note. For the past tense or past participle of some of these verbs, there is an alternative form which may be used instead of the one given in the table. For the other forms the student may consult the dictionary.

AGREEMENT BETWEEN SUBJECT AND VERB

463. A verb must agree with its subject in person and number. (For a general discussion, see Sec. 106.) In the following sections some special constructions are considered.

464. Compound Subjects. A compound subject connected by *and, both —and, not only—but also,* and similar conjunctions, requires a plural verb.

The soldier and the sailor *were* in uniform.
Chicago, Detroit, and Gary *are* industrial cities.
Both the house and the barn *were* destroyed.
Not only the captain but also his lieutenant *have* been captured.

Note. When the two parts of the subject refer to the same thing or person, a singular verb is used: "His teacher and friend *is* to be with him."

465. A compound subject connected by *or, either—or, neither—nor* takes a singular verb if the separate parts of the subject are singular; a plural verb if the separate parts are plural.

> The foreman or his assistant *is* always in the office.
> Either the miller or his son *was* responsible.
> Neither the employers nor the workmen *were* satisfied.

When the separate parts of the subject are of different **numbers or** persons the verb is usually made to agree with the nearer **part of the** subject.

> Neither the apple nor the *peaches were* ripe.
> Either Frank or *you are* guilty.
> Either you or *Frank is* guilty.

466. A Collective Noun as Subject. A collective noun sometimes takes a singular verb, sometimes a plural verb. The general rule is that a singular verb is used when the group indicated by the collective noun is acting as a unit; a plural verb when the members of the group are acting as individuals.

> The jury *has* agreed on the verdict (acting as a unit).
> The jury *were* divided in their opinions (regarded as individuals).

467. This rule, however, is not strictly observed. Often in a given sentence a singular or a plural verb may be used interchangeably without any serious difference in meaning.

> The army *was* (or *were*) scattered in every direction.
> The herd *was* (or *were*) grazing on the vast range.

In such instances the choice is determined largely by the writer's feeling as to which combination makes the better sound. In case of doubt it is usually safer to choose the singular.

468. "With" Phrase. A *with* phrase does not make a subject plural.

> The general, *with his staff, is* to be present.

469. "Everybody," "Each." The pronouns *everybody, every one, somebody, some one, anybody, any one,* and words modified by *every* or *each,* are always singular, and when used as a subject require a singular verb.

> Everybody in both classes *was* ready.
> Anybody *is* able to do the work.
> Every one of the details *was* perfect.

Every man, woman, and child in the town *was* present.

Each street and alley *is* paved.

470. "Some," "Half," etc. *Some, part, half, quarter,* and similar words take a singular or a plural verb, according to whether the meaning is singular or plural.

Some of the guests *were* late in arriving.

Some of the sugar *was* unfit for use.

Part of the soldiers *have* been discharged.

Part of the building *has* been wrecked.

Half of the questions *were* unanswered.

Half of the city *was* in ruins.

471. "None." *None* takes a singular or a plural verb, according to whether the meaning is singular or plural.

None of the sugar *was* wasted.

None of the men *were* punished.

Some grammarians hold that *none* is always singular, since it is a contraction of *no one,* and that a singular verb should always be used with it. This practice is permissible, but the resulting combination is sometimes awkward. The rule as given above represents the better usage.

472. "Number." *Number* takes a singular verb when it is preceded by the article *the;* a plural verb when preceded by *a.*

The number of members *was* increased to fifty.

A number of new members *were* elected.

473. "It." *It* always takes a singular verb, even when the verb is a linking verb followed by a plural noun.

It *is* a fact.

It *is* the citizens who are responsible.

474. "There." The expletive *there* (see Secs. 286–7) is followed by a singular or a plural verb, according to whether the real subject, which comes after the verb, is singular or plural.

There *is* a good *reason* for the change.

There *are* several good *reasons* for the change.

475. Plural Form, Singular Meaning. When the subject is plural in form but singular in meaning, the usage varies.

(1) With expressions indicating distance, amount, and the like, either a singular or a plural verb is generally permissible.

Ten pounds of sugar *is* (*are*) allowed to each customer.

A thousand dollars *has* (*have*) been spent in improvements.

Ten miles of concrete *was* (*were*) laid.

Four yards of material *is* (*are*) needed.

Fifty cents *is* the price of the book (here the verb must be singular).

(2) With the names of books, plays, etc., a singular verb is used.

"The Principles of Geology" *is* used as a text.

"Antony and Cleopatra" *was* the first play presented.

(3) With plural nouns used as words, not as names of objects, a singular verb is required.

Horses is a common noun.

(4) With certain nouns which have only a plural form, the usage is as follows (the list is not complete).

(a) A singular verb is used with:

molasses, news, physics, economics, mathematics, metaphysics.

(b) A plural verb is used with:

riches, proceeds, tongs, pincers, scissors, trousers, goods, athletics, nuptials, obsequies.

Note. With *athletics*, some writers use a singular verb, but the plural is preferable.

(c) Either a singular or a plural verb is used, according to the meaning, with *means, series, species,* and *statistics.*

this means *is, these* means *are; this* series *is, these* series *are; this* species *is, these* species *are; statistics is* a science, *these statistics are* correct.

Exercise 80

Supply the correct form of the verb to agree with the subject.

1. The city, with its suburbs, _____ a population of over two million (have, has).
2. The house and the furniture _____ to be sold by the heirs (is, are).
3. Every home, office, and shop _____ visited (was, were).
4. Neither Mary nor Alice _____ where you have been (know, knows).
5. The class in second-year Latin _____ reading Caesar (is, are).
6. Each of the candidates _____ confident of winning (feel, feels).
7. There _____ a number of exceptions to the rule (is, are).
8. In the last analysis there _____ only two questions involved (is, are).
9. None of the existing laws _____ this particular case (fit, fits).
10. We found that none of the property _____ injured (was, were).
11. The company _____ agreed to pay half of the damages (has, have).
12. Mathematics _____ required of all freshmen (is, are).

13. Only a third of the members of the committee ———— present (was, were).
14. The number of employees ———— increased (has, have).
15. A number of employees ———— been discharged (has, have).
16. You will find that either a dictionary or a book of synonyms ———— essential (is, are).
17. Everyone in the room ———— startled by this statement (was, were).
18. The principal and accrued interest on each bond ———— payable on August 15 (is, are).
19. Ten dollars ———— too much to pay for a ticket (is, are).
20. *We* ———— sometimes used editorially to mean *I* (is, are).
21. The chief-of-police, with two of his lieutenants, ———— going to St. Louis to bring back the prisoner (is, are).
22. There ———— a dresser and two chairs in each room (is, are).

Chapter XVI   ADVERBS

For preceding discussions of adverbs and adverbial phrases and clauses, see Chapter V, and Secs. 198 (3), 229 ff.

476. Any word or group of words used to modify a verb, adjective, or another adverb is an adverb.

The principal constructions that may be employed as adverbs are:

(1) Regular Adverbs: "He walked *rapidly*."

(2) Prepositions without Objects (see Sec. 183): "Come *up*." "They had been here *before*."

(3) Nouns denoting Time, Distance, Weight, etc. (see Sec. 28): "The sugar weighed *a pound*."

(4) Participial Phrases, in a Dual Relation (see Sec. 200): "*Hearing the cry*, he ran to the door."

(5) Infinitives and Infinitive Phrases (see Secs. 154, 198 (3)): "He came *to play*." "The visitors went *to see the house*."

(6) Prepositional Phrases (see Sec. 198 (3)): "The doors were closed *at noon*."

(7) Clauses (see Secs. 229 ff.): "He ate *because he was hungry*."

(8) Elliptical Clauses (see Sec. 292): "*While here*, he visited his uncle" (*while he was here*).

477. Nouns Ending in -s. In colloquial English a few nouns ending in -s and having, therefore, the appearance of plural nouns, are used as adverbs.

> He sleeps *nights*.
> They work *Sundays*.

Historically, these are not plural nouns. They are survivals of an Old English genitive case ending in *-es*, which, in addition to other functions, was once used in an adverbial sense to indicate time. In a later period of the language, the *e* was dropped from the ending, which became simply *-s;* and that process gave us the present forms. The same *s* appears in words like *always, nowadays* (from the old genitive case of the nouns *way* and *day*), which are now regarded as true adverbs.

Note. Our modern possessive case ending, *-'s,* is also a contraction of the former genitive case ending, *-es.* In this case, the apostrophe is used to show the omission of the *e.*

478. Pronouns with Adjectives. In sentences like the following, the expressions *his best* and *our hardest* are, in effect, adverbs of degree or manner, and may be parsed as such, each group as a whole being considered as the adverb.

He tried *his best* to please them.

We fought *our hardest.*

These expressions seem to be elliptical constructions resulting from the omission of cognate objects (see Sec. 300): "We fought our hardest *fight,"* in which *our* and *hardest* are adjectives modifying the cognate object.

For the use of *but* as an adverb, equivalent to *only,* in sentences like "They received *but* few presents," see Sec. 539 (2).

For constructions like "the more, the merrier," in which *the* is used as an adverb, see Sec. 379.

USES

For the ordinary uses of adverbs, see Sec. 173.

479. Modifying a Phrase or Clause. An adverb may modify an adverbial or adjective phrase or clause.

(1) Adverbial phrases and clauses:

We arrived *almost* at the appointed time.

He came to Boston *long* before the war.

He sat *exactly* under the window.

They left *soon* after the contract was signed.

I refused *only* because he was impudent.

(2) Adjective phrases and clauses:

A man *almost* in rags met us at the door.

He lives in the house *right* across the river.

We especially enjoyed the hour *just* before the sun went down.

480. Some grammarians regard these adverbs as modifiers of the connective, rather than as modifiers of the whole phrase or clause.

He sat *exactly under* the window.

They left *soon after* the contract was signed.

481. Independent Adverbs. The so-called Independent Adverbs modify the thought of an entire sentence, rather than any single verb, adjective, or adverb.

These adverbs usually stand at or near the beginning of the sentence, and in addition to their adverbial function, they have something of the nature of connectives, in that they help to make a smooth transition between the thought of the preceding sentence and that of the new one.

Happily, we were prepared for the emergency.
Obviously, this is a serious situation.
Unfortunately, he has lost his deed for the property.

482. To this class also belong *yes* and *no* when used as in the following sentences.

Yes, I will go.
No, you are mistaken.

Note. The difference between the independent adverb and the regular adverb may be seen by comparing the following sentences.

Happily, we were prepared for the emergency (independent).
Then they were *happily* married (regular).

483. An independent adverb may, through ellipsis, stand as a complete sentence. This construction is especially common in answer to questions.

Can you come? *Yes.* (*Yes,* I can come.)
Do you believe this? *Certainly.* (*Certainly,* I believe it.)

484. "Not." A peculiar use of the adverb *not* occurs in certain kinds of questions.

This is true, is it *not?* (*isn't* it?)
He has gone, has he *not?* (*hasn't* he?)
Will you *not* come in? (*won't* you?)

In these sentences *not* has no negative meaning; in fact, it anticipates an affirmative answer, an approval of the statement which precedes it. When the *not* is omitted, the attitude of the speaker is neutral: the answer may be either affirmative or negative: "This is true, is it?"

485. Sometimes the *not* is employed to express surprise that some expected or hoped-for occurrence has not come to pass: "*Hasn't* he gone yet?" Here the actual answer that is expected is "No," but the affirmative element is nevertheless present, for the implication is that the answer *ought to be* "Yes."

486. "Here." A curious use of *here* is seen in the following sentence.

Our life *here* is pleasant.

Here is a regular adverb, but it modifies the noun *life*. In this construction, *here* may be regarded as the remains of an adjective clause, *which we live here,* in which *here* was a pure adverb, modifying the verb *live*. Through ellipsis the rest of the clause was dropped, and only the adverb remained as the modifier of *life*.

There may be used in the same way: "Our life *there* was pleasant."

487. The Expletive "There." The use of *there* as a regular adverb of place should be carefully distinguished from its use as an expletive (see Secs. 286–7).

There is a real man (adverb).

There is a man in the room (expletive).

In the first sentence *there* is an adverb of place, meaning "in that place." In the second, it is an expletive standing for the subject.

488. Short Adverbs. In certain expressions, especially in brief commands and exhortations, a short form of the adverb may be used instead of the regular one ending in -*ly*.

These adverbs are identical in form with the corresponding adjectives (see Sec. 175).

Drive *slow* (instead of *slowly*).

Speak *louder* (instead of *more loudly*).

This construction is used because it gives emphasis to the command. Notice that in other sentences, where emphasis is not needed, the regular adverb is employed: "They drove *slowly* over the bridge."

These short forms are sometimes condemned on the ground that they are adjectives employed where adverbs are required. Historically, however, they are not adjectives, but are true adverbs. In Anglo-Saxon, a number of adverbs had the same form as the corresponding adjectives, except that the suffix -*e* was added. This ending was later dropped, with the result that the adverb and the adjective were identical in form. From these words our short adverbs have descended.

489. "Very" and "Very Much." *Very*, without *much*, is used regularly with ordinary adjectives and with present participles: as, *very sick, very* *cold, very tight, very dark; very exciting, very interesting, very annoying.*

She is *very sick.*

490. *Very much,* not *very* alone, is used regularly with past participles: as, *very much disappointed, very much excited, very much interested.*

I was *very much interested* in his reply (not *very interested*).

With a few past participles, however, which are so frequently employed as regular adjectives that their participial origin is forgotten, the *much* is regularly omitted: as, *very tired, very drunk.*

They were *very tired* when they reached home.

491. For the use of a predicate adjective, instead of an adverb, in sentences like "The flower smelled *sweet*" and "The prisoner looked *sullen,*" see Sec. 357.

For the use of an adverb as the object of a preposition, as in "I have not been there since *then,*" see Sec. 532 (3).

Exercise 81

Point out the special adverbial forms and uses described in Secs. 477 ff.

1. He could now walk almost without pain. (D. H. Lawrence.) 2. I was interested in it long before I was suspected of being a politician. (Woodrow Wilson.) 3. You saw the article in the *Tribune,* didn't you? 4. He left the house with his geometry conspicuously under his arm. (Willa Cather.) 5. The world will never be the better for it. (Nathaniel Hawthorne.) 6. There is the man who was formerly the alderman from the fourth ward. 7. There is no need for secrecy any longer. (E. E. Hale.) 8. That month we worked Sundays and holidays, and tried our best to finish our assignments. 9. The more he disliked him, the kinder he would be to him. (W. D. Howells.) 10. Come quick, and see the moon rise.

11. Besides, there was something engaging in his countrified simplicity. (Mark Twain.) 12. Her visit here was hurried and unsatisfactory. 13. But he woke even before the bugle sounded. (D. H. Lawrence.) 14. Naturally, he was not expecting a reply today. 15. He was surely expecting a reply today, wasn't he? 16. They are first seen, just above the horizon, soon after crossing the southern tropic. (R. H. Dana.) 17. We did the work exactly as you told us to do it. 18. No; but I don't know everybody yet. I haven't lived here quite two weeks. (Mark Twain.) 19. I gazed upon him with a feeling half of pity, half of awe. (E. A. Poe.)

CLASSIFICATION OF ADVERBIAL ELEMENTS

492. The classification of adverbial elements is difficult for two reasons. (1) They cover a wide and varied range of meanings. The meaning of an adverbial element may vary according to the context—the nature of the surrounding circumstances and especially the nature of the verb or adjective which it modifies; and since the context is capable of almost infinite variation, the shades of meaning expressed by adverbial elements are correspondingly numerous. (2) They may express a mixed adverbial relation, or may even have the dual nature of an adjective and an adverb.

493. Mixed Adverbial Relations. Adverbial elements sometimes have a mixed or overlapping meaning. In some of these instances there is only a suggestion of the secondary meaning; in others it is fairly prominent. A few typical examples are:

It was foolish to attempt this *when so many policemen were present* (time and reason).

The hour for closing having arrived, the employees left the office (time and reason).

It is colder now *than it was this morning* (degree and comparison).

It was so cold *that the water froze in the tank* (degree and result).

He strode through the house, *leaving a muddy footprint at each step* (accompanying circumstances and result).

The troops crept up the hill, *firing and then stopping to reload their muskets* (accompanying circumstances and manner).

He spoke *so that everyone could hear* (manner and result).

494. Dual Adverbial and Adjectival Relations. Frequently a construction has the dual nature of an adverb and an adjective.

Realizing the danger, the driver stopped. (The participle *realizing,* as an adjective, modifies *driver;* the whole phrase, as an adverb, modifies *stopped*—it tells why he stopped.) (See Sec. 200.)

Weak from his effort, John fell to the ground. (As an adjective, *weak* modifies *John;* as an adverb it tells why he fell.)

The beam was planed *square.* (*Square* is a predicate adjective modifying *beam,* but it is also similar in meaning to an adverbial clause of result: "until it was *square.*")

These overlapping relationships will be found frequently in the major classes of adverbial elements that are to be discussed.

ADVERBIAL ELEMENTS INDICATING TIME

For a previous discussion, see Sec. 231.

495. Typical forms of adverbial elements indicating time are shown in the following sentences.

They will come *today* (single adverb).
He is going *now.*
He will be here *Sunday.*
They work *at night* (phrase).
He has been here *since Thursday.*
The address being finished, the audience left the room (nominative absolute).
Breakfast over, we left the house (elliptical—*breakfast being over*).
They will pay you *as soon as they return* (clause).
While we were at dinner, the door bell rang.
Now that you have finished, you may help me.
Once you get the principle, the rest is easy.
While here, he called upon his former friends (elliptical—*while he was here*).
When last seen, he was wearing a borrowed overcoat.

Note. Some of these sentences carry a suggestion of *reason* or of *condition,* in addition to *time.*

496. The chief conjunctions used to introduce clauses of time are *when, while, since, before, after, until, as soon as, as long as, now that, once,* etc.

497. Modifications of the Time Relation. (1) Most adverbial elements of time answer the question *when?* and indicate the definite time when the action of the main verb takes place. Some of them, however, answer the question *how long?* and show the duration or extent of the action.

They watched *until the sun rose.*
He had been a gambler *from childhood.*

(2) In the following sentence the phrase shows the duration of the effect or result of the action (*for how long?*).

The flag was hauled down *for the night.*

Note. A time element used as an adverb is not to be confused with one used as an adjective to modify a noun which in itself indicates time (see Sec. 228).

They chose an hour *when the streets were deserted* (adjective clause modifying the noun *hour*).

ADVERBIAL ELEMENTS INDICATING PLACE

See also Sec. 232.

498. The following sentences show various kinds of adverbial elements indicating place.

> They live *here* (single adverb).
> He has gone *home*.
> He works *in the foundry* (prepositional phrase).
> They live *by the river*.
> He has a free hand *in the running of the factory*.
> We met them *going to town* (participial phrase).
> They discovered the fugitive *hiding in a barn*.
> They found the book *where they left it* (clause).
> I will go *wherever you wish*.

499. Adverbs of place may indicate *whence* (place from which) as well as *where*.

> They came *from the country*.

Note. Adverbial elements of place should be carefully distinguished from adjective elements modifying nouns which in themselves indicate place.

> This is the spot *where the house formerly stood* (adjective clause).

ADVERBIAL ELEMENTS INDICATING MANNER

See also Sec. 233.

500. Manner may be indicated as follows.

> He walked *rapidly* (single adverb).
> She lived *alone* in the big house.
> The manager spoke *with decision* (phrase).
> He obtained money *by writing books*.
> They counted the applicants, *left to right* (elliptical phrase—*from left to right*).
> The boy came *running* (participle in a dual relation—see Sec. 494).
> She acts *as if she were tired* (clause).
> He ate *as though he were hungry*.
> He did *as he was directed*.
> John served five years *as a soldier* (elliptical clause—*as a soldier would serve*).

Some participles and prepositional phrases showing "accompanying circumstances" have something of the value of adverbs of manner (see Sec. 527).

ADVERBIAL ELEMENTS INDICATING DEGREE

501. Adverbial elements expressing degree cover a wide range of meanings, but they are all distinguished by the fact that they tell *how much, how little, how far,* or some other *how* relation (excluding *manner*). They include various phrases and clauses which in addition to indicating degree also express comparison or result (see Secs. 234, 235). The distinction between degree, comparison, and result is, in many cases, so difficult to define that in the preliminary discussion in Part I, it seemed advisable to put them all into one general group. In the present classification they are treated separately, though in some of the examples given there may be an overlapping in meaning.

502. Degree may be indicated as follows.

He ran a *mile* (single adverb).
The fish weighed a *pound.*
She was *very* tired.
They are *almost* ready.
The boat was *entirely* submerged.
We have enough cloth *for a coat* (prepositional phrase).
His wardrobe was limited *to one suit and an old overcoat.*
He is too old *for this position.*
The picture is large enough *to fill the space* (infinitive phrase).
He is too small *to do this work.*
We have enough cloth *to make a coat.*
This burden is more *than I can bear* (clause).
He works as fast *as he can.*
He will come as soon *as possible* (elliptical—*as soon as it is possible for him to come*).

503. Clauses and phrases of degree are frequently used after *so, so much, enough, too,* or some similar expression.

ADVERBIAL ELEMENTS INDICATING COMPARISON

504. An adverbial element may indicate comparison between two actions, conditions, etc.

Life had been hard with him, *as it is apt to be with those who live on the frontier* (clause).
They plowed with oxen, *just as their forefathers had done.*
There are fewer here *than we expected.*

He was not as young *as I thought.*
She writes better *than she talks.*
John is larger *than his brother* (elliptical clause).
You are worse *than a thief.*
He was the least concerned *of all those present* (phrase).

505. Certain expressions indicating comparison show extreme ellipsis.
The sooner, the better.
The more, the merrier.

ADVERBIAL ELEMENTS INDICATING RESULT

506. An adverbial element may indicate the result of an action.
The railroads have been completely rebuilt, *so that it is now possible to travel in safety* (clause).
The wraps were strewn in confusion about the room, *the result being that there was considerable delay when the guests were ready to leave* (phrase—with a clause adjunct).
The ship was dashed upon the rocks, *with the result that the cargo was lost.*

507. This relation is common in participial phrases.
He fell over the cliff, *breaking his arm and otherwise injuring himself.*
The horse stopped suddenly, *throwing his rider to the ground.*
These constructions are sometimes difficult to distinguish from participles indicating accompanying circumstances (see Sec. 527).

508. An adverbial element frequently expresses both result and degree.
The audience was so noisy *that the speaker could not be heard.*
He arrived early enough *to catch the train.*
They were so kind *as to reserve a section for us.*

509. A subordinate clause of result introduced by *so that* must not be confused with a co-ordinate clause of consequence (see Sec. 219), or with a subordinate clause of purpose introduced by the same conjunction (see Sec. 515).

ADVERBIAL ELEMENTS INDICATING REASON

See also Sec. 236.

510. Reason or cause may be indicated as follows.
He was punished *for breaking the window* (prepositional phrase).
The senator died *of apoplexy.*

Because of his lameness, he was unable to march.
Seeing the danger, the driver leaped from the car (participial phrase).
The horse, *frightened by the explosion,* ran away.
The weather being warm, all the windows were opened (nominative absolute).
He was discharged *because he was dishonest* (clause).
As we were already late, we dared not wait any longer.
Since there is no alternative, we must accept his offer.

511. A clause of reason introduced by *that* may modify an adjective.

I am glad *that you escaped unharmed.*

512. The chief conjunctions used with clauses of reason are *because, as, since, for, for the reason that, on the ground that, in that, seeing that, considering that.*

513. Some adverbial clauses give the reason, not for the fact itself, as in the preceding examples, but for our knowledge of the fact: that is, they tell our reason for thinking that the statement is true.

Our neighbors have returned, *for I can hear them talking.*
It is a cold day, *for the windows are frosted.*

In the first sentence, for example, the fact that I can hear our neighbors talking is not the reason why they returned; it is the reason for my thinking that they have returned.

514. The thought expressed by a complex sentence containing a subordinate clause of reason, may also be expressed by a compound sentence containing a co-ordinate clause of consequence (see Sec. 219). Compare the following sentences:

As it was a long way to the next settlement, we camped for the night (subordinate clause of reason).
It was a long way to the next settlement; *therefore we camped for the night* (co-ordinate clause of consequence).

ADVERBIAL ELEMENTS INDICATING PURPOSE

See also Sec. 237.

515. Purpose may be indicated as follows.

They have come *for the money* (prepositional phrase).
We went West *with the idea of making a fortune.*
She ransacked her memory *for incidents of their early years.*
They came *to get their wraps* (infinitive phrase).

They drove fast *in order to catch the train.*
They took care *to avoid being seen by the officers.*
He worked late *so that he could finish the book that night* (clause).
They bought the house *in order that they might have a comfortable home.*
They took care *that the secret should not become known.*
Men sow *that they may reap.*
Take heed *lest you fall* (*lest* means *that—not*).

ADVERBIAL ELEMENTS INDICATING CONDITION

See also Sec. 238.

516. Condition may be indicated as follows.

Without a fire, you can do nothing (prepositional phrase, equivalent to *if you do not have a fire*).
With a little more capital, they would be sure to succeed.
To hear him talk, you would think that he was a man of importance (infinitive phrase, equivalent to *if you were to judge from his talk*).
The result, *considered from your point of view,* is satisfactory (participial phrase—equivalent to *if it is considered*).
They will finish the work tomorrow, *weather permitting* (nominative absolute, equivalent to *if the weather permits*).
If that is true, we have nothing more to say (clause).
Whether you are young or old, you will enjoy this music (*if you are young or if you are old*).
I will go, *provided he pays my expenses* (*if he pays*).
He cannot succeed *unless he works harder* (*if he does not work harder*).
If possible, he will go today (elliptical clause—*if it is possible*).
He will be here, *rain or shine* (*if it rain or if it shine*—see Sec. 136 (1), note *1*).

517. The chief introductory words are *if, unless* (means *if—not*), *whether—or, supposing that, provided, provided that, on condition that, in case that.*

518. The clause may be without a conjunction or other formal introductory word, in which case the order of the words is inverted.

Had he come, he would have seen me (*if he had come*).
Should the plan be successful, he will adopt it.

519. Sometimes the conditional clause is used alone as an exclamation, the main clause being omitted.

If he would only come! (*If he would only come,* I should be satisfied.)

520. A conditional element may give the condition under which a statement is made, rather than the condition under which an action is performed.

> The game, *as I remember it,* was played in Jackson Park.
> I was beginning to feel "groggy," *as it were.*

Thus the first sentence means "The game, *if I remember it correctly,* was played in Jackson Park." The second sentence is about equivalent to "I was beginning to feel 'groggy,' *if I may be permitted to use that expression.*"

Note. These constructions are often classified as parenthetical expressions.

521. Condition may be expressed by means of a co-ordinate clause having its verb in the imperative mood (this construction is to be classed as a main clause, not as an adverbial clause).

> *Ask him,* and he will tell you (*if you ask him*).
> *Bring me the package,* and I will pay you.

Adverbial Elements Indicating Concession

See also Sec. 239.

522. Concession may be indicated as follows.

> *With all his faults* I love him still (phrase—equivalent to *although he has many faults*).
> I would not exchange places with him *for all his money.*
> *Notwithstanding the obvious unfairness of the offer,* we were forced to accept it.
> *In spite of his boasted strength,* he was unable to move the weight.
> *Although he had the money,* he would not spend it (clause).
> *Though he was the king's messenger,* he was harshly treated.
> *Even if he is wealthy,* he is not happy.
> This rod, *though small,* is very strong (elliptical clause—*though it is small*).

523. Sometimes the order of words in the clause is inverted, in which case the conjunction may be within the clause or may be lacking.

> *Strange though it may seem,* the meeting was a success.
> *Strong as he was,* he could not lift the stone.
> *Try as he would,* he could not reach the goal.
> *Be that as it may,* I cannot go with you.

524. Clauses of concession may be introduced by the compound relative pronouns, or various other words ending in *-ever.*

Whatever we do, our opponent will be elected.
However much we give, it will not be sufficient.
Wherever he may try to hide, his enemies will find him.
Whichever road he takes, the journey will be difficult.

525. Sometimes, through ellipsis, only the introductory word remains.

Any reply *whatever* will be welcome (*whatever it may be*).
He objects to any noise *whatsoever* (*whatsoever it may be*).

526. The concessive relation is sometimes very similar to that expressed by co-ordinate clauses showing contrast (those introduced by *but, however,* etc. See Sec. 217). Compare, for instance:

Although he was large, he was not strong (concession—subordinate).
He was large, *but* he was not strong (contrast—co-ordinate).

ADVERBIAL ELEMENTS INDICATING ACCOMPANYING CIRCUMSTANCES

527. An adverbial element may indicate accompanying circumstances: that is, certain actions or circumstances that occur at the same time as the action represented by the verb.

He rambled on foot through France, *playing a flute for a supper and a bed.*
Then he went to Leyden, still *pretending to study medicine.*
His father died, *leaving a mere pittance.*
He remained there five years, *living the life of a country squire.*
His relatives, *with much satisfaction,* saw him leave the village.

528. A nominative absolute phrase may indicate accompanying circumstances.

The boat lay at anchor, *its flag flapping idly in the breeze.*

Note. Many of these constructions also have something of the nature of adjectives.

ADVERBIAL COMPLEMENTS OF ADJECTIVES

529. Most of the preceding classes of adverbial elements are used primarily to modify verbs, the most important exception being adverbs of degree, which regularly may qualify not only verbs but also adjectives and adverbs.

There are also a large number of adverbial phrases and clauses which modify adjectives. A few of these approximate in meaning some of the classes described above, but in general they show such a wide and varied range of relationships that it is almost impossible to bring them under any significant scheme of classification. Accordingly they are brought together into one general class and called simply "Adverbial Complements of Adjectives." A number of typical examples are given below.

(1) Prepositional Phrases.

It is very simple *in construction.*
He was hospitable *to strangers.*
The style is worthy *of the subject matter.*
This place is convenient *to transportation.*
The children are dependent *on charity.*
She was suspicious *by nature.*
His thoughts were free *from jealousy.*
James was angry *at his companions.*
The officer, eager *for revenge,* began an investigation.
The colonel, confident *of success,* ordered a general attack.
They found the guide dead *from exposure.*

(2) Infinitives or Infinitive Phrases.

This print is easy *to read.*
They were glad *to get the letter.*
He was quick *to resent the insult.*
We found the company about ready *to start.*
A man able *to do hard work* is needed at once.

(3) Clauses (see Sec. 240).

I am sure *that he is honest.*
We feel confident *that the plan will be successful.*
The clerk, jubilant *because he had been promoted,* started to work with a will.

Exercise 82

Point out the words, phrases, and clauses used adverbially, and name the kinds of adverbial relationship that they express. If any are elliptical, expand them to their full form.

1. They were all very joyful because, barring accidents, they would be home for Christmas. (William McFee.) 2. Once inside, the sightseer stands in the heart of utter desolation. (Rudyard Kipling.) 3. He stared at the house, thinking that there he was at last, after all these years. (John Masefield.) 4. Be it ever so humble, there's no place like home. 5. A Democrat in politics, Bancroft displayed a natural pride in the growth of American democracy. (Charles A. Beard.) 6. The congregation returned to the hotel, to put down their impressions in note books and diaries. (Rudyard Kipling.) 7. With

true Indian craft he always befriended the whites, well knowing that he might thus reap great advantages for himself. (Francis Parkman.) 8. Tired and discouraged, they were ready to give up the search. 9. The journey next day, short though it was, and the visit to his lawyer's, tired him. (John Galsworthy.) 10. It was such a cold, still night that the sliding windows of the car were almost shut. (Frank Swinnerton.)

11. No one will be vexed or uneasy, linger I ever so late. (George Gissing.) 12. The third attempt having failed, we decided to drop the plan for the present. 13. Had he died young, literature would have lost many glories. (Max Beerbohm.) 14. Gillespie came hurrying along to join them. (H. M. Tomlinson.) 15. To secure the quickest service, you should write to the main office. 16. Do what I can, I cannot keep my eye off the clock. (R. W. Emerson.) 17. Does he fail in gaining their favor, they will set his authority at naught. (Francis Parkman.) 18. I felt as though I were moving in the midst of a novel. (Rudyard Kipling.) 19. Popular magazines sprang up in the leading cities, spreading interest in literature and the arts. (Charles A. Beard.) 20. They were heavily overcoated, despite the heat. (Stephen Crane.)

21. The silence, for a time, was as perfect as the breathlessness. (William Beebe.) 22. Some feelings made less trouble, if unexamined. (H. M. Tomlinson.) 23. Tired as he was, he could not refuse the invitation. 24. His detractors, though outvoted, have not been silenced. (Thomas Macaulay.) 25. This done, she closed the door and locked it. 26. He leaned on the lee rail, amidships, watching a distant light. (H. M. Tomlinson.) 27. In the light of a calm and golden sunset it becomes lovely beyond expression. (Nathaniel Hawthorne.) 28. This time we did not heave to, as on the night before, but endeavored to beat to windward. (R. H. Dana.) 29. His dress was only a little less punctilious than the surgeon's uniform. (H. M. Tomlinson.) 30. In the carriage sat a school-boy, a book open upon his knee. (George Gissing.)

31. In a few minutes a heavier sea was raised than I had ever seen. (R. H. Dana.) 32. One must be a chemist to understand this reaction. 33. He is almost sure to be nominated in the April primaries. 34. A sailor and an artist, he had little sense of money. (John Galsworthy.) 35. Wolfe's malady had abated, and he was able to command in person. (Francis Parkman.) 36. Could numbers give assurance of success, their triumph would have been secure. (Francis Parkman.) 37. Sick or well, he will have to go.

Chapter XVII

For a preliminary discussion of prepositions, see Chapter VI.

530. Other Parts of Speech Used as Prepositions. (1) *Like* is used as a preposition in sentences such as:

> He looks *like* his father.
> In many respects she is *like* her sister.

In the first sentence, *like* is actually an adverb; in the second, it is an adjective; but in each instance it takes an object just as if it were a regular preposition. It may be considered as an elliptical construction with the preposition *unto* omitted: "He looks *like* (*unto*) his father."

Note. Like should not be employed as a conjunction to introduce a clause: "They walked *like* they were tired" (incorrect). Here the proper connective is *as if* or *as though:* "They walked *as if* (*as though*) they were tired" (correct). When used as a connective, *like* must be followed by an object, not by a subject and a verb.

(2) For a discussion of the following constructions used as prepositions, see the sections indicated.

> a. *But* in the sense of *except,* Sec. 539 (1).
> b. *Other than* in the sense of *except,* Sec. 547.

531. Constructions Used as Objects of Prepositions. The object of a preposition is regularly a noun or pronoun in the objective case.

> He works in the *factory.*
> They have had a letter from *him.*

532. Other constructions, when used as the object, are noun-equivalents. (1) A Noun or Pronoun in the Possessive Case.

> Ask for these goods at your *dealer's.*
> I prefer your book to *his.*

These constructions are the result of ellipsis: the real object is an omitted noun which is easily understood from the context: "at your dealer's *store,*" "to his *book*" (see Sec. 293 (3)). The form "at your dealer" should not be used. It is an incorrect and unidiomatic construction arising from an attempt to reduce the object of the preposition to the regular objective case.

(2) An Adjective.
This book is suitable for *young* and *old*.

This is another elliptical construction meaning "for young and old *people*."

(3) An Adverb.
They will come at *once*.
Where do we go from *here?*

(4) A Gerund or Gerundive Phrase.
They are fond of *singing*.
He objected to *buying the car.*

(5) An Infinitive or Infinitive Phrase.
She could do nothing but *wait.*
They had no choice except *to obey the order.*
We intended for *you to come early* (see Sec. 207).

(6) A Prepositional Phrase.
The water came to *within an inch of the top.*
He took the package from *under the table.*

(7) A Clause.
He is interested in *whatever he sees.*
I drew my own conclusions from *what you said.*
We cannot decide on *who should go.*

533. Special Uses of Prepositions. A preposition without an object may be used as a modifier after a noun.
He had come the day *before.*
They went the week *after.*
They live on the floor *above.*
The apartment *below* is for rent.
The life *beyond* is a veiled mystery.
They cautiously felt their way *around.*

These are elliptical constructions equivalent to "the day *before the one named,*" "the apartment *below this one.*"

534. A preposition without an object is commonly used as an adverb modifying a verb: "He walked *behind*" (see Sec. 183).

535. For a special type of apposition formed with some nouns by means of the preposition *of,* see Sec. 307.

536. A Preposition at the End of a Sentence. The old rule, that a preposition should never be placed at the end of a sentence, is now disregarded by many writers. It is a good rule for the novice to bear in mind, but the writer who has developed a feeling for sentence structure may safely put a preposition in this position when his judgment tells him that he will get a better effect.

As a matter of fact, this construc. n cannot be avoided in certain sentences, notably in short questions, without sacrificing naturalness and effectiveness. Thus, "What did you ask *for?*" is stronger than *"For what did you ask?"* Other examples are:

Where did you come *from?*
Which one are you interested *in?*
Which boy did he give it *to?*
What does it amount *to?*

Chapter XVIII   CONJUNCTIONS

For a preliminary discussion of Conjunctions, see Chapter VII. See also Secs. 220 ff.; 242 ff.

537. Conjunctions are divided into two general classes.

(1) **Co-ordinate Conjunctions,** which connect words, phrases, and clauses of equal rank: as, *and, likewise, in like manner, but, nevertheless, yet, however, on the contrary, or, nor, therefore, hence, accordingly,* etc.

(2) **Subordinate Conjunctions,** which are used to introduce subordinate clauses and to connect them with the words which they modify: as, *if, unless, although, though, that, as, since, for, so, so that, in order that, as if, as though,* etc.

538. Pure subordinate conjunctions, such as those enumerated above, are merely connecting words, and perform no other function in the sentence (see Sec. 243). Sometimes, however, subordinate clauses are introduced, not by pure conjunctions, but by

(1) **Conjunctive Adverbs,** which not only introduce the clause, but also have an adverbial function in the clause (see Sec. 244): as, *when, where, why, while, how.*

(2) **Relative and Interrogative Pronouns,** which serve as introductory words and also perform one of the functions of a noun in a clause (see Sec. 245): as, *which, who, that, what.*

539. "But." *But* is ordinarily a co-ordinate conjunction, but it may also be used in the following ways.

(1) As a Preposition, equivalent to *except.*
   All *but* John have gone (*except* John).
   They had no alternative *but* to go.
   He will do nothing *but* talk (see Sec. 434 (3)).

(2) As an Adverb, equivalent to *only.*
   We have *but* a few copies left.
   You have *but* to ask for it.
   They can *but* try.

The last sentence is not to be confused with "They *cannot but* try," in which *but* is a preposition (see (1) above). This expression seems to be due to ellipsis of "They cannot do anything *but* (*except*) try."

The expression *cannot help but* is an incorrect form resulting from a confusing of two correct forms: "They *cannot but* try," and "They *cannot help* trying."

(3) As a Relative Pronoun, equivalent to *that—not, who—not*.

There is no one *but* pities him (*who* does *not* pity him).

(4) As a Subordinate Conjunction, equivalent to *but that* or *that—not*.

There is no doubt *but* they are rich (*but that* they are rich).

I didn't know *but* you might be tired.

It never rains *but* it pours (*that* it does *not* pour).

He never goes to the theater *but* he regrets it.

540. "But that." *But that* is used as a subordinate conjunction.

I don't know *but that* I shall go.

I have no doubt *but that* he will come.

In these sentences, *but* emphasizes the idea in the subordinate clause—it implies greater certainty that what is said there is true or will occur. Compare the following sentences without *but*.

I don't know *that* I shall go.

I have no doubt *that* he will come.

Note. But what should not be used for *but that*. The sentence, "I don't know *but what* he will do it," is incorrect (say *but that*). In general *but what* is correct as a connective only when *but that which* can be substituted for it (*what* is equivalent to *that which* (see Sec. 68)): thus, "I do not know anything *but what* he told me" (*but that which* he told me).

541. "As." The word *as* presents many difficult problems. Some of its more important uses have been discussed elsewhere under different headings, as indicated in the references below. In most instances, *as* conveys at least a suggestion of an adverbial relation.

As may be used:

(1) To introduce a noun in a sort of apposition, as in "You, *as a stockholder,* must do your part" (see Sec. 306).

(2) To introduce a noun or an adjective used as an objective complement, as in "We selected him *as captain*" (see Sec. 312) and "We regarded him *as* entirely *trustworthy*" (see Sec. 361).

(3) As a relative pronoun, as in "Such papers *as* these (are) must be destroyed" (see Sec. 318).

(4) To introduce adverbial clauses of time, manner, degree, comparison, and reason.

> *As I was crossing the street,* I met a friend.
> They did the work *as they were directed.*
> A man is as old *as he feels.*
> They work as hard *as you do.*
> *As it was getting late,* I hurried home.

542. The following sentences contain adverbial elements, introduced by *as*, which are less regular in form. In some cases, a suggestion of an adverbial relation other than the one indicated is present. Many of the constructions are elliptical.

(1) Manner.

> He was regarded *as a vagabond* (as a vagabond is regarded).
> This tree will serve us *as a windshield* (as a windshield would serve us).
> Let us talk this over *as man to man* (as man would talk to man).
> They did the work *as ordered* (as they were ordered to do it).
> You must do *as seems best* (as it seems best to do).
> They went to class *as usual* this morning (as it was usual for them to go).
> The performance will be given *as advertised* (as it was advertised to be given).

(2) Condition.

> He has not yet, *as it were,* won his spurs as a writer. (*As it were* has the meaning "if I may be permitted to use that phrase." See Sec. 520.)

(3) Comparison.

> He succeeded, *as on other occasions,* in quieting the disturbance (as he succeeded on other occasions).

(4) Degree.

> He is not so foolish *as to say* that (degree and condition—"as he would be if he should say that").
> Come as early *as possible.*

543. "As to." *As to* and *as for* are equivalent to *regarding* or *concerning.*

> I can say nothing *as to* his bravery (*concerning* his bravery).
> *As for* his honesty, I can speak with conviction.

544. "As well as." *As well as* may be either a co-ordinate or a subordinate conjunction.

John *as well as* James will be there (co-ordinate).

You must do your work *as well as* you can (subordinate).

545. "Though." *Though* is sometimes placed at the end of a statement.

He offered me some money. I didn't take it, *though.*

They were unable to open the door; they certainly tried hard, *though.* In this construction, *though* may belong to a statement preceding the one which it follows. This preceding statement may be in the same sentence or in an earlier one. Thus the first example given above is equivalent to *"Though* he offered me some money, I didn't take it."

546. "Either." *Either* may be placed at the end of a statement, in order to express an emphatic negation.

I told him not to go, and he didn't go, *either.*

547. "Other than." *Than* is generally a conjunction, but the combination *other than* is used as a preposition equivalent to *except.*

No man *other than a knave* would do that (*except* a knave).

Chapter XIX

IMPROVING YOUR
                           VOCABULARY

548. Building an adequate vocabulary is a long—but interesting—task. It cannot be done in a few months or a year. Persistent effort and constant vigilance are required to eliminate bad habits in spelling and pronunciation; to learn the accurate meaning of words that you have been using more or less vaguely, or incorrectly; and to add regularly new and valuable words to the stock already at your command.

In the following pages a few fundamental principles are outlined briefly. They are presented as the beginning of a continuous campaign which should be carried on diligently—and daily—if any marked improvement in the command of words is to be made.

USE OF THE DICTIONARY

549. A good dictionary is, of course, indispensable to anyone who would know words and their use. It is the most accessible and authoritative source of information on words: their spelling, pronunciation, grammatical classification, etymology, definitions, synonyms, and antonyms.

550. For example, take the following item from Webster's *Collegiate Dictionary*, Fifth Edition. (Other good dictionaries, of a size adapted for desk use, are the *Winston Simplified Dictionary* and Funk & Wagnalls *College Standard Dictionary*. In these, the symbols and abbreviations vary in some respects from the ones used in Webster's.)

> **ab.rupt′** (ăb.rŭpt′), *adj.* [L. *abruptus,* past part. of *abrumpere,* fr. *ab-* + *rumpere* to break.] 1. Broken off; very steep, or craggy, as promontories. 2. Sudden; hasty; unceremonious. 3. Having sudden transitions from one subject to another; unconnected; as, an *abrupt* style. 4. *Bot.* Suddenly terminating, as if cut off.—**ab.rupt′ly,** *adv.*—**ab.rupt′ness,** *n.*

Syn. Unexpected, quick; headlong, impetuous, precipitate; rough, curt, brusque, blunt; disconnected; sheer, perpendicular, vertical, sharp.—**Abrupt, steep, precipitous.** Abrupt applies to a surface (as an acclivity or declivity) which rises or descends at a sharp pitch or angle. Steep implies such an angle as renders ascent, less frequently descent, difficult. Precipitous suggests steepness like that of a precipice.—**Ant.** Gradual; deliberate; gentle, smooth, suave.

551. Pronunciation. This is given in parentheses following the word. At the bottom of the dictionary page are listed the symbols used to indicate the various sounds of letters. See also the *Guide to Pronunciation* in the forepart of the dictionary.

552. Parts of Speech. The notation *adj.* indicates that *abrupt* is an adjective. Later, the corresponding adverbial and noun forms, *abruptly* and *abruptness,* are marked *adv.* and *n.,* respectively. (See the list of Abbreviations in the forepart of the dictionary for the meaning of other symbols: as, *v.i.,* for intransitive verb; *v.t.,* for transitive verb; and the like.)

553. Etymology. The entry in brackets tells you that the word *abrupt* is derived from the Latin (L. is the abbreviation) *abruptus,* past participle of the Latin verb *abrumpere.* This verb is then broken up into its parts: the prefix *ab-* plus the root *rumpere,* meaning "to break." For the meaning of the prefix, look back under *ab-.* Here you find that it denotes "away, off, from." Hence the Latin word *abruptus* meant "broken off."

(Other languages from which other words are borrowed are indicated by symbols such as, *Ger.* (German); *Gr.* (Greek); *Ir.* (Irish); *F.* (French); *OF.* (Old French); *AS.* (Anglo-Saxon); *ME.* (Middle English). For further examples see the list of Abbreviations in the forepart of the dictionary.)

(A statement like "OF. fr. L. fr. Gr." would mean that the word in question was borrowed into English from Old French, which borrowed it from Latin, which borrowed it from Greek.)

(When a number of words from the same root occur in a group, or fairly close together, the etymology is often given after only one—the basic word for all of them. Thus, in the group *compliable, com-*

pliance, compliant, comply, the etymology is explained after *comply,* the basic verb. Again, for *comprehend, comprehensible, comprehension, comprehensive,* the etymological information is presented only after *comprehend.*)

(In a list of words beginning with the same prefix, the meaning of that prefix is usually given only at the beginning of the list, and not after the other words in the series.)

554. Definitions. Four definitions of *abrupt* are given. The first considers the word as describing the physical characteristics of an object, such as a hill or promontory. The second defines the word in its relation to human actions or manners. The third refers to thought or speech. The fourth definition indicates the technical use of the word in one of the sciences, botany.

555. Synonyms. The list of fourteen synonyms for *abrupt* is divided into five groups (separated by semicolons), each consisting of those words which are most closely related in meaning. Thus, the three members of the second group all convey the idea of "rashness"; the four members of the third group emphasize "bluntness" in speech or manner.

Then three synonyms are differentiated in more detail to show the shades of meaning in each.

(Synonyms are usually listed in the dictionary under only one member of the group, with a cross-reference given under the other members. For example, under the word *steep,* elsewhere in the dictionary, there is a reference: "Syn. See ABRUPT.")

556. Antonyms. The final entry, marked **Ant.,** lists some words which are opposite in meaning to *abrupt.*

Note. For a complete guide in the use of the dictionary, see pp. xxii ff. in Webster's *Collegiate Dictionary.* The student should make himself thoroughly familiar with this material.

Exercise 83

(A) Look up the following words in the dictionary. Note the pronunciation, part of speech, etymology, one or two common present meanings, and several synonyms. Give the meaning of all abbreviations and of all symbols used to indicate etymology, pronunciation, etc.

adjacent	patience	educate
flourish	acrid	evade
heavy	blithe	force
delicacy	crooked	obtain
beseech	calm	strange
acme	erase	

(B) Look up the etymology of the following words. Explain the abbreviations used in the dictionary; and—if more than one language is involved—trace the course of the word through the different languages.

barometer	sherbet	sextet
bicycle	azure	pedagogue
knapsack	lilac	sheer
bask	horde	phlegm
zero	loyal	lagoon

ETYMOLOGY: THE BACKGROUND OF WORDS

557. The English vocabulary contains words borrowed from many different languages. The basic language is Teutonic or Germanic: the language spoken by the Teutonic invaders—the Angles and the Saxons —who conquered a considerable part of Britain in the sixth century A.D. These Angles and Saxons were people who lived along the shores of the Baltic and the North Sea. From them comes the name *Anglo-Saxon,* applied to the English; and from the name *Angles,* the words *English* and *England* are derived.

The chief additions to this basic language are borrowings from the French, Latin, Greek, and Danish. Many other languages, such as Arabic, Chinese, Hebrew, and so on, have also made smaller contributions.

The study of the etymology of English words covers their structure— the parts from which they are built; their earlier meaning in Anglo-Saxon (Old English), Latin, French, or other language from which they were derived; and their development to their present meaning.

558. Structure of Words. Words are built from three elements: roots, prefixes, and suffixes.

1. The root of a word furnishes the basic meaning.

2. The prefix, which is placed before the root, gives a particular modification to the root meaning.

3. The suffix, which follows the root, has chiefly an inflectional significance. It shows, in general, the grammatical classification of a word: thus *-ing* indicates a present participle or a gerund; *-ed* indicates a past tense or a past participle. Sometimes the suffix has a definite meaning also. Thus in *readable* the suffix conveys the idea of "able" (able to be read); and it also classifies the word as an adjective.

559. Take, for example, the word *contracting*. The root is *tract-*, from the Latin *trahere, tractus,* meaning "to draw"; the prefix is *con-* (Latin), which means "together"; and the suffix is *-ing,* which indicates that the word is a gerund or a participle. The word thus means "drawing together": as, "The *contracting* of the metal loosened the pin in the socket."

Again, in *retraction,* the root is the same as in the preceding example; the prefix *re-* means "back" or "again"; and the suffix *-tion* signifies "the act of" and indicates that the word is a noun. Thus *retraction* is a noun meaning the "act of drawing back."

Every word has a root. It may, or may not, have a prefix and a suffix, or it may have one and not the other. Thus:

come (root)	com-ing (root and suffix)
be-come (prefix and root)	be-com-ing (prefix and root and suffix)

Some words are made by a combination of two roots: as, *manufacture,* from the two Latin roots, *manus,* hand, and *facere,* to make.

560. Changes in Meaning. Some words retain their original meaning with little or no change. Thus *retraction,* in Sec. 559, still denotes "a drawing or taking back," just as it did in the Latin.

In other words, however, the meaning has changed, sometimes slightly, sometimes considerably. Thus *conspire,* which originally meant "to breathe together," now carries the idea of "plotting together," as if in whispers. *Advertise,* originally "to turn to," now means "to turn the attention of readers to something." *Hypocrite,* originally an "actor on a stage," now indicates a "person who pretends to be something other than what he is."

These changes are easily recognized. Other words, however, have undergone greater changes. Thus *focus,* which in Latin meant a "fireplace, hearth," now denotes a "central point, or a point where lines converge." At first sight, the relation between these two meanings may not be apparent, but it becomes clear when one remembers that the fireplace—in a home where it was the only source of heat—was the point about which much of the domestic life centered.

STRUCTURE AND CHANGE IN MEANING OF WORDS

561. Learning the structure of words and the meaning of the prefixes and roots from which they are built, is a valuable aid in improving your vocabulary. Not only does this knowledge furnish a clue to the meaning of many new words encountered in reading; but also it supplies a background for words which are already somewhat familiar, and thus it adds richness and significance to their meaning.

As an introduction to the structure of words, a few common Latin prefixes and roots which occur frequently in English are given below.

PREFIX	MEANING	ROOT	MEANING
a-, ab-	away, from	cedo, cessus	to go
de-	from	duco, ductus	to lead
e-, ex-	out	dico, dictus	to say
con-, com-	together, with	traho, tractus	to draw
in-, im-	in		
inter-	between		
pro-	forward		
pre-	before		

Exercise 84

In the following words name the roots, prefixes, and suffixes. Give the etymological meaning of each word as indicated by the root and the prefix, and show the relation between that meaning and the present meaning (for the latter, consult a dictionary, if necessary). (The suffixes need only be named, not explained.)

deduce, produce, conducive, induction, conductor, ductile
dictate, prediction, edict, dictum
proceed, excessive, preceded, interceding, concession
detraction, protracted, tractor, distract, extracting

562. Prefixes. Additional prefixes are listed below (for convenience in reference those given in the preceding section are included). The lists represent only a small percentage of foreign prefixes which occur in English. Others, as you encounter them in your study of words, should be looked up in the dictionary and added to the lists.

Most of the following prefixes are Latin.

PREFIX	MEANING	ENGLISH WORDS
a-, ab-, abs-	away, from	avert, abstain
ante-	before	antedate
anti-	against	antithesis
bi-	two	bisect
circum-	around	circumference
co-, con-, com-	with, together	coincide, confide, combine
contra-	against	contraclockwise
de-	from, away	debar
di-, dis-	separation, general negative	divert, displease
e-, ex-	out	eject, exclude
en-	in	envelope
in-, im-	in	invite, impress
in-, im-, il-, ir-	not	incorrect, improper, illegal, irregular
inter-	between	interstate
intra-	within, among	intrastate
non-	not	nonessential
per-	through	pervade
post-	after	postgraduate
pre-	before	premeditated
pro-	forward	protrude
re-	back, again	return
retro-	backward	retroactive
se-	away, away from	seclude
sub-	under	subordinate
super-	above	supernatural
trans-	across	transfer
un-	not	unnoticed

563. Roots. A Latin or a Greek root may vary somewhat in form according to the inflectional use of the word in which it occurs. Thus, the verb *capio* has an *a* in the present tense; an *e* in the perfect (present perfect) tense, *cepi;* and an *a* again, with an added *t,* in the past participle, *captus.* The noun *dux* (nominative case) becomes *ducis* in the genitive (possessive) case.

Sometimes, as in the preceding examples, the change is not very great.

In other instances, however, it is more marked. Thus, the Latin verb meaning "to direct" has the form *derigo* in the present tense, and *directus* as its past participle.

The same sort of change occurs, of course, in English words. Thus: *keep, kept; break, broke, broken; think, thought; tooth, teeth.*

564. A list of common Latin roots follows.

ROOT	MEANING	ENGLISH WORDS
ago, actus	do	agent, action
amo, amatus	love	amatory
annus	year	annual
audio, auditus	hear	audible, audition
bene	well	benefit
capio, cepi, captus	take, seize	capable, reception, capture
caput, capitis	head	capital
cedo, cessus	go	proceed, procession
corpus, corporis	body	corps
credo, creditus	believe	creed, credit
curro, cursus	run	incur, course
dico, dictus	say	predict
do, datus	give	donate, data
duco, ductus	lead	produce, conductor
facio, feci, factus	make	manufacture, effect
fero, latus	carry	transfer, translate
jacio, jeci, jactus	throw	ejaculate, eject
lex, legis	law	legal
locus	place	locality
malus	bad	maladjusted
manus	hand	manual
mitto, missus	send	emit, mission
pello, pulsus	drive	expel, repulse
pendo, pensus	hang	suspend
pes, pedis	foot	pedal
pono, positus	place	opponent, position
porto, portatus	carry	support
scribo, scriptus	write	scribe, script
sedeo, sessus	sit	sedentary, session
specto, spectatus	look	spectator
spiro, spiratus	breathe	inspire, inspirit
sto, steti, status	stand	status

teneo, tentus	hold	tenure, retention
torqueo, tortus	twist	extort
traho, tractus	draw	tractor
venio, ventus	come	convene, advent
verto, versus	turn	invert, reverse
video, visus	see	provide, vision
voco, vocatus	call	vocal, vocation

Exercise 85

Name the roots and prefixes. Give the etymological meaning of **each** word, as indicated by the root and prefix, and show the relation between that meaning and the present meaning (consult a dictionary, **if** necessary).

respiration	controversy	circumspection
abstract	projectile	donor
incredible	illegitimate	depository
incorporate	proposition	superannuated
postpone	benediction	contortionist
concurrent	export	composite
contradict	irrevocable	deportation
recur	audience	convoke
dejected	credulous	inspector
intervene	prospectus	convert
secede	invocation	tenant
decapitate	amateur	retrospection
propellor	antecedent	incredible
transmission	supersede	introvert
benefactor	subtract	
pedestal	excursion	

SYNONYMS

565. Synonyms are words which have the same or nearly the same meaning.

By the use of synonyms a writer or a speaker avoids tiresome repetition of the same word; and he also is able to express shades of meaning more accurately.

Some synonyms are practically identical in **meaning**: as *vigilant* and *watchful*.

Most so-called synonyms, however, convey different shades or degrees of a general meaning. Thus: *get, obtain, acquire, procure, earn, win. Get* is the most general word. *Obtain, acquire,* and *procure* emphasize the idea of getting *through effort*—the amount of effort implied increases in the successive words. *Earn* means to get something as a *reward* for work or effort. *Win* emphasizes the gaining of something in competition or against opposition.

Exercise 86

Give at least three synonyms for each of the following words; indicate the shades of meaning in the different synonyms; and use each in a sentence.

reply	small	rebuke
see	honest	decrease
brief	proud	develop
ask	healthy	odor
hate	stern	idle
annoy	vague	give
predict	busy	gaze
awkward	silent	say
obvious	talkative	infidel

Words Often Confused

566. The words in the following exercise are often confused, either because of similarity in spelling or because of faulty association. They are not interchangeable, and are not synonyms.

Exercise 87

Look up the following words in the dictionary, and use them correctly in the sentences.

1. accept, except
   In his calculations he _____ all words of doubtful origin.
   You should _____ the invitation at once.
2. affect, effect
   The long hours of work _____ his health.
   The company has _____ a reorganization of its plant.
   The _____ of the drug had worn off.

3. aggravate, annoy

He was _____ by the incessant noise.

Their carelessness _____ the judges.

His condition was _____ by the damp west wind.

4. almost, most

I have seen _____ all of the current plays.

They have _____ finished their work.

We were _____ interested in the modern paintings.

_____ everything has been arranged.

5. balance, remainder

For the _____ of the day he will be in the office.

The _____ in the bank was sufficient to cover the check.

6. beside, besides

They placed the package _____ the other presents.

Only two people were there _____ himself.

He has other income _____ his salary.

7. claim, say

He _____ that the stranger had robbed him.

He _____ his share of the proceeds.

They _____ that they had been deceived by his friendly attitude.

8. comprehensive, comprehensible

It was a _____ report, but much of it was not _____ to the average reader.

9. contemptuous, contemptible

A _____ smile showed his feeling toward this _____ trick.

10. credible, credulous, creditable

It was a _____ performance, but not a noteworthy one.

The story might have seemed _____ to a _____ listener.

11. distinct, distinctive

The sealed cap is a _____ feature of this pen.

One _____ advantage of the site is its accessibility to transportation.

12. disinterested, uninterested

The case will be tried before some _____ tribunal.

The only _____ spectator in the courtroom was a man half asleep near the door.

Since he is an (a) _____ witness, his testimony will carry weight.

13. egotist, egoist, egotism, egoism

Like most of us, John is an _____ but he is not an _____.

His _____ made him unpopular with his acquaintances.

14. expect, suppose, suspect

I _____ that he has forgotten his appointment.

We _____ that the sun will be shining tomorrow.

I _____ that his attitude is not wholly disinterested.

We _____ you to pay the money when due.

15. healthy, healthful

The island is noted for its _____ climate.

The boy was young and _____ and active.

Living conditions are _____ there, and consequently the natives are
a _____ race.

16. imply, infer

The speaker _____ that the plan was impractical.

From his letter we _____ that he was in difficulty.

From what you _____ in your note we _____ that you had been ill.

17. less, fewer

He has _____ friends than ever before.

We found _____ mistakes in the second report.

He boasts of having _____ money, and therefore _____ worries.

18. let, leave

_____ me do that work for you.

_____ me at the office, and _____ me finish the work.

You wouldn't want to _____ her go to the theater alone.

19. lie, lay, lain, laid

He likes to _____ in the sun.

After some hesitation, he _____ the book on the table.

After we had finished lunch, the guide _____ down to rest.

The fallen trees have _____ here all winter.

20. likely, liable

Every citizen is _____ to be summoned for jury service.

Business conditions are _____ to improve this year.

It is _____ to rain before morning.

21. luxurious, luxuriant

The furnishings in the room were _____ and expensive.

They lived _____ly in a penthouse on the boulevard.

The house was surrounded by _____ shrubs and flowers.

22. practical, practicable

Both plans seem _____ but this one is more _____.

He prides himself on being a _____ man.

23. principle, principal

This is a well recognized _____ of law.

The _____ reason for his failure was laziness.

He had an excuse signed by the _____ of the school.

He is entitled to both _____ and interest.

24. unique, unusual
    It is the most _____ feature of the book.
    Each watch is individually engraved with some _____ design.

SOME TROUBLESOME ADVERBS

567. Many adverbs end in *-ly*, and have no other form (*intensely*). Others have no form in *-ly* (*fast*). Still others have both a short form and one in *-ly* (*late, lately*).

In the first two classes, the correct form should be learned, or may be found in the dictionary.

For words in the third class, the dictionary usually indicates the difference in meaning between the long and the short form: thus, *late* is defined as "after the usual or proper time"; *lately*, as "not long ago." ("They came home *late*." "He has been more careful *lately*.") Sometimes, however, the difference is largely a matter of good usage, and the student must train himself to observe what that usage is.

Note. The short form of the adverb, which is the same as the adjective form, is often defined under the adjective entry in the dictionary, instead of in a separate entry.

For the distinction between adverb and predicate adjective, see Sec. 357.

Exercise 88

In the following sentences use the correct forms. Consult the dictionary, if necessary; and see Secs. 357, 488.

1. He could learn to write _____ if he tried (good, well).
2. The workmen ate their lunch _____ (fast, fastly).
3. He treats his employees _____, and pays them next to nothing (bad, badly).
4. He makes the trip to the city _____ on Saturday (regular, regularly).
5. She comes to the office _____ every day (almost, most).
6. Living conditions now seem to be _____ better (some, somewhat).
7. The class was _____ prepared for the examination (ill, illy).
8. In those early days horses ran _____ on the prairies (wild, wildly).
9. The frightened child ran _____ down the street (wild, wildly).
10. They finished the work as _____ as they could (quick, quickly).
11. The promoters are _____ concerned over this new development (much, muchly).

12. The room was furnished quite _____ in the modernistic manner (artistic, artistically).
13. You can finish all this work _____ in half a day (easy, easily).
14. After dinner he went _____ to his office (straight, straightly).
15. The judges were interested in the boy's picture and commented very _____ on it (favorable, favorably).
16. The mayor was _____ surprised at this new criticism (very, very much).
17. Surely the law was passed more _____ than that (recent, recently).
18. He must live _____, or he wouldn't be so healthy (right, rightly).
19. The trail up the mountain was _____ steep and we were _____ exhausted when we reached the top (real, really; near, nearly).
20. Talk _____, and don't mumble your words (louder, more loudly).
21. He needs the money and the house will be sold _____ (cheap, cheaply).
22. The audience was not _____ interested in the speech (very, very much).
23. The Wrights have _____ more money than the Smiths (considerable, considerably).
24. The car runs very _____ and needs but little oil (smooth, smoothly).
25. He is working _____ now at the postoffice (steady, steadily).
26. He stood _____ (erect, erectly).
27. The chairman remained _____ (firm, firmly).
28. The post remained _____ imbedded in the sand (firm, firmly).

SPELLING

568. The following words are frequently misspelled. Pick out those which give you trouble, and *learn* how to spell them. Some perhaps you have been misspelling regularly for years; a little concentration should correct that bad habit.

A number of rules for spelling are given under the heading "Orthography" in the forepart of Webster's *Collegiate Dictionary*.

absence	all ready	analysis
accidentally	all right (never,	analyze
accommodate	*alright*)	article
accumulate	altar	ascend
acquainted	alter	athlete
across	altogether	believe
already	all together	benefited

boarder
border
born
borne
bridal
bridle
business
calendar
canvas
canvass
capital
capitol
cavalry
cemetery
changeable
cloths
clothes
coarse
course
column
coming
committee
complement
compliment
conceivable
confidant
confident
conquer
conqueror
conscientious
convenience
consul
council
counsel
defendant
dependent
descend
desert
dessert
desirous
dining

disappear
disease
decease
eighth
embarrass
equipped
etc.
extraordinary
fascinate
February
forbade
foresee
formally
formerly
forth
fourth
grammar
guard
harass
height
incidentally
ingenious
ingenuous
instance
instant(s)
its
it's
judgment
laboratory
lacquer
lead
led
legal
leisure
lightening
lightning
loose
lose
maintenance
misspelled
necessary

nickel
noticeable
occasion
occurring
pamphlet
parallel
permissible
perspiration
Philippines
planing
planning
possess
prairie
precede
preparation
privilege
procedure
proceed
quiet
quite
recommend
repetition
seize
separate
siege
similar
sophomore
stationary
stationery
statue
stature
statute
supersede
their
there
undoubtedly
who's
whose
your
you're

PRONUNCIATION

569. An adequate vocabulary is one which is effective for speaking, as well as for writing. Hence it is obviously important that words be pronounced correctly.

There are two common causes of mispronunciation.

1. The speaker does not know the correct pronunciation; therefore he gives the wrong sound to letters (such as ī instead of ĭ), or he places the accent on the wrong syllable.

2. Even though he knows the correct pronunciation, he carelessly slurs or omits syllables.

The following exercises contain words which are frequently mispronounced. Practise saying them *aloud*, so that the ear will become accustomed to the correct sound of the words.

Exercise 89

Pronounce the following words *correctly*—observing the proper sound for each letter and placing the accent on the right syllable.

alias (ā'lias)	genuine (gen'-u-ĭn, not gen-u-ine')
athlete (ath'lete, not ath-a-lete)	grimace (grimace')
combatant (com'batant)	guardian (guard'i-an, not guar-dēēn)
comparable (com'parable)	
corps (cōr)	height (hīt, not hītth)
diphtheria (dif-ther'ia)	impious (im'pious)
dirigible (dir'igible)	indisputable (indis'putable)
elm (not ellum)	irreparable (irrep'arable)
exquisite (ex'quisite)	irrevocable (irrev'ocable)
film (not fillum)	mischievous (mis'chĭ-vous, not mis-chēv'i-ous)
genealogy (-ălogy, not -ŏlogy)	preferable (pref'erable)

Exercise 90

Pronounce the following words *distinctly*—observing the particular points specified in the directions (the words should be spoken aloud).

(A) Give full value to *-ing:* thus, com*ing,* not com*in'.*

running	carrying	reading and writing
singing	trying	coming and going
reading	going	talking about going

writing	practicing	weeping and wailing
hurrying	driving	buying and selling

(B) Give full value to *-ally*: thus, gradu*ally*, not gradu'*ly* (remember that the *a* in *-ally* is short, as in *account*, and should not be accented).

literally	usually	rationally
finally	naturally	habitually
accidentally	continually	casually

(C) Give full value to the second word: thus, found *them*, not found-*um*.

We set them	We fought them	We strapped them
We saw them	We got them	We sank them
We do them	We caught them	We struck them
We sent them	We clipped them	We picked them
We dropped them		

(D) Give full value to all syllables.

reg-u-lar (not reglar)	gov-ern-ment (not goverment)
prob-a-bly (not probly)	quan-ti-ty (not quanity)
par-tic-u-lar-ly (not particurly)	soph-o-more (not sophmore)
sat-is-fac-tor-i-ly (not satisfac- turly)	lit-er-a-ture (not litertoor)
	un-doubt-ed-ly (not undoubtably)
fac-to-ry (not factry)	stū-dent (not stoo-dent)
boun-da-ry (not boundry)	dū-ty (not dooty)
crim-i-nal (not crimnal)	new (nū, not noo)
Arc-tic (not Artic)	ma-tūre' (not ma-toor)
Feb-ru-ary (not Febuary)	dū-ly (not doo-ly)
can-di-date (not canidate)	per-form (not pre-form)

(E) Read the following sentences aloud; pronounce each word distinctly.

1. We were riding slowly, looking at the scenery which was particularly pleasing at that time of year.
2. They were probably studying the records of the candidates for government offices.
3. We usually begin thinking about going home before the new moon gets unduly bright.
4. Bring them here and set them on the desk so that the other students can see them.
5. We arrived in this Arctic country just at the beginning of February.
6. The amateur generally does not produce as good a book as the mature professional writer does.

570. In the following discussion two main factors are considered in determining the punctuation to be used in a given place: the kind of relationship between groups of words, and the position of groups in the sentence. The importance of the first factor will be apparent as the discussion proceeds; the second needs some explanation.

In general, groups of words have two positions in relation to each other.

(1) Logically related groups may be *placed together,* so that the thought runs naturally from one to the other. Here our problem is to indicate the kind of relationship that exists between them.

(2) Logically related groups may be *separated* by other elements which interrupt the natural flow of the thought. In this case, the problem is to set off the interpolated element, so that the reader can readily see where the thought is interrupted and where it is taken up again.

571. A few general characteristics of the marks used in punctuation also need to be kept in mind. A *semicolon* is stronger than a *comma,* and indicates a more remote connection in thought. A *colon* gives notice that a specific enumeration or explanation is to follow a general statement. A *dash* marks a decided break in thought, or adds emphasis to the statement that follows.

572. In the following discussion, note the basis of the classifications. In *Series of Elements of Equal Rank,* related groups are together; in *Main and Subordinate Elements,* some are together, others are separated; in *Interruptions,* the related groups are separated; in *Enumerations and Explanations* and in *Direct Quotations,* the relationships are of specific types.

SERIES OF ELEMENTS OF EQUAL RANK

Main Clauses in Series

573. Two classes of main clauses are to be noted: (1) those which are connected by the conjunctions *and, but, or,* or *nor;* (2) those which have no conjunction or have some connective other than those named, such as *therefore, however, nevertheless.*

574. Main Clauses Connected by "And," "But," "Or," or "Nor." Here the punctuation varies with the length of the clauses, and the closeness of relation between them.

575. *Comma.* A comma is regularly used between clauses of fair length and fairly close connection.

A second door is thrown open, and the visitors advance into a large, square room blazing with gas. (Rudyard Kipling.)

My heart is with them, but my mind has a contempt for them. (Woodrow Wilson.)

These small disturbances will have to be curbed, or there will be a serious outbreak before morning.

She had no desire to attend a girls' school, nor did she want to go to the state university.

576. *Semicolon.* A semicolon is regularly used between long clauses, especially if there are commas within these clauses.

She had studied music in Vienna, had been a social worker in London, and had traveled extensively in the East; and now she was coming back home to Iowa to take up the old life again.

The people are sick, perhaps, with toil; but below that sickness there is a lust for enjoyment that lights up every little moment of their evening. (Thomas Burke.)

577. *No Punctuation.* If the clauses are short and closely connected in thought, the punctuation may be omitted.

It was Sunday and the street was very quiet.

578. Main Clauses Not Connected by "And," "But," "Or," or "Nor." These clauses may have no connective, or they may be joined by connectives other than those named, such as *therefore, nevertheless, however,* and the like.

579. *Semicolon.* A semicolon is used in this group, regardless of the length of the clauses.

The photographer reproduces nature; the painter interprets nature.

By nature he is a dreamer; by training he has made himself a practical man of affairs.

There is no occasion for worry about the larger banks; in fact, they are now in a better financial condition than ever before.

We had been told that the natives were suspicious of strangers; there-fore, we were surprised at their friendly interest in us.

They did not leave home until nearly noon; nevertheless, they were in Buffalo before dark.

Exercise 91

Punctuate the main clauses, and tell why you use each mark of punc-tuation.

1. He had lived for many years in Paris but he never thought of it as home.
2. The article is instructive moreover it is interesting.
3. The moon was shining and the stars were out.
4. Many of the buildings were poorly ventilated and inadequately heated and in other respects as well they were unsanitary.
5. John is a freshman his brother is a junior.
6. He had never had any experience in this sort of work nevertheless he ·was confident that he could do it.
7. We were now about a mile from the place where we were to camp and the trail was becoming steeper and more difficult at every step.
8. The investigator may work for months on a case or if he is fortunate he may find the solution to be unexpectedly simple.
9. Today the secretary may be in London or in Berlin tomorrow may find him in Rome or in Paris.
10. He was the last of a long line of soldiers, diplomats, and explorers and, as might be expected, he was vocally proud of his family.
11. A few of the warriors were full-blooded Indians the others were half-breeds or renegade whites.
12. He has promised to be at the conference therefore he must go.
13. At Detroit you can continue your trip to Buffalo by boat or you have the option of finishing the journey by rail.
14. This law will correct some of the abuses in the system but it does not go to the root of the trouble.
15. It was miles to the nearest village or filling station and the gas was running low.

SERIES OF WORDS, PHRASES, OR SUBORDINATE CLAUSES

580. Comma. A comma is regularly used to separate the members of a series of three or more words, phrases, or subordinate clauses of equal rank.

The majority of these venders are immigrants from *Greece, Italy, and Turkey.*

The first chapter gives a *concise, interesting, and unprejudiced* account of the events leading up to the war.

In the dining room she deftly *arranged the silver, straightened the napkins, and picked a faded flower from the bouquet.*

The trip may be made *by automobile, in canoes, or on horseback.*

The treasurer reported *that twenty new members had been added, that all current bills were paid, and that a substantial reduction in the mortgage on the club house could now be made.*

Some writers omit the comma before the last two members of the series when they are joined by a conjunction.

The majority of these venders are immigrants from *Greece, Italy and Turkey.*

The preferred practice, however, is to use a comma here, as well as between the other members of the series.

581. *Semicolon.* A semicolon is used if the members of the series are long, or if they contain other members set off by commas.

Before us we saw a *weary, bedraggled woman, leading a grimy urchin about eight years old; two men, surly and half-drunk; and a spruce officer of the law, who had evidently taken them in charge.*

SERIES OF VARIOUS TYPES

582. Commas are used between the members of the following groups, which are series of one sort or another.

(1) A long compound predicate.

I *took* down a thick quarto volume curiously bound in parchment, and *seated* myself in a great armchair by the fire.

(2) A declarative sentence followed by a short question.

You will come early tonight, *won't you?*

(3) Contrasted statements, positive and negative.

He was referring to the sailors, *not to the marines.*

His advantage lies, *not in his weight,* but in his speed.

(4) Parts of addresses, dates, names and titles, and similar groups of data.

He was born on *April 24, 1902,* in *Huntington, West Virginia.*

Early in *June, 1786,* the settlement was attacked by Indians.

They have moved to *1628 Oakton Street, Keesport, Ohio,* for the summer season.

For further details you may consult *A. G. Tyler, "Life Among the Cannibal Tribes," Vol. II, p. 65.*

The lecture will be given by *Dr. Frank E. Billings, A.B., Ph.D., president of Gridley College.*

(5) Words in apposition.

The library, *a magnificent building of Gothic design,* is his latest gift to the school.

Sixty miles further on there was another place of call, *a deep bay with only a couple of houses on the beach.* (Joseph Conrad.)

He is visiting his uncle, *Mr. Simpson,* this week.

In (4) and (5) note the punctuation after the last member of a series which is in the middle of a sentence.

Exercise 92

Punctuate the following sentences, and give your reasons.

1. In Jacksonville Florida the plan has been tried with marked success.
2. They hoped for a settlement by arbitration not by war.
3. F. W. Street a prominent lawyer of Chicago was made chairman of the commission.
4. It was on May 12 1924 that the treaty was signed by France Italy and Spain the three nations chiefly concerned.
5. The country people flocked into town in wagons on horseback and on foot.
6. You see now how important the question is don't you?
7. The main building a three-story modern fireproof structure is located at 335 West Adams Street Mansfield Indiana in the main business district.
8. Those trees with the white bark are birches not poplars.
9. I had often read about the grace and the beauty of the albatross and was glad to see one at close range.
10. He told us what he wanted when he wanted it and how he wanted it made.
11. The first three places in the contest were won by Albert Fletcher of Toledo Ohio Frank Murphy of Canton Iowa and Giles Overstreet of Alton Illinois.
12. Early in November 1837 he made his first visit to Chicago then a small struggling frontier town.
13. The stevedores had already finished unloading the cargo of the first steamer and were lounging on the dock until the next boat arrived.
14. His companion a younger more active man took him forcibly by the arm and hurried him up the steps.
15. The chief wealth of the country lies in its mines of lead iron and gold

its agricultural products such as wheat and barley and its great forests
of rare woods suitable for the finest cabinet work.
16. He found a long straight tough branch of an oak tree and made a cane
of it.

MAIN AND SUBORDINATE ELEMENTS

583. In this group, punctuation is needed if the main and the subordinate elements are not closely related in thought, or if the subordinate element is so placed that it appreciably delays or interrupts
the normal flow of the thought. A short element that makes only a
slight interruption is not usually punctuated.

ADVERBIAL CLAUSES AND PHRASES

584. Interruption of the Thought in the Sentence. A comma is regularly used to set off an adverbial clause or phrase (1) preceding a main
clause; (2) placed between the subject and the verb of the main clause;
or (3) placed between the verb and its object or predicate noun.
In the first case, the subordinate element delays the statement of the
main thought; in the other two cases, the subordinate element interrupts the regular flow of thought in the sentence, from subject—to verb
—to object or predicate noun.
(1) Before the Main Clause.
> *If I did not believe that,* I would not believe in democracy. (Woodrow
> Wilson.)
> *While ever careful to refrain from wronging others,* we must be no less
> insistent that we are not wronged ourselves. (Theodore Roosevelt.)
> *Having no love for the public,* I have often accused that body of having
> no sense of humour. (Max Beerbohm.)

When the subordinate element is short and closely related in thought, the
comma is sometimes omitted.
> *On our trip* we visited seven countries.
> *Where there is smoke* there is fire.

(2) Between the Subject and the Verb.
> This village, *when the French missionaries first visited it,* was the chief
> town of the Illinois Indians.
> Jukes, *straddling his long legs like a pair of compasses,* put on an air
> of superiority. (Joseph Conrad.)

(3) Between the Verb and the Object or the Predicate Noun.

> He had, *even at this early age,* an unusual faculty for analyzing his own emotions.

585. No Interruption of the Thought. An adverbial element which is placed after the verb and does not separate the verb from its object or predicate noun, is not usually punctuated. In this case there is no interruption of the thought in the sentence.

> You do not love humanity *if you seek to divide humanity into hostile camps.* (Woodrow Wilson.)
>
> He walked round it *till he came to what had been a gate.* (John Masefield.)
>
> Only a slight ripple of applause was heard *when the speaker finished his address.*

586. Exceptions. Certain kinds of adverbial elements are regularly punctuated even when they follow the verb.

(1) A clause of reason introduced by *for* or *as,* and a clause of concession introduced by *though* or *although.*

> We had many things to do that night, *for we were starting before dawn the next morning.*
>
> He is keeping up the house in the country, *though he expects to spend most of the time in the city.*

Moreover, any adverbial clause following the verb may be punctuated if the writer wants to give it special emphasis.

(2) A participial phrase which belongs to the subject and is somewhat removed from it; or a nominative absolute phrase.

> (1) He made his home in the old manor house, *living the life of a country squire.*
>
> He spent his afternoons down town, *calling on his friends in the insurance offices.*
>
> (2) The old woman leaned against the wall, *her crutch trembling in her hand.* (Dorothy Canfield.)

Both of these constructions frequently perform the dual function of an adverb and an adjective (see Sec. 200).

Exercise 93

Punctuate the adverbial clauses and phrases when punctuation is needed, and give your reasons.

1. If this procedure is impractical under the present law then the law should be changed.

2. Spanish was the common ground on which we all met for everyone knew more or less of that language.
3. Each applicant as he entered the waiting room of the recruiting office was given three forms to be filled out.
4. He belonged to the aristocracy of the country his family being of pure Spanish blood.
5. The other driver realizing the danger swung sharply to the right.
6. Measuring off twenty yards from the first marker the surveyor drove the stake where he wanted the excavating to begin.
7. Whether he writes about the situation in Europe or in the Far East he shows the same thoughtful restraint.
8. The captain was pacing the bridge watching the storm as it swept toward the ship.
9. Although they had driven steadily since noon it was after midnight before they arrived at the station.
10. You can be in Denver tomorrow morning if you go by plane.
11. Women and children were hurried to places of safety as no one knew when the next attack would be made.
12. Disturbed by the continued decrease in sales the directors doubled their appropriation for advertising.
13. He was well qualified for the position having been an assistant in the department for twenty years.
14. I always felt when the president was speaking that he was not entirely sincere.
15. These rumors are greatly exaggerated although there seems to be an element of truth in all of them.
16. The motion having been seconded the question was open for discussion.

Adjective Clauses and Phrases

587. Restrictive Elements. Restrictive adjective clauses and phrases are not punctuated.

This new controversy touched everybody *who read a book or heard intelligent conversation.* (H. G. Wells.)
The picture *which hangs over the fireplace* was painted by Sargent.
The candidate *who spent the most money* was usually the one *that got the nomination.*
The man *riding the black horse* is the governor.

588. Non-restrictive Elements. Non-restrictive adjective clauses and phrases are set off by commas.

That year he had spent in Paris, attending to some business for his father, *who had a plantation in Cuba.*

This book, *which was written by an eye-witness,* is the only authentic account of the catastrophe.

St. Marks Church, *erected in 1564,* is now in ruins.

Note. A *restrictive* clause or phrase is one which points out what person or thing is meant: that is, it restricts the statement to that person or thing. It cannot be omitted without changing the meaning of the sentence.

A letter *which is written with a pencil* is hard to read.

A *non-restrictive* clause or phrase is descriptive or explanatory, and can be omitted without changing the essential meaning of the sentence. It is not needed to show what person or thing is meant.

His first book, *which was written in 1916,* was a story of the sea.

589. Notice that a restrictive element is so closely connected with its main element that it is not punctuated even when placed between the subject and the verb, where it interrupts the flow of the thought. A long restrictive element thus placed, however, may be *followed—but not preceded*—by a comma, to show where the main thought is resumed.

Any plan *which does not take into account the conditions underlying the industrial unrest,* is doomed to failure.

Exercise 94

Punctuate the adjective clauses and phrases when punctuation is needed, and give your reasons.

1. All the trees that were blown down in the storm have been removed.
2. The driver of the east-bound car who was responsible for the accident escaped without serious injury.
3. John Thurman who was then our consul in Hamburg investigated every complaint which came to his attention.
4. The doctor smiling his best professional smile began to question the patient.
5. The *Columbia* which was the flagship of the fleet was anchored in the inner harbor.
6. A part of the crew slept here in hammocks swung fore and aft from the beams.
7. The man standing outside the main entrance was the sergeant-at-arms whose duty it was to examine the credentials of all who applied for admission.

8. The young prince standing stiffly at attention watched the troops file by the reviewing stand.
9. We could find no one whom we could trust to carry the message to headquarters.
10. The lord mayor dressed in his official regalia had come in person to welcome the rajah who seemed pleased at the attention.
11. A skyscraper constructed of steel and concrete might have withstood the shock.
12. His uncle who was a director of the corporation had insisted on his promotion.
13. The novel was written by Samuel Clemens whom we know better as Mark Twain.
14. It was a story that was told to me by an Englishman who had spent many years in the East.
15. The Telford Inn where Washington once had his headquarters will be restored by the local historical society which is collecting funds for that purpose.

NOUN CLAUSES AND PHRASES

590. As a general rule, noun clauses and phrases do not require punctuation.

For some time we had noticed *that his memory was failing.* (Object of the verb.)

I think they were *what are called failures in life.* (H. M. Tomlinson.) (Predicate noun.)

What you do in the examination will determine your standing for the semester. (Subject of the verb.)

591. A comma is generally used to set off a clause which is the object of the verb but which is placed at the beginning of the sentence, or a clause which is the subject of the verb and ends with a verb that makes an awkward combination with the main verb.

Whatever was needed, the commissary would supply. (Object of the verb.)

What he will do, cannot be predicted. (Subject of the verb.)

INTERRUPTIONS: PARENTHETICAL AND INDEPENDENT ELEMENTS; DIRECT ADDRESS

592. Elements such as parenthetical and independent expressions and words in direct address delay or interrupt the normal flow of a sentence, and are outside its regular grammatical structure. For that reason, they need to be definitely set off from the context.

593. *Comma.* These elements are regularly punctuated with commas.
(1) Parenthetical and Independent Elements.

This demonstration, *one might suppose,* would set us definitely ahead in the solution of the problem. (C. D. Stewart.)

His son, *it seems,* had never been greatly interested in the business.

Our report, *of course,* gives only a general survey of the field.

Fortunately, the fire was discovered before it did much damage.

Both students, *curiously enough,* had arrived at identical conclusions.

It was not, *however,* to describe the country that I began this letter. (G. Lowes Dickinson.)

He had, *too,* something of the austerity of the early Puritans.

Nevertheless, we must meet the issue squarely.

His father, *alas,* is no better.

Note. An emphatic interjection is set off by an exclamation point.

Nonsense! he won't hurt you.

(2) Direct Address.

Liberty does not consist, *my fellow citizens,* in mere general declarations of the rights of man. (Woodrow Wilson.)

He will not deny the charge, *Mr. Crane,* when you show him the evidence.

John, will you get me a copy of the treasurer's report?

MORE EMPHATIC INTERRUPTIONS, AND COMPLETE BREAKS IN THOUGHT

594. *Dash.* A dash is frequently used to indicate a more emphatic interruption in a sentence, or a complete break in the thought.

The Duke—*we called him that because of his grand manner*—was in reality a grocery clerk.

At that time—*this was in the days of crinoline and hoop skirts*—women had not thought of invading the business office and the barber shop.

I will never speak to him again, and I—*but what's the use of talking about him?*

You come to me, and you say that they—*why, you surely don't mean that.*

"*You asked me what we*—" I began.

"He *told—promised me that—that* he would be here," she wailed.

595. *Parentheses.* Parentheses may be used instead of dashes, to set off emphatic parenthetical expressions. Modern writers, however, usually prefer the dash.

The Duke (*we called him that because of his grand manner*) was in reality a grocery clerk.

596. Parentheses are regularly used to enclose certain minor routine explanations and details.

The Fourth Ward is represented in the Council by E. G. Quinlan (*Republican*) and James Quinn (*Democrat*).

In the previous chapter (*see p. 465*), this subject is discussed in greater detail.

In the accompanying diagram (*Fig. 6*), the annual fluctuations in price are indicated.

Exercise 95

Punctuate the parenthetical and independent elements, and the words in direct address.

1. Similar conditions we may be sure prevail in many American cities.
2. Consequently the assignment is usually made at least a month before the paper is due.
3. The president was irritated too by the rising tide of criticism against his policies.
4. His wife she was a Bradford from Boston had been active in founding the Society for the Promulgation of Culture.
5. Queerly enough he had never been in an airplane before that eventful trip.
6. This in fact has been the subject of much argument during the past month.
7. His stupidity yes my friends it was stupidity was responsible for his candidate's defeat.
8. Here John is the latest edition of the *Times.*
9. His success was largely due of course to his political affiliations.
10. The building was not completed however until after the exposition was opened.
11. A. C. Fabri spelled with an *i* instead of a *y* is their representative in this country.
12. Unfortunately sir your remark was misinterpreted by many who heard it.
13. "No yes well I suppose so," he stammered.
14. Nevertheless the project will have to be abandoned.

15. No doubt you are right Mr. Sabin but there are you must admit some arguments on the other side.

ENUMERATIONS AND EXPLANATIONS

597. A colon is regularly used before a formal enumeration of details following a general statement, or before a specific explanation of a general statement (see Secs. 215–16).

The enumeration or explanation may be introduced by words like *namely, viz., for example,* and *that is;* or may follow the phrases *as follows* or *the following* in the preceding clause; or may have no introductory connective.

(1) Enumerations.

The outline contains three main divisions: *namely, the introduction, the body, and the conclusion.*

The income of the club is derived from *the following* sources: *initiation fees, annual dues, and special assessments.*

The furnishings in the room were meager: *a bed, a dresser, a straight-back chair, a worn rug, and nothing more.*

(2) Specific Explanations.

Our orders were explicit: *we were to be at the cabin by ten o'clock, and bring the papers with us.*

He had dressed up for the occasion: *that is, he had added a collar and a tie to his every-day clothes.*

Note that a comma is used *after* introductory words like *namely, for example, that is,* etc.

598. For special emphasis or clearness, enumerations and explanations in the middle of a sentence may be punctuated—both before and after —with dashes.

Three officials—*the president, the secretary, and the treasurer*—have been indicted.

The first rumor—*that the ship had sunk*—was false.

Exercise 96

Punctuate the following sentences, and give your reasons.

1. There were three men in the party a physician a lawyer and a banker.
2. Four broad classifications namely Excellent Good Fair and Poor are used in grading the themes.

3. This disease can be cured that is it can be cured if it is taken in hand in the early stages.
4. He had one enviable gift the ability to make and to hold friends.
5. Your practice is inconsistent for example you begin one quotation with a capital *L* and the next one with a small *t*.
6. The following cities were included in our itinerary Salisbury Bath Exeter and Plymouth.
7. His excuse for missing class was a stereotype he had been studying late and had overslept that morning.
8. The telegram read as follows "Contract signed—letter of confirmation follows."
9. Two books a dictionary and a book of synonyms were always on his desk.
10. On his desk he always had two books namely a dictionary and a book of synonyms.

DIRECT QUOTATIONS

599. A comma or a colon is used before a formal direct quotation. The present tendency is toward the use of the comma unless the quotation is long.

> We opened our gates to all the world and said, *"Let all men who wish to be free come to us and they will be welcome."* (Theodore Roosevelt.) They can look out over these broad stretches of fertility and say: *"We made this, with our backs and hands."* (Willa Cather.)

600. Before expressions like *he said,* a direct quotation is followed by a comma, unless a question mark or an exclamation point is required by the thought.

> *"We were at the convent together,"* the girl said. (John Masefield.)
> *"Who brought you the news?"* said the planter. (Rudyard Kipling.)
> *"Stop her!"* bellowed Mr. Rout. (Joseph Conrad.)

601. When *I said, he replied,* etc., are placed within a quotation, the punctuation at the end of these expressions may be a comma, a semicolon, or a period, the choice depending upon the closeness of connection between the two parts of the quotation.

> "I believe," he replied, "that I am right."
> "No," I said, "you can't do that."
> "She can afford it," I replied; "she has plenty of money."
> "We will not go," she said. "We were not invited."
> "Why did he come?" she asked. "He knew that he was not wanted."

602. A quoted phrase or word introduced informally into a sentence does not require a comma before it.

> Under the new system, success in life is described as "getting by." (Stuart Sherman.)

(See also the examples in the following section.)

603. Miscellaneous Uses of Quotation Marks. Slang; names of ships; titles of books, poems, and magazine articles, are often enclosed by quotation marks.

> The opposing pitcher was certainly "hot" today.
> The "Majestic" will sail tomorrow.
> Whittier pictures his early life on the farm in "Snowbound."

604. Many writers prefer italics to quotation marks in names of ships, and titles.

> The *Majestic* will sail tomorrow.
> Whittier pictures his early life on the farm in *Snowbound*.

When the name of a magazine or a book and the title of a chapter in the book or an article in the magazine occur together, the former is put in italics and the latter is enclosed in quotation marks.

> This month's *London Courier* contains his latest article, "The Triumph of Reason."

605. Quotation Within a Quotation. A quotation within a quotation is enclosed by single quotation marks.

> "When she said, 'I won't go,' we thought she meant it," replied Mary.

606. Capitals and Small Letters. A formal direct quotation begins with a capital letter; an informally quoted word or phrase begins with a small letter—unless, of course, the first word is a proper name.

> His reply was, "The book is lost."
> The opposing pitcher was "hot" today.

Exercise 97

Insert quotation marks and make any other changes that are needed; and give your reasons.

1. Why did you choose this kind of work they asked him.
2. But you should go at once he argued.
3. After a moment's hesitation she replied you know what I mean without my explaining further.
4. Stop the car he shouted as he saw the obstruction ahead.
5. In his sports stories a baseball is always a spheroid or a pill.

6. When I received your telegram come at once I lost no time in starting he said.
7. For the classic critic Shakespeare is tops as a dramatist.
8. Then we read Longfellow's Evangeline and compared it with Masters' Spoon River Anthology.
9. Well he replied this is what I want to do
10. Shall we go I asked the train starts in half an hour.
11. The word accommodate is frequently misspelled.
12. Then I asked him why did you do it

Exercise 98

Explain why each mark of punctuation was used in the following sentences. Each use is covered by one of the rules given in the preceding discussion.

1. He lived a long life, and his complete works are but a modest dozen volumes. (John Macy.) 2. That, too, is a mistake. He is not really wise; he is only intelligent. (C. Gauss.) 3. In each county, besides the reserve officer in charge, there is a junior and a medical officer. (*Atlantic Monthly.*) 4. Everybody was subconsciously sorry for everybody else, and wanted to be kinder. (*Reader's Digest.*) 5. They were given an additional year in which to transfer their possessions, if they wished to move. (*Survey Graphic.*) 6. In one wing of the White House, the State Bank and the Savings Bank have their offices; in the opposite wing is the State prison. (*Harper's Magazine.*) 7. When no flowers are to be found, this is the quickest way to find a bee. (John Burroughs.) 8. Wherever Mrs. Pankhurst turned in protest, she met the scornful opposition of aldermen, clergymen, statesmen. (*Washington Post.*) 9. And there are only three qualifications for tenants: that they own good implements, be reasonably free from debt, and have interest in ultimate farm ownership. (*Reader's Digest.*) 10. Adventure would come; and for the moment he was at ease, lingering on its threshold. (J. B. Priestley.)

11. In their pioneer days—only a scant few years ago—news broadcasters, who were mostly ex-newspapermen, tried using city-room methods. (*Collier's.*) 12. It amazed me that she had noticed, for she had seemed so far removed from the present. (J. P. Marquand.) 13. Considered aside from its moral implications, such a policy does not make much practical sense. 14. The ship, after a pause of comparative quietness, started upon a series of rolls, one worse than another. (Joseph Conrad.) 15. A complicated technical structure should be run by engineers, not hucksters. (Stuart Chase.) 16. I don't expect it to be solved in my lifetime, but I expect it to be solved

sometime, because it is the fundamental problem of man's existence on earth. (C. F. Kettering.) 17. Moreover, they have been, on the whole, poor linguists, and so they have dragged their language with them, and forced it upon the human race. (H. L. Mencken.) 18. If anyone working for the company is in financial straits, and a superintendent finds out about it, this is reported, too. (*Reader's Digest.*) 19. Viewed from a balcony, the whole thing would doubtless have been weirdly picturesque. (Stephen Crane.) 20. On the contrary, however, there is excellent reason to hold that a man of thirty, forty, or even fifty can learn nearly anything better than he could when he was fifteen. (*Atlantic Monthly.*)

21. The Danube, between its stone embankments, was chalky gray. (Joseph Hergesheimer.) 22. The rumor reached Denby, who maintained a culpable silence. 23. Going in, we found nearly all the people of the town—men, women, and children—collected and crowded together, leaving barely room for the dancers. (R. H. Dana.) 24. The reason for this change is clear enough, and can be stated in four words: last November's election returns. (*Collier's.*) 25. Waterloo ended the rout; it left Napoleon without support and without hope. (H. G. Wells.) 26. It was a broad platform, and the boy walked cautiously, lifting his bare feet and putting them down with extreme deliberateness on the hot, dry, cracked planks. (Sherwood Anderson.) 27. The political sciences, since they deal with conduct, must rest upon some positive conception of human motives. (Walter Lippmann.) 28. In fact, I always felt, when with him, that I was with no common man. (R. H. Dana.) 29. Life's second lesson—at least for me—is that few people are wholly evil. (André Maurois.)

Exercise 99

This general exercise covers the preceding rules. Punctuate each sentence, and give the reasons.

1. The news spread over the town quickly growing as it traveled.
2. A month was a long time to wait for a reply but it would not necessarily be fatal to our plans.
3. A chain of high hills protected the harbor on the north and west and ran off into the interior as far as the eye could reach.
4. He decided therefore to support the Republican candidate who had been endorsed by the Non-Partisan League.
5. The club now has only a small membership and therefore it has less political influence than it once had.
6. When her husband was ill there were few people who came to visit them hence she became lonesome and despondent.

7. Hours later or so it seemed to me we were back at the main entrance which we now found locked and bolted.

8. A babel of sounds the clatter of dozens of telegraph keys the shouts of clerks and traders the shuffle of hundreds of feet greeted me on my first visit to the Board of Trade.

9. Opening the door quickly he heard someone running up the stairs.

10. The tropical moon shone through the casement windows flooding the room with a soft mellow light.

11. The story opens in Manchester the birthplace of the hero William Fenn and the scene of his early struggles against a sordid environment.

12. As the clouds in the west grew blacker and more threatening the less hardy fishermen pulled up anchor and hurried to shore.

13. They made good time that morning although the roads were somewhat heavy from the recent rain.

14. Living conditions had improved for the laboring man moreover he and his class now had representation in Parliament.

15. Nevertheless everyone likes Jack for he is an innocent harmless amiable fellow.

16. The man was arrested as he was trying to enter the house of W. E. Griffith 1128 Canfield Avenue an official of the telephone company.

17. These people do not ask whether the practice is ethical they want to know how much they can profit by it.

18. Mr. Adams do you know my friend Mr. Compton?

19. Shakespeare makes us see the sharp contrast in the two characters crafty villainous Iago simple honest Othello.

20. Some hours later after the returns had been checked it was found that the First Ward which had been strongly Democratic had elected a Republican alderman.

21. The defeat of the bill was assured when the constituents back home the farmers the merchants the bankers began to write caustic letters to their congressmen.

22. When his father moved to the village it consisted of a small country hotel a general store a blacksmith shop and a scattering of houses but now it is a thriving city the center of a prosperous farming community.

INDEX

A, indefinite article, 42, 157, 159; distinguished from *an*, 42; for *each*, 160

About, in verb-group (*about to go*), 164, 166

Absolute use of noun and participle, 14, 77, 94, 181; pronoun and participle, 21; noun and infinitive, 185

Abstract noun, 6; article omitted with, 159

Accompanying circumstances, adverbial element of, 219

Accusative case, see Objective case

Active voice of verbs, 69; defined, 69; forms of, 56, 58, 62; infinitives, 73-4; participles, 76

Addresses, dates, etc., punctuation of, 249

Adjective, 41 ff., 152 ff.; defined, 41; pronominal adjective, 41; the articles, 42, 157 ff.; predicate adjective, 43, 91, 92, *note*, 153 ff.; objective complement, 43, 156, 180; object of preposition, 84, 223; modifying a gerund, 91; used as noun, 121, 141. Constructions used as adjectives, 152: noun, 15, 41, 139; pronoun, 41; infinitive, 73, 154, 184; participle, 77, 154, 180; phrase, 93, 184; clause, 105; various constructions, 152; *ten-foot, five-mile*, 152. Comparison of adjectives, 44; position of, 43, 153; modified by adverbial clause, 108; as adjunct in a phrase, 91; adverbial complements of, 219. Dual relation of adjective and adverb, 93, 211

Adjective clause, 105, 152; as predicate adjective, 154; punctuation of, 253

Adjective phrase, 93, 152, 184; as predicate adjective, 154; as objective complement, 156; punctuation of, 253

Adjuncts in phrases, 91; in the complete subject, 122; in the complete predicate, 123

A dozen, 160

Adverb, 81 ff., 206 ff.; defined, 81; classification, 81, 211 ff.; forms, 82, 209; comparison, 82. Constructions used as adverbs, 206: noun, 15, 139; infinitive, 73, 184; phrase, 93, 94, 180, 184, 212 ff.; clause, 106 ff., 212 ff.; preposition, 85; nouns in *-s* (*nights*), 206; *the*, 161; *but*, 225; various constructions, 206. Adverb used as object of preposition, 84, 223; in verb-group, 163; to modify infinitive, participle, or gerund, 91; to modify phrase or clause, 207. Conjunctive adverb, 111; independent adverb, 130, 208; short adverb, 209; some troublesome adverbs, 241; adverb distinguished from predicate adjective, 155; dual relation of adverb and adjective, 93, 211

Adverbial clause, 106 ff., 212 ff.; position of, 109; punctuation, 251 ff.

Adverbial complements of adjectives, 219

Adverbial elements, various types, 206, 211 ff.; mixed and dual relations, 211; elliptical, 227

Adverbial phrases, 93, 212 ff.